THE FLYING PRINCE
Alexander Obolensky

THE FLYING PRINCE
Alexander Obolensky

The Rugby Hero Who Died
Too Young

Hugh Godwin

HODDER &
STOUGHTON

First published in Great Britain in 2021 by Hodder & Stoughton
An Hachette UK company

1

Copyright © Hugh Godwin 2021

A CIP catalogue record for this title is available from the British Library

Hardback ISBN 978 1 529 37288 5
eBook ISBN 978 1 529 37289 2

Typeset in Adobe Garamond Pro by Palimpsest Book Production Limited, Falkirk, Stirlingshire

Printed and bound in Great Britain by Clays Ltd, Elcograf S.p.A.

Hodder & Stoughton policy is to use papers that are natural, renewable
and recyclable products and made from wood grown in sustainable forests.
The logging and manufacturing processes are expected to conform to the
environmental regulations of the country of origin.

Hodder & Stoughton Ltd
Carmelite House
50 Victoria Embankment
London EC4Y 0DZ

www.hodder.co.uk

*To my dear wife Violeta – thank you for your love
and grace and patience and positivity.*

CONTENTS

ACKNOWLEDGEMENTS

My sincere thanks to the relatives of Alexander Obolensky, all of whom encouraged me to tell his story and helped in every way they could: Alexandra Hulse (née Obolensky), Serge Beddington-Behrens, Felizitas Obolensky, Nick Obolensky and Alex Ranicar. With fond memories of Stuart Hulse, dear husband of Alexandra – his understanding and enthusiasm set me on the way.

To those whose support, advice and cajoling kept me going, thank you: to my dear late sister Louise, who reviewed the clumsy first draft, and to John Richards and Camilla Richards, Katya Galitzine and her family, Huw Richards, Julian Godwin, Adam Hathaway, Tim Glover, Richard White, John Griffiths, Ron Palenski, Michael Heal, Brendan Gallagher, Stephen Cooper, Ally McKay, Donald Trelford, Steve Tongue, Andy Bull, Michael Aylwin, Michael Calvin, Rory Scarfe and Anne Turner.

For their knowledge and their willingness to share it: Katya Galitzine's colleague Elena at the Prince George Galitzine Memorial Library and historian friend Nikolai Rodin; George Galitzine; Margaret Kononova (Institute of World History at the Russian Academy of Sciences); Julian Disney; Shaun Disney; Charles Percy and Averill Gordon; Robin Darwall-Smith; David Pinney and Ann Randell at Trent College; Georgina Edwards and Helen Sumping (Brasenose College); Mark 'Disco' Discombe of the Battle of Britain Memorial Flight; Malcolm Barrass (Air of Authority); Vic Skeet; Robert Dunnett, Alan Smith and Tarkey Barker (Martlesham Heath Aviation Society); Kris Hendrix and Bryan Legate (Royal Air Force Museum at Hendon); Julia Boyd;

Rachel Kiddey; Reg Gadney; Rory Underwood; Alan Thomas (Air Historical Branch, RAF); Jessica Thurtell; Geoffrey Archer; Yvonne Allen Fox (née Gaunt); Victoria de Lempicka and Marilyn Goldberg; Simon Kidner; Martin C. Harris (Harris Ice Hockey Archives); Michael Owen-Smith; Alex Bray (East India Club); Phil McGowan and Jayne Linaker (World Rugby Museum at Twickenham); Patricia Mowbray (RFU); Dai Richards (Rugby Relics); Ruth Cahir (British Pathé); John Hamilton-Curzon (Oxford University Russian Society); Niels Sampath (Oxford Union Library); Elizabeth Back (Oxford University Archives); Amanda Corp (London Library), Tom Sprent (St Edmund Hall, Oxford); Karen Farr (Wadham College, Oxford); Charlotte Berry (Magdalen College, Oxford); Oliver Mahony (St Hilda's College, Oxford); Katrina Rowbottom (Scotch College Adelaide); Elizabeth Back (Oxford University Archives); Anthony Brems and Sophie Hurden (University of Oxford Student Registry); Helen Drury (Oxfordshire History Centre); Terence Pepper and Clare Freestone (National Portrait Gallery); Adam Goodwin (Record Office for Leicestershire); Adam Tyrer and David Whittam (Rosslyn Park FC); Vera Narishkin; Stuart Farmer; Tim Stevens (Oxford University Rugby Football Club); Dave Green (Nottingham RFC); Heather Edwards-Hedley (Haileybury); Sir Brian Harrison; Will Mawhood (DeepBaltic. com); Alistair Roach (Society for Nautical Research); Bill Treadwell (ERIC); Mario Sebastiani (National Central Library of Rome); Peter Boyle; Robert Finan; Noelle Worthington; Jane Goddard (*Derby Telegraph*); Peter Moore (504 Association); Paul Bolton; Paul Mawhinney; Philip Goodman; Grahame L. Newnham; Andrea Zsubori and Wojciech Janik (School of Slavonic Studies); Konstantin Shlykov (Russian Embassy in London); Eriks Jekabsons; Linas Jegelevicius; Toms Kikuts (National History Museum of Latvia); Klavs Zarins; Igor Polski; Selina Pearson (Ipswich Borough Council); Anna Stone (Aviva); John Porter (Prudential); Annette Brownhill; Terry Gotch; Rita Bailey; Carly Collier (Royal Collection Trust); Len Outridge (Tangmere Military Aviation Musem); Joshua Freedman; Peter Cholerton; Jon Culley; Trevor Sharpe (Chesterfield RFC); Robert Chugg; Brough Scott; Cornelius Lysaght; Sue Montgomery.

ACKNOWLEDGEMENTS

Thanks to everyone who works at the British Library, Bodleian Library, National Archives, St Petersburg Archives, London School of Economics Library, New Zealand Rugby Museum, and numerous other libraries, museums and collections . . . We are very lucky to have them.

Last, but not least – David Luxton and Rebecca Winfield at David Luxton Associates; and at Hodder & Stoughton, the mighty Roddy Bloomfield, Morgan Springett, Lewis Csizmazia and Katy Aries, plus Sadie Robinson and the copy-editors supreme Tim Waller and Penny Isaac.

PICTURE ACKNOWLEDGEMENTS

The author and publisher would like to thank the following for permission to reproduce photographs:

Section One: Reserved; collection National Portrait Gallery, London; Illustrated London News Ltd/Mary Evans; Fox Photos/Hulton Archive/Getty Images; PA Images/Alamy Stock Photo; Associated Newspapers Ltd; Associated Newspapers/Solo Syndication; AP Archive/British Movietone; Prince N Obolensky; the Richards Archive; the Beddington-Behrens Archive.

Section Two: www.world-rugby-museum.com; The Photographic Collection at the Royal Air Force Museum; the Felizitas Obolensky Collection; the Beddington-Behrens Archive; the Alexander Obolensky family archive compiled by Stuart Hulse.

Special thanks is given to the Obolensky family and their friends, who have kindly given permission to reproduce photographs from their archives.

All other photographs are from private collections.

Every reasonable effort has been made to trace the copyright holders, but if there are any errors or omissions, Hodder & Stoughton will be pleased to insert the appropriate acknowledgement in any subsequent printings or editions.

PROLOGUE

ALEXANDER SERGEEVICH OBOLENSKY climbed aboard the bus carrying the England team from central London to the Cole Court Hotel in Twickenham for an early lunch. From there it would be a 15-minute walk to the stadium. Alex was excited and nervous and mad-keen to get on with the match, but there were still four agonising hours to go.

Seventeen men in club ties and worsted-wool suits bounced gently in their seats; there were 15 starters and two reserves; athletes of every shape and size, ranging in age from Alex, the baby at 19, and in his second year at university, to Charles Webb, the 33-year-old Plymouth-born lock forward, nicknamed 'Tank'.

The air reeked of aftershave and cigarettes, and brilliantine and shoe polish, as the bus chugged through Shepherd's Bush and Hammersmith into that part of the capital's south-west outskirts where residential streets were probing for the first time into the countryside of Middlesex and Surrey: row after row of terraced and semi-detached houses, each with a little front garden as a green emblem of a house building boom.

On this first Saturday of January 1936, Christmas decorations still twinkled in bay windows. Kick-off was set for 2.15. Those without tickets could try alternative entertainment nearby: the Richmond Theatre had performances of *Cinderella* at 2.30 p.m. and 7.30 p.m., and the local 'Kinema' would soon be showcasing seven-year-old Shirley Temple in *Our Little Girl*.

Alex sat next to Hal Sever, who was doing his best not to feel jittery. Both of the England wings were about to make their international debuts. The 25-year-old Sever had spent the past fortnight fretting about tripping over the pavement or pulling a muscle.

Alex lit a cigarette and jiggled his legs to keep the muscles supple. His eyes flitted to the people on the pavements – mostly men, and almost all wearing overcoats and hats. The captain, Bernard Gadney, came down the aisle of the bus from the back seats. Later Sever recalled how he soothed their worries: 'He talked anything but rugby.'

The England players had gathered the day before for practice at the Honourable Artillery Company (HAC) rugby club, an oasis of grass between the offices and residences of London's City Road. The HAC put some men up for the forwards to scrummage against, while England's goal-kickers, Peter Cranmer and Philip 'Pop' Dunkley, took shots at the posts.

The training was perfunctory – some stretching, a few passes thrown, basic routines practised. Twenty-four hours before the biggest match of the season and, in many cases, of their rugby-playing lives, the players were keen only to avoid injury. John Daniell, the chairman of the England selectors, was confident his team would win, provided the big fellows in the second row did not blow up. There again, it was a selector's job to be confident.

All the players had met at least once during the England trial matches in December, but Alex knew only a few of his new team-mates well. He had played with Gadney seven times for Leicester, while Cranmer was an idol of his at Oxford. Just 21 years old, but precocious and bright-minded, Cranmer had already played two international seasons. Alex had glimpsed Dunkley and a couple of the others during his short experience on the senior club circuit.

England's opponents were a great deal more attuned to each other. The All Blacks had arrived from New Zealand for their tour 23 weeks before, and this would be their 28th and final match. Thirteen of the England team had met the New Zealanders before; the exceptions being Cranmer and the full back, Tuppy Owen-Smith. The latter had a misleadingly careworn look on the field, with creases on his forehead and bandages on his knees. Alex knew it was in Tuppy's nature to take risks. That was fine – Alex was prepared to take a few himself. He had done well against the All Blacks, first with the

Midland Counties and then with Oxford, when his controversial try rattled the tourists in their one-point win.

After training, the players felt gently keyed up as they repaired to the Metropole Hotel on Northumberland Avenue, within sight of the Thames. Its clientele included 'travellers from Paris and the Continent; officers attending the levees at St James; colonial and American visitors; and Ladies going to the State Balls at Buckingham Palace'.

On this occasion, the All Blacks were in residence too. They were supposed to have prepared in Brighton, but a booking error diverted them to Porthcawl, 200 miles away in south Wales. Now they were back in London, and staying at the place where the England team were having dinner. Gadney would have preferred the contact to be reserved for the next day, but he shared in the laughs as an England player walked to a New Zealand table by mistake.

Come the Saturday morning, the newspapers ran extensive previews of the match. Colonel J.P. Jordan, the 'rugby football expert' in the *Daily Mail*, was on to something when he wrote next to a huge photo of Alex with his blond hair ruffled and broad, angular nose prominent: 'Obolensky has already captured the imagination of the crowd. Given the chance, he might easily win the game for England and so help to break a 30-years-old spell.' The reference was to the All Blacks' spectacular record of 57 matches unbeaten on English soil across three tours since 1905.

The local *Richmond & Twickenham Times* predicted good things for Alex, if not necessarily for his team: 'Their forwards are a solid enough bunch, but mere weight in the scrum is not everything. More favourable is the English backline. Prince Obolensky and Peter Cranmer will give E.V. Tindill and T.H.C. Caughey plenty to think about.'

The stadium opened at midday, and within half an hour there were 10,000 spectators inside. By kick-off a capacity crowd of more than 70,000 would be packed in. A hum of conversation became a hubbub that would turn into 'the most deafening cheer ever raised at Twickenham'.

At the gates of the huge West Stand, the guest of honour arrived: a clean-shaven man in his early 40s, with bags under his eyes and an easy smile, dressed in a heavy grey overcoat over a grey checked suit, and a blue muffler concealing a collar and tie. Edward, the Prince of Wales, known as David to family and friends, had a red rose in the buttonhole of his wide left lapel.

Alex – nicknamed Obo by his teammates – entered England's changing room underneath the West Stand, removed his suit and pulled on the pristine white jersey made by Lillywhites. An oblong patch bearing the Rugby Football Union's red rose was stitched onto the left breast. A shout went up for the players to go out to the pitch for the team photograph. The heavy rain of recent days had abated, and the straw piled a foot high around the touchlines had done its job in warding off any frost.

With the commemorative photo duly snapped, the players returned down the tunnel for a final smoothing of the hair or a trip to the loo. John Daniell, the chairman of England's all-powerful selectors, sidled up to Cranmer to reiterate a point discussed earlier. 'Peter, we want you to play left centre today, so the ball can get to Obo,' Daniell said. The theory was the ball travelling from a set-piece scrum or lineout on the left of the field would reach Alex in his position on the right wing more smoothly if Cranmer was the first receiver from Peter Candler, the fly half, in preference to the other centre, Ronald 'Gerry' Gerrard.

A few minutes before kick-off, there was another call to the team. The guest of honour had let the RFU know he didn't want the players standing around in the cold, so they lined up outside the changing rooms, instead of on the pitch as was the custom.

The Prince of Wales entered the corridor to be met by Gadney, who then guided him along the line of white jerseys, introducing each player by name. When they reached Alex Obolensky, the eyes of the two princes met.

'By what right do you play for England?' said Edward Albert Christian George Andrew Patrick David Windsor, the immediate heir to the British throne.

'I attend Oxford University, sir,' came the reply from Prince Alexander Sergeevich Obolensky, sire of the line of Rurik, founder of Russian nobility.

Was the Prince of Wales's remark a haughty put-down made by a confident man-about-town enjoying his hereditary status and his sporty day out, unaware he would become leader of the British Empire before the month was out? His father George V was gravely ill, and his death on 20 January would set in train a tumultuous reign of just 10 months for Edward VIII, with no coronation, before he was succeeded by his brother Bertie as King George VI.

And if the words were an admonishment, how should we judge Alex's reply? Challengingly defiant or respectfully acquiescent? This Oxford undergraduate, referred to as 'Obo the Slav' in parts of the press, derived from a much longer royal line than the Windsors'. Did Edward frown angrily at Alex's insolence – or did his twinkly-eyed features break into a grin of empathy?

More likely is that the Prince of Wales was aiming to make the young man in front of him feel at ease. Edward was a former Oxford man himself, and a passionate follower of rugby, and it was his father's first cousin, Princess Marie Louise, who had welcomed and helped the Obolensky family when they arrived in London as penniless émigrés in 1919.

The formalities continued. A quarter of an hour before kick-off, Sydney Coopper, the grey-haired secretary of the RFU, raised his bowler hat outside the committee entrance in the forecourt behind the West Stand and said calmly to those within earshot: 'Ladies and gentlemen, please take your seats.'

The Prince of Wales had the best of those, in the West Stand above the standing terrace. He motioned his guest, the Crown Prince of Egypt, to sit next to him. Men in adjacent seats removed their hats in deference. Other men with megaphones were imploring the crowd on the terraces to stand closer together, to allow latecomers in.

Down below, the teams entered the field: New Zealand first, striding purposefully, then England, led by Gadney.

Alex Obolensky, third from last to emerge, skipped up the steps, his slim, muscular frame camouflaged by baggy white shorts reaching almost to the knee. He smiled as he ran. The sky was overcast as the teams stood facing each other, five yards apart, for the national anthem, 'God Save the King', played by the band.

The Sunday newspaper writers have taken their seats in the press box, perpendicular to the halfway line. Scribbling notes and bashing on noisy typewriters, their reports of the action will be relayed by phone to sub-editors back in the office. There is commentary on live radio, too. Crucially, for this story, there are cameras filming for cinema newsreels as well.

The early exchanges are tight and exciting. Gadney breaks through from a lineout and spins a pass out to Alex on the right wing. The crowd roars but, before Alex can work up full speed, Nelson 'Kelly' Ball brings him down. This is a shock. 'We thought Obo would have the legs of everyone,' Gadney says to himself.

About 25 minutes have been played when there is a scrum in midfield in England's half. The forwards heel the ball smartly, Gadney slings it to Candler, who gets his backs moving. Candler passes to Cranmer, who passes to Gerrard just before he is hit by a tackle from Caughey. The redoubtable Gerrard absorbs the impact as he passes to Alex, who has held his depth intelligently so as not to overrun his teammate.

Alex takes a straight line onto the pass, 15 yards infield from the touchline, with a daunting 60 yards to get to the All Blacks' goal line. He cradles the ball in his right arm, as he was taught to at school. He is young, yes, but he possesses the foot speed and has developed the instincts of a natural-born wing – even in this sport that is a mystery to almost everyone in the country of his birth.

These are the opportunities he has been picked for. This is why the venerable duffers of the Rugby Football Union voted down a spiteful motion aimed at denying England's adopted hero his shot at glory. The actions of Prince Alexander Obolensky now and in the minutes that follow will captivate lovers of sport for decades to come.

CHAPTER 1

FROM WARLORDS TO REFUGEES

THE LITTLE BOY with blond hair gripped the hand of his mother as they clambered up the wooden gangplank, trying not to scuff his tiny brown shoes on the cross-joists designed to help their ascent. His nose wrinkled at the stench of the engine oil, and the tips of his ears were stung by the freezing wind. He trembled at the cold, but also with a nervous excitement that made him want to let out a scream of exhilaration. A life-ring to his right bore the name of the vessel, HMS *Princess Margaret*: a royal name for a less than regal escape, although the irony was lost on Prince Alexander Obolensky. He was one month short of his third birthday, and had no comprehension of the voyage awaiting him or of the hatred and horror he was leaving behind.

On the deck of the ship, moored on the Daugava River, the boy tried to pull away from his mama and sprint ahead, but Princess Lubov held firm. A man in a blue uniform beckoned them towards a wooden door. The Royal Navy minesweeper, which had been converted from a Canadian pleasure boat, heaved on its anchor chain. A blast of a horn briefly drowned out the shouts of the British sailors to their colleagues on the quayside.

Lubov turned to see her mother-in-law, Maria Trigoni, wearing a woollen shawl over wispy grey hair, and sister-in-law, Pelageya Maksutov, shepherding Alexander's older sister, Maria, soon to be four, and 16-month-old Irena on to the deck. The three children's father, Prince Sergei Alexandrovich Obolensky, known as Serge, was away on his military posting.

No one could tell them when the ship would be leaving, because no one could be sure. The Obolenskys belonged to one of the oldest noble families in the land, but they had lost control of their fate almost two years ago, when revolutionaries swarmed through Petrograd, their home city, and now they were being forced into exile.

In the moonless dark of this late-December evening in 1918, the *Princess Margaret* and the harbour were illuminated intermittently by the ship's searchlights. In large parts of the world people were still celebrating the end of the Great War, seven weeks earlier. Not here, though. The capital of the newly independent Latvia was in a state of anarchy, a boiling outpost of the vast, unravelling Russian empire. Gunshots could be heard from hidden snipers, and bands of looters roamed the streets. A bloody and brutal civil war was raging in Riga and far beyond.

The howl of the wind was shut out as the Obolenskys stepped into a cabin with bunk beds fixed round its bare, patchy walls. Lubov took a blanket from a pile, draped it on a warm pipe running along the floor and then around Irena's shoulders. The soft furnishings, pictures, mirrors and pretty bathroom fittings belonging to the pleasure steamer had been put into storage, and the first-class smoke room stripped of the timbers of the original design based on an English country house.

Lubov shivered and wondered whether the heat from the oil-burning turbines rumbling beneath them would ever permeate the room. She hoisted Maria onto one of the top bunks. 'Bless her,' Lubov said to herself. 'Bless all the children. What have they done to deserve this?'

Footsteps clattered outside as Maria Trigoni fussed over little Alex. 'Keep still, Alexander Sergeevich,' said Lubov as she looked with love into her weary son's pale blue eyes. Licking the tips of her fingers, she smoothed Alex's white-gold fringe into a neat line across his forehead. Her fingers traced down to the hem of her dress, and the angular outlines of the possessions she had escaped with: a few small jewels and a Fabergé cigarette case. Then she touched the rounded bulge above her waist. She was six months pregnant with her next child.

Serge Obolensky married Lubov Narishkin in Petrograd, known then as St Petersburg, in February 1914. The groom was a mounted captain in the Imperial Horse Guard; he was coming up to his 35th birthday, the bride had just turned 24. Their first child, Maria, arrived in January 1915. Alexander, the 'gift of heaven' as Lubov called him, was born in Petrograd in February 1916, the day before his parents' second wedding anniversary.

The wedding had been exciting and exhausting. The Russian Orthodox service lasted well over an hour, and Lubov was laden with jewellery and wearing a dress of satin and lace. Priests and deacons stood in silver and gold robes, and sang beautifully in a vaulted church glowing with gilded icons and eternal candles. There were no bridesmaids, just groomsmen who were mostly Serge's brother-officers in scarlet uniforms. Serge was lean and neatly moustachioed; a fine figure in his white parade uniform with long boots, carrying a gold helmet topped by the imperial double eagle. The groomsmen held gold crowns over the couple's heads for luck, and Serge and Lubov held wax candles decorated with white ribbons and orange blossom.

As with all Russia's noble families, substantial tracts of inherited land and wealth were part of the deal. Serge received 75,000 roubles as his wife's share of her birth father's money. He bought a property for Lubov in St Petersburg.

Serge was born in Moscow in 1879, the middle of five children and the only son. His father, Alexander Sergeevich, graduated from the Cadet Corps in Moscow, but spent most of his life as a local government administrator and magistrate. He had been born in Arsamas, a town founded by Ivan the Terrible, 250 miles east of Moscow, joining a line of Obolenskys that was longer than the Romanovs who ruled the Russian empire.

The Obolenskys' lineage ran back unbroken to the ninth century and Rurik, a Viking warlord who renounced Christianity and was invited by the Slavic tribes of what is present-day European Russia to impose peace on their squabbling chieftains. 'Our land is great and abundant, but there is no order in it,' they said. 'Come and rule over us.' So Rurik and his seafaring raiders from Scandinavia sailed their long ships down the mighty rivers to the Black Sea and took control. These were the beginnings of Russia as an organised state and one of the largest and most powerful nations on earth.

Rurik's son Igor became Grand Prince of Kiev, which was the capital for the next few centuries, and his power radiated through a network of semi-autonomous princely seats. In the year 1097 this power became hereditary and the seats subdivided, eventually creating 10 'grand principalities' and more than 100 'principalities'. In the 11th generation after Rurik came a Christian martyr named Michael, who was tortured to death but canonised in 1246. It was his grandson, Constantine, who became the first Prince Obolensky, taking his name from his seat in the town of Obolensk. The brothers Ivan and Semyon Obolensky helped inflict a decisive defeat on the Tartars in 1380, and Semyon's reward for ridding Moscow of a rogue courtier who gouged out the eyes of Grand Prince Vassili was the village of Tolstikovo and a landed estate – the first in the Obolensky family.

Over time the grand princes of Moscow become the tsars – the supreme rulers – of all Russia. In the 17th century, the first tsar from the Romanov line rose out of the internecine struggles that had left the 'Kievan Rus' prey to Genghis Khan and his successor invaders from central Asia. There were 276 of Russia's princely families at one time, together with another 40 who were considered 'noble' but had no title. The number had fallen to 28 by the fateful revolutionary year of 1917.

The title of 'prince' in tsarist Russia denoted royal origin, and it also served with 'count' and 'baron' as an honour for distinguished military or civilian service. The descendants of Rurik belonged to the princely category.

The Obolenskys through the ages had more often been soldiers or statesmen or farm owners than courtiers. The family crest contains a black imperial Chernigov eagle, holding a cross in its beak to commemorate the forebears who introduced Christianity into Russia, and the archangel St Michael. There are also the two hunting birds granted by the shah of Persia to an ambassador who was an Obolensky, in recognition of his work for peace. Each bird holds a Persian arrow in its beak and an imperial orb in an upturned claw, symbolising plenipotentiary powers granted by the tsar. At the top of the shield, a closed crown with four arches indicates the Obolenskys are a princely family. The red coat of ermine wrapped around the periphery denotes a family that at some time held kingly powers.

Serge was an expert horseman from a young age, and he entered the Life Guards Equestrian Regiment as a volunteer, aged 19. Successive promotions made him a non-commissioned officer, a standard-bearer, a cornet and, in 1903, having temporarily commanded the fourth squadron, he became a lieutenant. He was aide-de-camp to a series of Moscow governor-generals (the equivalent of the city's mayor), and survived an assassination attempt on one of them, when he was riding in a horse-drawn sleigh with Sergei Constantinovich Gershelman. A female socialist-revolutionary threw a bomb she had concealed in a basket of fish, killing the horses and ripping their hooves off; yet Gershelman and Serge survived.

As a formal acquaintance of the grand dukes who headed the army and navy, Serge and his wife Lubov were accustomed to parties, where the men wore dazzling uniforms and the women glittered in sapphire brooches and diamond tiaras. When Serge was stationed at Luga, south of St Petersburg, Lubov was said to be the centre of social life. On state occasions, Serge was one of the hundreds of perfectly turned out horsemen riding proudly behind the tsar through the city streets.

Lubov, whose name could be alternatively anglicised to Louba or Luba, had been born the illegitimate daughter of Alexander Dmitrievich Narishkin and a peasant girl named Matashilova, in St Petersburg in January 1890. Narishkin then had an illegitimate son, Vadim, with a Lydia Volkova, in December 1891. When Lubov was only four, her father died, and she and her two-year-old half-brother

Vadim were adopted by their aunt Maria and her husband, Feodor
Galitzine. An imperial decree allowed Lubov and Vadim to keep the
Narishkin name – the family had been known at the Russian court
since the time of Peter the Great – and a coat-of-arms in which the
Narishkin royal eagle was replaced by a bear denoting the Galitzines.
So Lubov was both illegitimate and orphaned of her father, and her
children would be descended from three noble lines entwined, or
should we say entangled, by marriage.

Lubov grew to be one of several ladies-in-waiting to the Tsarina
Alexandra Feodorovna and a friend to the Grand Duchess Xenia,
Tsar Nicholas II's sister. Lubov's chin-held-high demeanour is evident
in an early photo at a fancy-dress party at the tsar's Alexander Palace.
She was about 5 feet 6 inches tall and uncomplicatedly pretty, with
high cheekbones and blue eyes with irises like a cat's.

Serge viewed his duty in life as being first to God, through the
Orthodox Christian faith, and then to the tsar and his empire, and
then to his family line.

In certain ways, however, the Obolenskys were as much European
as they were Russian. The city of St Petersburg owed its beginnings
in the early 18th century to Peter the Great's dream of a new Russia,
embracing Western ideals. It replaced landlocked Moscow as the
capital, and transformed Russia into a naval as well as a military
power. The court relocated to St Petersburg on the shores of the
Baltic Sea, and many an aristocratic family followed. Everyone in
the court spoke French as a cultural preference – hence Serge's use
of the French version of his name, not Sergei.

A few months after the wedding of Serge Obolensky to Lubov
Narishkin, the First World War began. A few months after that, St
Petersburg was renamed Petrograd – 'Peter's City' – to excise the
German words Sankt and Burg.

Little Alex would hear all about it from Lubov one day: the patriotism that swept Russia as the tsar blessed the departing troops from
the balcony of the Winter Palace. But the war was a disaster. Three

out of four of Russia's soldiers were killed or wounded, and the death toll was two million – around a fifth of the worldwide total. Peasants grew to believe they were being put into the army simply to be slaughtered by Germans. Food ran short and the economy collapsed.

Pockets of dissent had fomented across Russia for years until, in February 1917, the powder keg exploded in Petrograd with a strike by female textile workers and spontaneous food riots. Anti-government protesters marched with banners demanding 'Bread and Peace!' One afternoon a mob of protesters was fired on by troops in the main street, the Nevsky Prospect, with many dead. The streets emptied and electricity was cut.

Serge and Lubov Obolensky had been living in Moscow in 1915 and 1916. Now they and their eldest children, Maria and Alex, were in Petrograd, and Lubov was pregnant again. The family and their domestic staff occupied most of a six-storey house on Nadezhdinskaya Street, a 10-minute walk east of the Fontanka River. It brought them close to Serge's parents and four sisters on Potemkinskaya Street.

In the fashionable quarter where Serge and Lubov lived – normally busy with cars, trams and smart carriages – night-time was eerily quiet. A few hours later, government buildings and the law courts were set on fire, and trucks drove down streets full of dissenting soldiers and 'disreputable women' waving red flags.

Serge placed his faith initially in Russia's history of failed rebellions. He was distantly related to Prince Eugene Obolensky, one of the leaders of the Decembrist uprising against Nicholas I in 1825. They had demanded a parliament and more rights for serfs, but the movement was suppressed by the tsar. Much the same had happened during the mass unrest of 1905.

On 15 March 1917, Nicholas II abdicated, signing power over 'as simply as one hands over a cavalry squadron to its new commander', an astonished general said. Nicholas intended his brother Grand Duke Michael to succeed him; when Michael refused power unless it was proven to be the will of the people, 300 years of Romanov rule was at an end.

At this point, liberals and constitutional democrats took charge, led by Prince Lvov and later the lawyer Alexander Kerensky, and they were trusted by the likes of the Obolenskys. The leader of the hard-left Bolshevik Party, Vladimir Lenin, was still in exile. But the Germans had spotted an opportunity, and dispatched Lenin in a sealed train that arrived in Petrograd in April. The workers' and soldiers' councils known as soviets were organising to take power in Petrograd and Moscow. On 1 August, Tsar Nicholas and his family left for Siberia.

The second wave of revolution came in October, as insurgents moved against the provisional government. Kerensky escaped to New York, the Council of People's Commissars became the new government, and Lenin declared all land as belonging to the people without payment. The Bolsheviks occupied strategic locations in Petrograd, a 'Red' army held power bases around the country and opposing 'White' forces mustered on the periphery. 'Citizen' was the only title permitted now, the banks were nationalised and religion was under attack: the Bolsheviks denounced God as an invention of the bourgeoisie.

In Britain, the revolutions were reported amid the greater priority of the war. On 22 December 1917, the chessboard was flipped over as the Bolsheviks met delegates from Germany, Austria-Hungary, Bulgaria and Turkey to arrange peace. Russia recognised the rights of Poland and agreed the independence of Lithuania, Courland, Livonia and Estonia – territories mostly occupied by the Germans. On 3 March 1918, the Treaty of Brest-Litovsk was signed, and Russia was simultaneously out of the Great War and plunged deeper into its own vicious civil strife.

The Whites continued to fight for the pre-revolutionary system and held governments in many parts of the empire. In the capital Petrograd, the 'Red Terror' that led to the flight of the Obolenskys began.

CHAPTER 2

THE RED TERROR AND THE TRAIN TO RIGA

THE LAST PHOTOGRAPH of the Obolenskys together on Russian soil, taken at their holiday estate near Kazan in the summer of 1918, bears witness to the troubled times. Behind the family lies a sprawling façade – a main building flanked by an outbuilding on either side – with attractive sash windows. Alex, aged two and a half, wears a short-sleeved smock as he squints in the sun. Next to him, Maria smiles shyly, holding a flower. Mother Lubov's brown hair flops over her blue eyes as she holds baby Irena in her right arm. An unidentified friend or cousin completes the group. But the idyll ends there: a fence of barbed wire runs the width of the mansion, and the barrier appears to have been erected in a hurry, with three-foot-high tree branches for fence posts and the wire criss-crossed haphazardly between them. This was no happy family scene; the 'privileged' classes were now in extreme danger.

The Obolenskys returned from this holiday to Petrograd to find themselves at the heart of a civil war that was savage even by the standards of Russia's long and violent history. The chaos and brutality unfolding were epoch-making for the Obolenskys and their kind. It was a perilous time, too, for British expatriates: insular, conservative, and led by Sir George Buchanan, the British ambassador.

In July 1918 came the shocking news of the execution of the Romanovs, shot and bayoneted in Yekaterinburg in the Urals. To the nobility of Russia, Nicholas II and his wife Alexandra and their children became martyrs – and the Bolsheviks the anti-Christ.

In August, Lenin was wounded by a gunman in Moscow, and

then came the greatest flashpoint. Moisei Uritsky, head of the Petrograd Cheka – the secret police – was shot dead, and thousands of prisoners and political opponents were executed, including 500 in Petrograd, where some were thrown into the River Neva. Four grand dukes, including an uncle of the tsar, were shot in the Peter and Paul Fortress.

The slaughter was made more terrifying by its unpredictability. As the historian Douglas Smith wrote in *Former People*: 'There simply is no way to explain why some perished and some survived. It was chance – or, as many Russians would have it, fate.'

Petrograd rapidly emptied of people. The population reduced by more than two-thirds, from 2,400,000 in 1916 to 740,000 in 1920, as military personnel and government staff relocated to Moscow, while able-bodied men joined in the civil war or absconded to the countryside. Bread and milk were scarce and food prices rocketed. When cart horses collapsed of exhaustion in the street – eyes bulging and sides blown out – they were butchered in moments. The smart houses and apartments of Peter the Great's beautiful city reeked of stewed cabbage, herrings or other salted fish, supplemented with potatoes. Electricity was rationed to two hours a day, there was no coal, and the tramway service was suspended.

Lubov watched as trusted neighbours packed up and moved out. An acquaintance sold a 300-year-old suite of ebony furniture for a decent price. Soon, though, pawnbrokers, jewellers and clothing shops were paying derisory amounts for anything the well-off families could offload. Walking with a parcel risked confiscation by Red Guards, who lurked in black cars on street corners.

Money in the bank was out of reach. Lubov was summoned to be told her family's gold in coins, jewellery and ornaments was to be requisitioned. She bowed her head in pretend politeness as a commissar weighed her brooches and rings and pearls, some of them heirlooms. To lose them without payment made her blood boil.

Lubov and Serge had always lived in the comforting belief that noble landowners were enlightened and helpful to the peasants. Now they were branded as evil exploiters. Three members of a single branch of the Obolensky family perished, including a Vladimir, murdered at his estate in Ryazan in February 1918, and an Alexander, an artillery officer shot at the Peter and Paul Fortress at the end of August.

While Serge was away on duty, Lubov and her children spent nights in Petrograd nervously on edge, listening to shooting and peering at menacing silhouettes through the curtains. A daytime walk on the pleasant streets near the Neva revealed boarded-up windows, bullet holes on walls and sad figures selling shoelaces and matches.

Armed Bolshevik confiscators roamed from house to house, lecturing anyone who refused to hand over belongings on their 'lack of consciousness'. Years later, when Lubov explained to Alex why the family chose to flee, she described a confrontation with a murderous invader. It was a story Alex passed on to his friends at Oxford University: how his 'mama' was 'held up at the point of a revolver in the hand of a fanatical revolutionary', a commonplace event in the febrile atmosphere of the times. Men wearing peaked caps on their heads and stubble on their chins rifled through cupboards and drawers, swiping possessions as they pleased and making snide comments about 'offerings to the dead tsar'.

Some time during the autumn of 1918, the Obolenskys decided to escape.

Gallingly to Serge, he was paid a degree of respect by the Reds due to his military service, and because the family name had a kind of political cachet derived from Eugene Obolensky's role in the Decembrist revolt of 1825. Eugene was exiled to Siberia to 'count trees' and eventually pardoned to join the army as a plain soldier, earning a commission for his bravery and the return of his title with 2,000 serfs.

Serge's valet said he had an 'in' with the powers-that-be, and offered a pass signed by Lenin that would enable Serge to fill a truck with his family's possessions. Serge spat out his refusal. 'I'd rather lose everything than make a deal with these traitors,' he said. Four decades later, when Nikita Khrushchev was president of the Soviet Union, and Serge was living in London, he received an official invitation to 'come and visit' his old estates. Serge ripped the paper up, saying: 'I shall never accept a Bolshevist invitation to my own home.'

There were several possible escape routes. The Germans' presence in Kiev to the south-west attracted some families from Moscow, while others looked south to the Crimea. Many in Petrograd looked north to Finland and then Sweden. The Obolenskys were guided to Riga in Latvia – and in this mad, mixed-up world, they found themselves in the hands of the Germans, who were in control of the Baltic states.

How Lubov and her family, without Serge, made their way to Riga is not documented, but the most likely method was by the '*regelmäßiger baltischer Flüchtlingszug*' ('regular Baltic refugee trains'), reported by Latvian newspapers as departing from Petrograd every weekend and organised by the German Baltic Committee. To secure a place it was necessary – as Stella Arbenina explained in her 1929 book, *Through Terror to Freedom* – to find Alexander Roth, a member of the committee, in his office on the Fontanka embankment. Lubov's connections in Latvia through Serge's mother probably assisted with the travel documents. 'The general opinion is the Bolsheviks can't last more than two or three months, and you might be back in Petrograd by Christmas,' Roth said. 'But things are sure to get worse before they get better.' Roth had 3,500 applicants, when 3,000 should have been the limit. He told the travellers not to take too much luggage as the 'unlucky' trains were being raided by the Communists. The émigrés would be quarantined in a *lager* camp upon reaching Riga.

The three generations of the Obolenskys packed sparingly: clothes, underwear and a couple of thin mattresses tied up with string. Luxuries such as oil paintings were left behind or sold quickly at pathetic prices. The family dressed shabbily, hats over their eyes. We do not know the day of departure, but it would have been early morning when they set off for the Warsaw Station near the Griboyedov Canal in the south-west of Petrograd.

Well-off families used to sweep through the grand entrance of the Warsaw Station to take *'trains-de-luxe'* to Paris, or the French beach resorts, or London. The Obolenskys also knew the Nicholas Station as the starting point for trips to Moscow on what was said to be the straightest railway track in the world, because Tsar Nicholas I had placed a ruler on a map and said: 'That's the way I want it.' Bells would ring at intervals in the minutes before a train's departure, then three times just before the train began to move.

There were no cheery bells now, just a huge courtyard seething with people and suitcases and bits of property from kitchen utensils to iron bedsteads. The refugee trains were formed not of pretty passenger carriages but dark red cattle vans, in which wooden boards were wedged onto beams to make two 'floors' of makeshift bunks. Each van was packed with up to 36 travellers.

Almost from the day they were invented, railways have transported the downtrodden and desperate. The train chugged out of the station late at night, its chain-links clanking. There was one route from Petrograd, at the eastern end of the Gulf of Finland, to Riga, roughly 350 miles to the south-west, via Pskov and a small patch of Estonia. Ordinarily it was an overnight journey. It took the refugee train four days and four nights.

The train crept along for an hour or two, and then stopped for a similar period, and the occupants stretched their limbs in fields and emptied their bladders. Bemused babies and toddlers cried, and the air inside the vans grew increasingly foul. At some of the stops Bolshevik troops boarded and demanded documents. A passenger muttered: 'We know the Bolshevik army is well organised – Lenin has forced the old generals to lead it.'

Families got talking, swapping stories. If there was any worth to the revolutions or the rhetoric of the Communists, these people did not care. They had been denounced along with the so-called alien classes, which included priests, teachers and Cossacks, to be robbed and murdered while the proletarians or 'toilers' were gifted the good things in life. A new creed had replaced God and monarchy, and it was: 'Rob the robbers!'

At every stop, Lubov peeked through the van doors to see if they would be getting out. At one, there was a shout from a German officer, and the refugees were led to sheds where long tables were laid for dinner of a bowl of soup, a chunk of black bread and some meat.

Each person was given a parcel on which was written: 'A gift of welcome from the Kaiser.' The German national anthem was played and the refugees were obliged to stand. They all blamed the German Kaiser for the Great War; now they observed the singing of his praises. 'Every time I see a German uniform, I want to spit,' said a passenger. 'Yet I am grateful to them, too.'

There were more German troops at the Latvian frontier, then at last they reached Riga, and the *lager* of barns, each containing hundreds of people perched on two levels of straw-covered benches. The noise and smell were overpowering.

The Obolenskys waited for the next move, probably for a couple of weeks. On 29 December they were told to go down to the Daugava River, where they found the *Princess Margaret* easily enough, close to a spot next to Riga Castle where German warships had stood five abreast a few months earlier. The family joined the queue for the gangplank and their British deliverance to an uncertain future.

CHAPTER 3

VOYAGE TO FREEDOM

To LUBOV OBOLENSKY, the ship resembled the steamer the tsar had once toured Russia in, although a giveaway clue was the exterior paintwork of the Royal Navy's 'dazzle' camouflage of irregular stripes and swirls.

The *Princess Margaret* and her sister vessel, the *Princess Irene*, had been built by the Canadian Pacific Railway Company in 1914 for pleasure trips they would never undertake.[1] Following the outbreak of war in Europe, they were taken and converted into minelayers by the Royal Navy, which needed vessels larger and quicker than the British cross-Channel steamers to lay mines in the North Sea. By early 1915, each of the Princesses was refitted with two 4.7-inch guns, two 3-inch guns and the capacity to lay 400 mines.

The ship should have been carrying cheery tourists on the waterways of Vancouver and British Columbia. Instead, of the five decks for passengers and crew, the upper and main decks were mostly cleared to accommodate the huge, bulbous mines, which rolled on tracks out of holes cut in the stern.[2] It was perilous work, and the *Irene* blew up in the Medway Estuary in May 1915, with the loss of 300 lives. Now her surviving sister's 127 cabins were filled with 392 passengers, including 169 women and 80 children, from almost every European nation. Some of the refugees were obliged to sleep between decks.

How the British came to be in Riga was a saga symbolising the complexity of European politics at the time.

There had been Baltic Germans in Latvia since the 13th century, and Russia had been shot through with German influences for decades. There was a fear that even if the Great War ended in an

Allied victory, Germany might absorb the vast territories of Russia and Siberia, and build again to dominate Europe. The Russian empire had been Britain and France's most important ally.

Then there were the royal family ties between the competing powers. Britain's King George V was a first cousin and near doppelgänger of both Tsar Nicholas II and Kaiser Wilhelm II. The Tsarina Alexandra, Nicholas's wife, was a German by birth, and a granddaughter of Britain's Queen Victoria. She was Alix of Hesse and by Rhine before her inception into the Russian church.

In 1914, when Britain went to war, there were anti-German riots and attacks on German products even though the Saxe-Coburg-Gothas were residents of Buckingham Palace. In July 1917, George declared the 'discontinuation of all German titles', and he and Queen Mary created the House of Windsor.

By spring 1918, the Allies were straining to defeat the Germans on the Western Front and they were horrified when the Brest-Litovsk treaty allowed Germany to transfer forces across from the east. Meanwhile, King George approved a plan for his Russian cousin Nicholas to escape to asylum in Britain, only to withdraw the offer over fears the mere presence of the tsar might spark a workers' uprising. Antipathy towards the Bolsheviks was heightened by a Cheka raid on the British embassy in Petrograd on 31 August and the killing of Captain Francis Newton Allen Cromie, the much-decorated naval attaché who was the most senior diplomat left in the city.

When the German army had taken Riga in September 1917, thousands of Latvians fled into Russia. Some formed riflemen units in the army and some of those were radicalised to the Bolshevik cause. When the First World War ended with Germany's surrender in November 1918, the Bolsheviks vowed to regain Russia's lost lands. Lenin declared: 'The Baltic must become a Soviet sea.'

The British government wanted Estonia, Latvia and Lithuania to be independent, and the First Armistice demanded Germany evacuate its troops from occupied Russian lands – but only as soon as the Allies deemed it appropriate. Latvia proclaimed independence while, in Estonia, government leaders were released from prison to resume power. Britain wanted to defend its position, but not with an infantry campaign so soon after the Armistice, and the War Cabinet sent the Royal Navy instead. So began a supposedly post-war period up to January 1920 in which the Royal Navy was operational in the Baltic.

In December 1918, the Bolsheviks were advancing on Riga, and the Germans, who had a volunteer National Guard, the *Landeswehr*, decided to withdraw. The British began to conceive the idea of an evacuation of refugees – and it had to happen before the eastern Baltic froze over.

On the 17th, Rear-Admiral Edwin Alexander Sinclair led two cruisers, seven destroyers and the *Princess Margaret* towards Riga. They entered the Daugava and began to unload weapons to the Latvians, although Sinclair cautiously retained 15,000 of his 20,000 rifles on board. Eventually, *Princess Margaret* landed marines on 27 December and, accompanied by an armed party from the *Ceres*, they marched through the town. The following day frightened British subjects began to board the *Princess Margaret*.

On 29 December, HMS *Ceres* opened fire on the barracks of Latvian mutineers who were hoping to merge with the Bolsheviks; the Bolsheviks had closed to within 10 kilometres of the city. The British continued to land armed parties on defensive patrols and launch star and lyddite shells, while keeping anxious watch for the approaching ice. The purpose now was to collect as many fleeing British subjects and White Russian aristocrats and supporters of the Latvian provisional government as they could, as quickly as they could. *The Times* reported on 2 January 1919: 'A panic feeling is manifesting itself at Riga.'

The departure of the *Princess Margaret* was set for 3 January. The night before, the British patrolled for the last time, before Sinclair withdrew them at 8 p.m. and left the city to looting and arson.

It was 6.30 a.m. when the *Ceres* cast off, followed 22 minutes later by the *Princess Margaret*, proceeding at 10 knots past the low-slung skyline of Riga, distinguished in the Old Town on the east bank by the domed steeples of the cathedral and St Peter's Church. Together with the destroyers *Wolfhound* and *Windsor*, they joined the *Cardiff* and began a 700-mile voyage west to Copenhagen.

At 9.30 a.m. on Sunday 5 January, nearing Copenhagen, a pilot came aboard and some of the refugees disembarked. Rear-Admiral Sinclair regretted leaving Riga to the Reds, but he felt Britain had 'taken the measure' of the Bolsheviks' fleet, Estonia was on the road to freedom, and security in Finland had been increased. At Copenhagen, the fugitives presented a large silver cup to Captain Smyth for his crew's kindness.[3] The next landfall would be in Scotland.

On Friday 10 January, the *Princess Margaret* made a stop-start departure due to thick fog, but the mood on board lightened. The British sailors arranged concerts and dances, and played with little Alex Obolensky and the other children, and the passengers arranged the striking of medals as further tokens of thanks. Able Seaman Samuel Wegg, 33 years old, Belfast-born, and recipient of the Distinguished Service Medal in October 1917 for laying mines off German ports, was one who received the 'Princess Margaret's Medal' made of white metal in the shape of a lifebelt, with the name Princess Margaret embossed on it, and the inscription: 'Riga–London 3rd Jany. 1919–17th Jany. 1919 From the Grateful Passengers in Remembrance of their Deliverance from the Bolsheviks.'

At midnight on Saturday 11 January, the crew and passengers put their clocks back half an hour, and at 11 a.m. the ship dropped anchor in Leith roads. Scottish crew members disembarked before the ship set off for its final leg south to London.

The Obolenskys' cabin had been their home for 17 days, 13 of them at sea, but they were made to wait for the final relief. At 10 a.m. on 15 January, they were at Gravesend Reach near the wide mouth of the Thames. At 11.25 a.m. they proceeded upriver to Millwall only to be ordered to return to Tilbury. There, the dock entrance was closed so they waited at Rosherville Pier on the opposite bank, then dropped anchor in Gravesend Reach again. Tower Bridge lay 20 miles upriver, with the mysterious, mighty city beyond.

The ship's logbook, preserved in the National Archives at Kew, gives no explanation for this hiatus. The page for 16 January refers to 'hands employed cleaning ship' at 6.30 a.m., and 'hands to make and mend clothes' at 1.30 p.m. At 6 p.m., an 'alien examination officer left [the] ship' – probably after an inspection of papers. A generally tolerant approach to immigration during the 19th century was hardened in the early 20th century after the 1905 Aliens Act, although refugees were given asylum for religious and political persecution, and subsequent Acts continued to admit favoured members of royalty and the aristocracy and politicians and academics, who were categorised as 'desirable aliens' or 'special cases'.

An 'alien examination officer' was on board again at 11 a.m. on Friday 17 January. A tug boat steered the *Princess Margaret* into Millwall Docks. The passengers could see grubby chimneys and cranes and jetties and barge piers punctuating the river's retaining walls. Then, more waiting, as it became clear they would be aboard for one more night.

The ship moved off again on Saturday 18 January and, just after 9 a.m., the gangplank was finally lowered at Millwall. The sailors said their goodbyes in a spirit made more festive by the knowledge that they were about to receive their quarterly pay and take long-postponed leave. The Obolenskys – Lubov and her mother-in-law, sister-in-law and three children – gathered their pile of belongings and walked tentatively down and onto British soil.

As Alex Obolensky blinked in the morning light of a new country, he stood on the threshold of an unexpected fate: a life to be shaped by forces his family could not predict or control. Of his history and bloodline and heritage, only the legends and the name remained.

CHAPTER 4

PRINCESSES AND PATRONAGE

A S THE OBOLENSKYS settled into London in the spring of 1919, the now three-year-old Alex was introduced to the wider world by a photograph in the *Sketch* and the Scottish *Sunday Post* newspaper. It showed him in a white sailor suit in the garden of a smart house in Onslow Gardens, South Kensington, alongside his sisters Maria and Irena and their parents Serge and Lubov, plus the new arrival Theodore – to be known always as 'Teddy' – who had been born a month earlier. Serge had made it to London via Murmansk or Odessa; his surviving descendants have never been sure which.

The occasion was Teddy's baptism in the house of Hardman Earle and his wife Edith, and the guest of honour was a statuesque lady with close relations in at least eight of Europe's royal families.

Princess Marie Louise was Queen Victoria's granddaughter, daughter of Helena and her husband Prince Christian of Schleswig-Holstein, and first cousin to King George V, Germany's Kaiser Wilhelm II, Queen Victoria Eugenie of Spain, Queen Marie of Romania, Queen Sophie of Greece, Queen Maud of Norway, the Duke of Saxe Coburg and – most relevantly for this ceremony and the Obolenskys' future in exile – the Russian Tsarina, Alexandra Feodorovna. The previous summer, it had been Marie Louise's grim task to take the news of the Romanovs' murder to her cousin Victoria, the tsarina's sister, on the Isle of Wight.

Marie Louise was regarded as a working member of the British royal family and an altruist who had devoted her life to charitable works and patronage of the arts since her marriage to Prince Aribert of Anhalt was annulled 19 years earlier. She and her mother Princess Christian (as Helena was styled) were godmothers to Teddy, and Marie Louise stood, long-nosed and stern-looking under a broad-brimmed hat, and wearing a simple white dress with a decorative bow, to observe the christening ceremony.

In a drawing room decorated with white flowers, Teddy was lowered into a font draped with white fabric, alongside an altar bearing a saintly ikon and several pictures picked out in gold leaf, and lit by candles in silver candlesticks.

For several months now, the British newspapers had carried reports from Petrograd – the old St Petersburg which would be renamed Leningrad in 1924 – of 'people dropping dead' from exhaustion. Medicines were running short, and the peasants producing food refused to take the paper money poured out 'like water' by the Bolsheviks. The only produce reaching the city was snatched by the Red Guards, usually violently.

Hardman Earle, an Eton-educated son of a baronet who had worked in electrical engineering in Russia, had agreed to be a bene-factor to the Obolenskys, but the family needed income and somewhere to live, and Marie Louise was keen to help.

Connections made in old St Petersburg were going to be useful, and Lubov renewed her acquaintance with Lady Georgina Buchanan at the Russian Embassy, Chesham House, in the heart of Belgravia. They had first met at a reception given at Alexander Palace, by Tsarina Alexandra, when Lady Georgina's husband, Sir George Buchanan, was the British ambassador. Before the war the embassy had hosted some of London's most brilliant entertainments. Now its stately ballroom was a kind of sweatshop for the nobility, filled with dozens of female refugees from the Russian civil war being paid six shillings a day to knit and sew 'comforts' – warm clothes, bandages and other Red Cross material – for White Russian troops and pris-oners of war. These ladies' plight was reported in a pathos-laden piece in the *Sunday Post*, and illustrated by the photo of little Alex and his family.

Lubov met Elizabeth Craig, the author of the piece, and volunteered her tale of 'escapes from death' at the hands of the Bolsheviks. 'I saw the Princess . . . just after the christening of her baby,' Craig wrote. 'Delicately fair, with Dresden colouring, she was keenly interested in what her fellow countrywomen were doing, and highly praised Lady Buchanan for the work she was carrying on at the Russian Embassy.'

The work was emergency subsistence instigated by the frizzy-haired Lady Georgina, who had been a rare foreign recipient of the Order of St Catherine for services to Russia, before she and her husband and their daughter Meriel fled in January 1918.

From three refugees at Chesham House in the autumn of 1918 there were now 260: tiny girls learning to knit alongside schoolteachers and princesses who had revelled in the high life when St Petersburg outdazzled most cities in Europe. Many spoke no English; others whispered a half-sentence: 'The things I have seen . . .'

In one corner was a baroness aged 74, and in another three young Russian girls whose family had lived in the Winter Palace but who were now living in one room until they could sell their few remaining jewels. One woman was 'hopelessly disfigured with nervous eczema'; another had 'a look like a hunted animal in her staring eyes'. To Craig, who was the daughter of a Scottish Presbyterian minister, and accustomed to reporting on London fashion and weddings, they looked like 'a hive of white-capped bees'.

The clacking of knitting needles paused for lunch of a bowl of stew or soup with bread and a pudding, prepared in the conservatory turned welfare kitchen. Lady Georgina was looking for funds to continue the work, as her 'salaries' exceeded £200 a week. 'I am incredibly moved by these women's pitiful stories,' she said. 'Some of them hid for days without food in cellars or holes in the ground. One refugee came to me with 100,000 roubles in notes that were worthless. The banks would not look at them.'

Others had met a much worse fate. In February 1919, Lady Georgina received a letter describing the murder of the 30-year-old Princess Nina Galitzine by the Bolsheviks, killed as she attempted to cross into Finland. Her body was found with the fingers and ears cut off, and 300 roubles (£30) untouched in her clothing.

The *Sunday Post* headlined the piece 'Society Queens in Exile – Russian Aristocrats' Humble Life in London', and Craig wrote: 'It is a far cry from Petrograd to London, a still farther cry from mansion to humble circumstances. But the Bolsheviks, with their cruelty, have broken the heart of loyal Russia, and, desperate, her noble sons and daughters have fled to us for refuge. It is a pathetic situation . . . the refugees are flooding in daily. Another safe haven, British-controlled Malta in the Mediterranean, is hospitable but full.'

By summer 1919, Lady Georgina had 530 refugee women in the scheme and she only abandoned it, with regret, when Sir George took a posting in Rome. In September, *The Times* reported 'wholesale executions at Moscow' when the 'Cheka' had summarily shot 67 people, including an unspecified Prince Obolensky. Between 1918 and 1920, there were an estimated 300,000 political executions.

Overall, the emigration from Russia was on a mind-boggling scale, with the League of Nations estimating 1.5 million refugees by the early 1920s. Taking into account the 6.5 million Russians killed or wounded in the Great War, the degree of tumult is staggeringly apparent.

Lubov Obolensky was feisty by nature and she grew only tougher and more opinionated as time went on.

While historians often pay more attention to primogeniture and the male line of a family, various descendants confirm Lubov as the dominant figure in Alex's early years and the family in general. Her challenge in exile was to re-establish the family home she had been creating in Russia – her third daughter and namesake, Lubov, would arrive in February 1921, to be joined eventually by the Obolenskys' sixth and final child, Michael (known as 'Misha'), in 1926.

In early 1920, Lubov took her then four children to Portman

Square, off Baker Street, for portraits at Elliott & Fry, a well-established studio producing photographs of leading figures in London's social scene, the arts, science and politics.

Lubov wore a plain dress of chiffon and silk, with high-heeled shoes. No jewels adorned her neck or wrists, and the laurel wreath around her soft curls of hair was a prop provided by the studio. She took the 10-month-old Teddy on her lap, and perched two-year-old Irena on the side of the chair. Standing to the right were Maria, in a plain white dress with matching ankle socks and shoes, and the four-year-old Alex, his hair newly cut in a straight fringe and his upper lip pouting over protruding teeth. He wore the dark blue sailor suit beloved of many a mother in London since Queen Victoria had dressed her sons in the same.

To look at the photos now is to guess at the family's feelings. Little Irena – who was born in Luga 19 months after Alex and would be his closest sibling in terms of emotional character – has her eyebrows raised, as if in surprise. Five-year-old Maria, or 'Masha', fixes her attention on the man with the camera. She is destined for a life troubled by depression. Baby Teddy is the only one apparently at ease. Alex has a nonplussed or even mournful look, as if worried or disconcerted. The feet that will one day fly across the turf at Twickenham are cocked awkwardly at the ankles as he leans into his 'mama'.

Lubov's eyes are doleful but there is defiance and maybe anger, too. Always in the background was the knowledge that her life might have been very different. A few years before her marriage to Serge, a grand duke's son named John Constantinovich was infatuated with Lubov. He called her 'Lyubochka' and decided she loved him, and the Russian law about marrying out of one's royal station could go hang. 'I fell in love with many, but this is the first time in my life that a girl fell in love with me,' he wrote to his father. Constantin Constantinovich opposed the union, however, and John married the daughter of a Serbian king instead.

A photo of Lubov from the Elliott & Fry shoot appeared in a March 1920 edition of *Tatler* and on the gossip page of the *Daily*

Mirror, captioned: 'Princess Obolensky, who escaped from Bolshevist Russia after terrible experiences, is very popular in London.'

Popular, maybe, but the family were almost penniless, too. Alex would write later of how his parents initially believed or hoped it would be a 'matter of weeks or, at the worst, months before Russia would stop bleeding and resume her normal healthy state'. While they waited, Serge started life again in a Britain whose attitude to Russia's civil war was non-interventionist amid the dread of a spread of Bolshevism, with the domestic Labour Party rising to the anthem of 'The Red Flag'. The Obolenskys were free to work, and to reside wherever they liked, but they were in a poor position to exploit those rights. Lubov felt no affinity with the thousands of Russian-descended Jews in London's East End, despite their shared experience of a flight from persecution in the 19th century. She urged her husband to take matters in hand. 'How about seeing Vladimir Emmanuelovich?'

Vladimir Galitzine and his wife Countess Ekaterina Gräfin von Carlow were living at Chessington Hall in Surrey and had a farm nearby with pigs and poultry. Ekaterina, or Catherine, also tried establishing a finishing school for girls. They had fled Russia via Constantinople in April 1919 on the British ship HMS *Grafton*, a day after HMS *Marlborough* carried away what was left of the imperial family.

Vladimir, a squat man with a bent nose and a thick, dark moustache, invited Serge to spread straw and feed geese and pick turnips, and the royal pair were filmed as obvious curiosities by Pathé News: 'Russian princes and generals working as farm hands in Surrey!'

When the pigs contracted foot-and-mouth disease, Vladimir gave up the farm and became an antiques dealer in Paris. In any case, going back to nature was not Serge's line of country. He clung to memories of parties and parades and everything else that had been his gift and duty to bequeath to his son. He looked up another old friend: Eugene Sabline, chargé d'affaires at the Russian Embassy and a contemporary when they graduated from the Lycée Impérial Alexandre in St Petersburg in 1898. Temporarily, Serge worked in the Department of Personal Composition and Economic Affairs, then in October 1921 Sabline typed a letter of commendation:

> To all whom it may concern, I beg to certify hereby that Prince Serge OBOLENSKY is personally well known to me and I do not hesitate to recommend him as being a thoroughly reliable and trustworthy person.
>
> After having successfully terminated his studies in one of Russia's best Universities – the Lycée Impérial Alexandre in Petrograd – he joined the Army and served in the Imperial Horse Guards.
>
> During the revolution Prince Obolensky was obliged to escape from Russia with his wife and children, taking refuge in England in very precarious material circumstances.
>
> For more than a year he was employed at the Russian Embassy in London where his services have been much appreciated.
>
> The Prince speaks several European languages fluently.

The Obolenskys continued fretting until a request from the Grand Duchess Xenia Alexandrovna, made via Princess Marie Louise, drew a response from a wealthy industrialist-philanthropist from Yorkshire.

Francis 'Frank' Green was the grandson of an ironmaster who had made a fortune patenting 'Green's Economiser', a system of recycling wasted heat from boilers that was shown at the Great Exhibition at Crystal Palace in 1851 and soon used in many countries, including Russia. When Frank's father, Sir Edward, died in York in 1923, his brother Edward Lycett Green succeeded to the title of second baronet and Frank became chairman of the family company.

By 1920 Frank was aged 59, eccentric and well-connected. A smartly dressed dandy, fond of floppy bow ties, he collected powerful friends and motley antiquities. At his Treasurer's House in York in 1900 he had hosted the Prince of Wales, soon to become Edward VII, his wife Alexandra and their daughter – enabling Frank to proudly rename the rooms they stayed in as the King's Room, the Queen's Room and Princess Victoria's Room.

Frank donated to good causes and public works, including the upkeep of York Minster, and in his spare time he drove Rolls-Royces round Europe. He never married but he mentored young people. When he went to live in Somerset in 1930, he gifted Treasurer's House to the National Trust and left his Rolls-Royce to his chauffeur, who operated it as York's first black cab.

Green owned properties around England and, to the relief of the Obolenskys, he moved them into Beresford Manor, a pretty 17th-century house near the village of Hartington on the border of Staffordshire and Derbyshire in the English Midlands.

Green also struck a deal with Serge Obolensky that changed the family's lives, ensuring Alex would be educated in the English public-school system and put on the road to his sporting success.

The arrangement between Green and Serge was fundamentally pragmatic. Hereditary nobles in Russia had bought and handed down vast estates and forests and farms all over the empire, and Serge's mother Maria Nikolaevna Trigoni inherited an *osobnyak*, or large wooden house, plus 200,000 roubles from an aunt in Moscow. Over the years Maria invested in various properties and estates, but in 1912 or 1913 she made her most successful purchase: the estate she bought for Serge in Alexandrovka in the Urals, with a mortgage and 200,000 roubles borrowed from Nina. It ranged over 27,000 acres – around 42 square miles – and it was flourishing with a distillery, a brickyard, a brewery and a railway. Serge agreed to 'pre-sell' this estate to Green, who would pay an allowance in return every month.

According to Felizitas Obolensky, née Joerchel, who became the second wife of Alex's youngest brother Michael in 1967, Green and an associate (possibly Hardman Earle) had a plan – a gamble, really – that their monthly outlay would eventually be paid back at a handsome profit by gaining the ownership of the land, assuming its return to Serge under some as yet unknown transformation in Russian politics.

Instead, the defeat of the White Army and the establishment of the Soviet Union meant the gamble came to nothing. Serge eventually told Green the estate would never be coming back and that the payments ought to cease. In the meantime, the Obolenskys existed on the allowances, and Serge took a job as a representative of Green & Son engineers in France. He and Lubov moved there in 1925, only returning to London in late 1936. Family records of their time in France are sketchy, but it appears Michael was born in Lille, in 1926, and the family also lived in Paris and at Rue du Pensionnat in La Mulatière, Lyon.

Alex would later mention visits to all three cities, including ad hoc Russian places of worship in the attic of a large house in Lille and two rooms in a block of flats in Lyon, but his formal education was always in England.

Green also began paying for the schooling of the Obolensky children, and when Alex was seven years old, in 1923, he was sent to the Ashe Preparatory School for Boys in the village of Etwall, 27 miles from Beresford Manor and seven from Derby.

CHAPTER 5

PREP SCHOOL AND GUARDIANS

T O JU D G E B Y the photo of Alex wearing his uniform at Ashe School, he could be any English prep-school boy, in his striped tie and simple blazer with a crest on the pocket depicting the leaves of an ash tree, with his side-parted hair cut to a regulation short back and sides. The establishment set in a moderately stately Victorian manor house, in 18 acres of grounds, attracted Serge and Lubov Obolensky with its proximity to Beresford Manor and its Christian ethos – but it was also a school in love with sport.

Cornelius John 'C.J.' Corbett, the headmaster during Alex's time, had been an accomplished county cricketer for Derbyshire and a very good hockey player, too: a centre-forward for Derby Mercians and the Midlands, who represented England in 1910 and 1911. The son of an Oxfordshire vicar, he served in the Honourable Artillery Company in the Great War, then took on the headship at Rycote School in Derby.

Alex played football in the winter season, and it would be claimed by the *Sunday Express* sports reporter Leo Munro in 1938 that while Alex was at Ashe he 'wanted to play soccer some day for Derby County'. Finding his feet literally and metaphorically, Alex may well have dreamt of joining the nearest professional club. Derby County were promoted to the top division of the Football League in 1926, and runners-up in 1929–30. Alex enjoyed cricket, too, in the Ashe team expertly looked after by C.J. Corbett.

Quite when Alex started out in rugby is unclear, although there is a brief clue in an edition of the *Isis* – one of two long-standing

Oxford University periodicals – from January 1936: 'Alex's first game of Rugger, at his prep school, was not a success: for two months afterwards he had to go about with his arm in a sling.'

In pre-revolutionary Russia, Alex's life would have been moulded by servants and a sprawling family replete with aunts and great-aunts. He would also have been looked after by a *diadka* – a sort of valet crossed with a personal fitness trainer – and in summers he would have frolicked among 'courtyards flooded with sunlight, circular lawns with scorched grass, yellow charabancs with coachmen in canvas coats'.[1]

He would probably have followed his father to the Lycée Imperial Alexandre and into the cavalry, or become a government martinet. Above all, perhaps, he would have been raised as a Russian-Orthodox Christian, learning the catechism in class, attending Vespers on Saturdays and Mass on Sundays, and going to confession without fail before Easter.

At his pastoral and semi-rural Derbyshire prep school, Alex's upbringing was overseen by male clerics and teachers. On any given Sunday, he would don a round straw hat and make the one-mile march with his school pals down Ash Lane and over the Etwall Brook to St Helen's Church in the village, and the Church of England service held there. Six steps led up to the entrance of the squat, rectangular building, and an imposing stone column topped by a cross. Alex could trace his finger over an inscription chiselled into the plinth: 'TO THE GLORIOUS MEMORY OF THE MEN OF THIS PARISH WHO FELL IN THE GREAT WAR 1914–1918.' There were 19 names on the other side of the plinth, and another six would join them after the Second World War.

Alex would only comprehend it later in life, but Ashe's Anglican code made him wrestle subconsciously with the different branches of the Christian faith.

He would write: 'The silver spoon was in my infantile mouth in 1916 when I was baptised in the Greek Orthodox Church [historically, the term "Greek Orthodox" was used as a catch-all for every Eastern Orthodox Church, as a nod to their roots in the Byzantine Empire].

'Barely three years later, my parents landed in England deprived entirely of former wealth and position, but still in possession of young Alex who then little realized that the silver spoon had been rudely and roughly torn out of his mouth, never to be replaced.

'Every good orthodox Christian child goes through a fairly extensive course of religious instruction. This was not to be my lot, especially in a foreign land which contained but one Russian Church [in London].'

Russians in exile clung to their religion as the 'centre of everything'.[2] It was also a vicarious antidote to their impoverished state, as Orthodox places of worship tended to be lavishly decorated, with Russian music ever-present. Alex probably rose to bouts of classroom teasing. 'My family owns two estates back in Russia, I'll have you know! One of them is the size of Yorkshire!' But he had not seen this land since he was two years old, and never would do again.

It is not clear from the records kept by Alex's surviving relatives how often he was able to cross to France to be with his parents, but they spent long periods apart and, considering they were already coping with their dislocation as refugees, it was far from a settled family life. Whether this made Lubov, in particular, more or less protective towards Alex is open to question.

During at least some of the school holidays, Lubov and Serge passed Alex into the care of an altruistic and devoutly Christian couple living a mile outside the village of Chaddesden, 10 miles from Etwall. Charles Carlin was an ecclesiastical artist, a staunch Catholic who had served overseas and run concert parties in the Royal Army Medical Corps. His wife, Lilian, was the Anglican daughter of Sir Thomas Isaac Birkin, a wealthy lace manufacturer, and she had been made an OBE for her Red Cross work during the Great War. Together the Carlins were arch-philanthropists, who looked after convalescing children from poor homes for a couple of weeks at a time.

Today the Carlins' house at Moor Grange on the Morley Road is a convent; the *Derbyshire Daily Telegraph* in 1930 described it as 'eight acres of fairyland' overseen by 'two people of love and imagination . . . not for themselves, although they share it, but for a succession of white-faced children, in order to bring roses back to their cheeks . . . nearly 300 children in the past seven years since the fairy godfather and godmother decided Moor Grange was just the house they wanted to make a dream come true.'

To the 10-year-old Alex, Moor Grange was a surrogate estate, and the fascinating home and eclectic family of Lilian Carlin, who was 50 years old when he first came to stay, would do much to open his eyes to the stimulations and moral vagaries of the wider world. He made a number of visits throughout his schooldays and into his first year at university, and learnt that his altered circumstances as a refugee need not be a bar to mixing in glamorous company.

Screens in the rooms of Moor Grange were decorated with the tale of Goldilocks and the Three Bears, painted by Charles. The walls and furniture were decorated in blue for peace and happiness, and gold for sunshine. There were meadows of buttercups, a walled garden, pavilions, an apiary and an apple orchard. A signpost on the road outside read: '20 miles from anywhere' and '50 miles to nowhere'. Live-in pets included a parrot, an enormous black cat, and Prince, a war horse rescued from being sold off for meat. Ducks and chicks were penned in the orchard. A renovated lodge housed 'weary and lonely business girls' in the summer. A statue of St Francis of Assisi overlooked games of croquet, swings and a see-saw, and a stretch of smooth lawn across which Alex jumped and sprinted. Daily prayers were said in a small chapel, with an organ played by Lilian and an altar on which Charles had painted a copy of Da Vinci's *Last Supper*. Their motto adapted from the gospel of Matthew was: 'Inasmuch as ye have done it to one of the least of these little ones, ye have done it to me.'

The Carlins gave Alex his first tiny taste of celebrity status. In January 1929, there was a fundraising bazaar at St Mary's, and on a kind of theatre bill printed in the local newspaper, 'Prince Alexander Obolensky' had a line of his own. There were elements of society and sporting glamour in Lilian's wider family. Her nephew Peter Birkin was captain and later president of Nottingham rugby club (known then as Notts), which was probably the route to Alex eventually playing a few matches for them while he was at secondary school. Lilian's godson, Sir Henry Birkin, nicknamed 'Tiger Tim' in the press, raced fast cars and represented an English ideal of power, speed and daring. One of her nieces was Winifred May Birkin, better known by her married name of Freda Dudley Ward – mistress of David, the Prince of Wales.

Whenever Alex was described later in life as possessing a lightness of spirit, part of it must be ascribed to the Carlins and their connections. In November 1948, the Bishop of Nottingham presented the couple with Papal awards. Lilian received the Cross 'Pro Ecclesia et Pontifice' and Charles was made a member of the Order of St Gregory the Great (Civil Division).

CHAPTER 6

TRENT AND TRIES AND LESSONS IN RUGBY

WHEN IT WAS time for Alex to leave Ashe, his family lacked the funds and connections to contemplate a top public school like Eton or Harrow; he was sent to the all-boys' Trent College, in Long Eaton near Nottingham, 30 miles from Beresford Manor. The fees of £120 a year were taken care of by Frank Green, a donation from C.J. Corbett and a large scholarship.[1]

Alex arrived aged 13 in September 1929, to be met by the encouraging sight from the driveway off Derby Road of a pristine cricket field. Behind that were the main buildings, centred on a huge, ornate chapel and imposing clock tower. The chapel's wooden door was where Trent College's fantastically successful rugby team would pose for group photographs, underneath an inscription carved into an arch of yellow stone: 'Seek the Lord and his strength – Seek his face evermore – for the Lord never faileth them that seek him.'

Around the corner, and at the bottom of a short slope, the flat and lush rugby pitch would be Alex's stage as the try-scoring star of the Trent College first XVs of 1932–3 and 1933–4, whose record-breaking feats have never been bettered at the school. Across those two seasons Trent played 37 matches, with 34 wins, one draw and two losses, scoring 1,028 points and conceding 98. And when you consider the team's record from 1914 to 1969 was 236 wins and 344 losses, the outstanding success during Alex's two years in the sixth form is obvious.

There were four principal influences on this success and the nurturing of Alex's talent, and the greatest of these was Geoffrey

Bell, the headmaster. The son of an Old Trident (a former pupil of Trent), he held a Military Cross from the Royal Artillery Regiment in the Great War and he had been head boy at Repton School under two headmasters who became archbishops of Canterbury. In 1927, at the age of 31, Bell was Trent College's first lay headmaster since the school's foundation in 1868. Nevertheless, Trent was solidly Church of England.

Bell had won a blue for cricket at Oxford (sportspeople who represented either Cambridge or Oxford won the right to wear the university colours, dark blue for Oxford and light blue for Cambridge), and played briefly for Derbyshire. He was a passionate enthusiast for sport; an advocate of the power of teamwork and a shared sense of purpose. With his full head of hair tapering sideways to a faintly foppish point, and puffy bags under his eyes, he was a regular spectator in his greatcoat on the touchlines of Trent's rugby matches, cheering the team on.

Bell brought modern methods from teaching at Christ's Hospital and in Canada, and he admired Kurt Hahn, the German-Jewish refugee who founded Gordonstoun School. Still the overriding tone at Trent was the 'muscular Christianity' that had dominated English public-school education since the early 19th century. At the morning and evening services in the chapel, Bell's writings and sermons were serious and moralistic. He steered the school through the Depression following the Wall Street Crash of October 1929, as numbers fluctuated up and down from 152 to around 200 by the time he left in 1936.

Trent's facilities were a mix of the spartan and handsome: large dormitories with no curtains or carpets and washbasins lined up at one end, gas lighting on the blink, and boys earning certificates as 'navvy millers' by levelling the sports fields, wheeling big barrows of soil. Alex mucked in with the construction of a new library, digging the earth and heaving bricks to the site.

He was given the Trent handbook, stuffed with rules: 'The lavatories are out of bounds except for the business for which they are intended'; 'The headmaster's garden is out of bounds, except on

Sundays, or on weekdays for purposes of tennis or photography'; 'Boots must be on and properly laced up by 7 a.m.', 'Wearing stockings without garters is penal', and so on.

Physical exercise was hard going. 'The rule of a dip under cold water in the morning which so closely concerns the manhood of Tridents, is absolute,' the rulebook stated, and those dips in the open-air pool were often taken naked. A picture of dispirited boys at a cross-country run appeared in the *Nottingham Guardian* on 1 April 1931, captioned: 'Not a trio of Bedouins but competitors who found protection from the icy blast in heavy motor rugs.'

Less onerously, there was a well-equipped engineering shop, a full-sized snooker table and a heavily stocked armoury.

From reveille at 6.30 a.m. to lights-out for Middle School at 9.15 p.m. or Upper School at 10 p.m., Alex's curriculum covered English, mathematics, history, modern languages, science, French, music, reading and Divinity – and it was all founded on Christian principles.

Bell's right-hand man was the Reverend G.J.S. Warner, second master and chaplain from 1901 to 1951, and a venerable, dog-collared figure known by Alex's time simply as 'Daddy', whose study was a treasure trove of pictures, tobacco pipes of all sizes and, formerly, Barnabas, a tame boa constrictor.

Warner directed the Trent boys' energy into treks to Land's End and John O'Groats, and skating parties and the building of bridges over the nearby river. Spiritually, he explained to Alex, the Church of England had no objection to this son of the Orthodox church taking Communion in the school chapel. 'It was delightful not to be considered a heretic,' Alex wrote later.

Alex knew Holy Communion in the Russian Church could be taken only after a confession had been made and the priest had given absolution, and he thought there was something 'very sacred' about that service, and it was of more spiritual value than the Protestant equivalent where 'the Communion is merely a symbol of the Last Supper'.

In his mid-teens Alex went through what he termed his 'atheist stage', partly out of resentment at the order to attend chapel twice a day when he preferred the voluntary Communion early on Sunday mornings. 'I feel sure that if the words "you should" were substituted for "you must", a far better effect would be produced,' he said.

Alex and a pal wrote an article aimed at exposing the supposed irrationality of the Bible. They picked out what they regarded as absurd texts and attempted to debunk them. 'Let's disprove the Nativity,' said Alex. 'It only needs us to ask our generation what they would hold if a virgin gave birth to a child.' He thought the article would have a profound effect on those privileged to read it.

Warner possessed the certainty of faith to dismiss Alex's misgivings, but in one end-of-term sermon, he exhorted Trent's students not to neglect their church attendance when they went out into the world. Warner said: 'I am afraid that some of you will only enter a church twice more – when you are married and when you are buried.'

Rugby union in the 1930s was characterised by play that was 'excessively defensive. Forwards were spread out all over the field to counter any move of the backs and only men of genius . . . could make any real impression on these blanket defences'.[2]

The Trent team can be said to have possessed collective genius. They went through the 1932–3 season unbeaten, playing 18 matches with 17 wins and one draw, scoring 539 points and conceding just 22. Alex scored 36 tries and revelled in his appearance in reports in national newspapers, even though they named him variously as 'Oberlinsky', 'Ovolensky' and 'Oberlinski'. In the following season of 1933–4, he racked up a school-record 49 tries. Boys from nearby schools scampered in from the Derby Road to watch matches when they knew Alex was playing.

The school's teams in cricket, hockey and rugby were reported in *The Times* and the *Manchester Guardian*, among others, and Alex was involved in them all. In cricket, he was a good wicketkeeper/batsman, eventually in the first XI looked after by M.A.J. Tarver, a balding man with tattooed arms and a fondness for daily cold baths who was also the master of Alex's school house. An innings of 51 by Alex was reported in *The Times* in June 1933, and it helped him earn full colours in the lower sixth. Trent's quarterly magazine, *The Trident*, described him in summer 1933 as 'very useful behind the stumps, but probably would improve with a style which allows quicker movement. Has played several good innings, and has a good drive.'

Alex ran the 100 yards in a school-record time of 10.2 seconds when he was 16 in 1932. By way of context, Jesse Owens in 1933 equalled the world record with 9.4 seconds. In April 1933, Alex represented Trent at the Public Schools Athletics Championships at White City Stadium in London. He had won the inter-house under-15s' quarter-mile in his first year, on 1 April 1930.

The scene is an autumnal afternoon on the rugby field at Trent College. The 15-year-old Alex Obolensky turns an oval-shaped ball over in his hands, watched by a dozen of his teammates. A biting breeze flicks at his blond quiff as Alex lowers his chin slightly and stares warily from his hooded eyes at the overbearing man standing in front of him.

'Now, Obolensky – run straight at me,' barks the Reverend P.C. Matthews, setting himself in a half-stoop, his arms stretched out in front of his body. A dozen of Alex's schoolmates stand by, agog to see what happens next.

Matthews was a housemaster in his mid-thirties with a harsh reputation: stern and Welsh and unmarried, a master of Classics from Brecon with a first-class degree; a martinet given to dreary sermons, and to punishing a minor misdemeanour with six swipes of the cane. Matthews was also devoted to rugby. His colts team of 1930–1, and an unbeaten year of 1931–2, was the source of the great Trent College side to follow. His byword for the game was 'a desire to play it hard and well'.[3]

On this day, the boys were playing a small-sided practice and Matthews was about to mete out a lesson. Alex's remarkable sprinting speed made him a natural choice to play on the wing. He had developed the upright running style for which he would become world-famous, but was less well known for his ability to tackle. Having watched him allow opponents to brush past him, Matthews, who was refereeing, whipped off his bottle-thick spectacles, called the game to a halt, threw Alex the ball and issued his 'run at me' instruction.

Alex barely took a step forward before the teacher slammed a shoulder into his chest, his head to the side of one hip, arms wrapped round the body. As Alex's feet went one way, vertically upwards, his body was slammed to the ground with a heavy thud. 'That's how to damned well tackle,' muttered Matthews in his south Wales accent, as he replaced his glasses.

Alex was winded, but he made no fuss. A couple of the boys helped him up. 'That's the spirit, Obo,' his pals whispered, using the nickname they had coined for their exotic friend.

Alex's reputation grew steadily as he passed into the lower sixth form of 1932–3, and Matthews passed the colts team to M.A. Tulloch, the coach of the first XV.

Tulloch was a former captain of rugby at Bedford School who had played for Durham University. Another persistent taskmaster, he ran gruelling drills every day of the rugby term, from September to December.

The object of the game, as Tulloch saw it, was to attack and to score tries. With the flying Prince Obolensky in his team, it was a sensible theory. Trent's forwards were told to provide the ball quickly and hone their dribbling, while the half backs perfected their passing. 'Always remember Adrian Stoop,' Tulloch said, evoking the words of the much-admired former England fly half. '"The duty of the forwards is to smash up the opposition and get on with the game."'

Tulloch had a practice drill called the 'quick heel', involving the entire team and imaginary opponents. 'Right, you forwards,' Tulloch told the pack, as Alex looked on from the wing, 'I'll toss the ball up, you need to get to it as soon as possible and form a loose scrum then heel it as quickly as possible to the scrum half.' The scrum half was Reginald Sverre 'Reggie' Blix – a tall, lanky lad and one of three big blond brothers educated at Trent who were Norwegians born to an English mother in a family based in Shanghai. The eldest was Peter Blix, the quietly spoken captain of this team.

After the first crack at the task, Tulloch blew his whistle, demanded the ball back and hurled it in a different direction for the forwards to repeat the exercise. This continued for 10 minutes in heavy boots on a heavy pitch, and the physical effort made it seem an eternity. But the exercise reaped rewards in a season that started modestly with an 11–0 win over Ilkeston on 1 October 1932, with tries by the centre John Harrison and Alex's fellow wing, Goodrich, and a goal kicked by Peter Blix. This win was followed in kind against Mr Tulloch's XV (39–5), Derby RFC A (28–0), Derby Borough Police (a 'powerful and heavy side' overrun 35–0) and Broughton Park A (17–5) – Trent's opponents were a mix of school teams and men's sides from Midlands clubs – before a 0–0 draw with Nottingham University on a day of pelting rain.

The unpretentiousness of rugby was seeping into Alex's soul. After training or matches, the boys drank mugs of cocoa and ate sausages and toast and jam, and talked nonsense and the news of the day. Teammates turned into friends, and Trent were a happy side on and off the field.

They included 'Coo' Gerrish, a diminutive defensive rock of a full back and ever-smiling comedian, never upset at the post-match tease: 'Good heavens, Coo, you've done it again – your shorts are as gleaming-white as when you put them on!'

Gerry Bishop, known as 'Bish', was an understated fly half who could catch even the most awkward pass from Reggie Blix, while 'Mac' Sedgwick was a skilful hooker, and the flanker John Kennington was a formidable breakaway forward. Harrison's fellow centre Errol Button was praised by the *Yorkshire Post* in March 1933 for his 'pace, thrust and a devastating tackle'. The same report credited Alex with 'great pace and a remarkable swerve'.

As Alex grew and gained in strength, he filled out in the chest and thighs, and quickened in pace. Everyone knew he owed a good deal to Button's bursts through the midfield, engineering the space for Obo to finish the try with often only the opposing wing and full back to beat. Alex learnt the necessary angles, the swerves inside and out, the straight run and sidestep, the bluffing of an opponent into thinking space had been shut down before realising too late the door was ajar. Harrison was another great foil, rarely passing outside if he had not carved out a good opening. Button and Harrison came very close to England honours in later years, which in itself was unusual for Trent.

The successes continued in November 1932 with five tries for Alex in a 21–3 defeat of Nottingham A, followed by RAF Cranwell's 2nd XV (72–0 with seven tries for Button). The inter-schools fixtures began with Oakham beaten 35–3 and Worksop College 33–0, with Alex scoring four times, followed by various wins including Southwell RFC (54–0; six tries for Alex) and Ratcliffe College, 99–0, when the referee blew for full time five minutes early.

Trent had around 40 boys aged over 16, and when they faced Birmingham's King Edward's School – an institution six times bigger – the scoreline of 16–0 caused consternation at BBC Midlands. The radio announcer exclaimed 'My God!' as he read the result out.

Old Tridents and Weymouth College (Trent's 'sister' school in Dorset, also owned by the Evangelical College and School Company Ltd) were beaten, and in the second of these at Richmond FC in London, Alex dropped a goal in a 14–0 win. A photo appeared in the *Daily Mail* and *Daily Mirror*, and the *Morning Post* praised Tulloch's preparation: 'When a school team comes through a football season unbeaten, and scores over 500 points, it must possess some special qualities . . . They revealed the perfect training which brings a boy back at the gallop to pack down towards the end of the game, and the equally perfect confidence with which a boy can rely on the next man to cover up any "bloomer".'

Tellingly for Alex's prospects, the paean continued: 'There were other traits that should serve them well . . . in senior football. They had been taught to play the ball quickly; they had practical ideas on varying the attack; they never grieved or got rattled over mishaps.'

The team celebrated the end of term with a Christmas 'Rugger Dinner' of grapefruit, roast turkey with bread sauce, potatoes, Brussels sprouts, and Christmas pudding, cream, trifles, cheese and biscuits, and coffee. Alex signed a menu card for a younger pupil with a flourishing underscore.

Pals asked Obo how this compared with Christmas in Russia. 'There would be a big family meal on Christmas Eve with 12 courses to represent the 12 apostles of Jesus. And the pantry would be full of sweets and gingerbread and tangerines and nuts and all sorts.' And he knew Russia's version of Father Christmas was *Ded Moroz* – Father Frost – who had his granddaughter Snegurochka to help. But Alex had not been at home for Christmas since he was two.

CHAPTER 7

CARVING HIS NAME WITH PRIDE

DADDY WARNER HAD a pet project at Trent every November: a huge bonfire to mark Guy Fawkes Day on the 5th by burning the 'villain of the year'. The one in 1933 took Alex and his upper-sixth cohort two weeks to construct, and the identity of the villain tells of the wicked world beyond the school grounds.

It was a 60-foot-high steeple of poplar and birch wood cut from the school's arboretum (itself established by Warner) and bolstered by reclaimed telegraph poles. Alex, now a strapping 17-year-old, shinned up and down to bang in dozens of nails and hang rubber tyres off the sides.

Lashed on near the top was the 'guy' – a wooden figure with splayed arms and a painted-on face. It was Adolf Hitler, the Chancellor of Germany, and the name Warner and his boys gave to the bonfire, in a sign hung from its side, was 'Hitler's Hades'. Twelve months later the tower would be topped with a fresh villain and dubbed 'Mussolini's Madness'.

Geoffrey Bell watched the burning of 'Hitler's Hades' from the nursery and felt 'the awe of watching it slowly catch fire, flare up and fall with a tremendous crash of flames and sparks'.

The Trident tiptoed round the subject: 'Though we are well aware who was intended by the guy, we refrain from giving his name. One never knows in these days who will get a passionate enthusiasm for whom, and there might be reprisals.' Maybe this was to protect the boys already growing up among family and teachers chilled by the lingering shadow of the Great War. A typical example was John

Harrison. His father, 2nd Lieutenant Jack Harrison of the East
Yorkshire Regiment, had already been decorated with the Military
Cross when he was killed charging at a German machine-gun post
at Oppy in France in May 1917, and posthumously awarded the
Victoria Cross. His widow Lilian was supported by a fund for John
to attend Hymers College, followed by Trent.

John would follow his father as an officer cadet at the Royal
Military College at Sandhurst before gaining a commission in the
Duke of Wellington's (West Riding) Regiment. When war broke out
again in 1939, Harrison was in the British Expeditionary Force in
France, and killed in action during the evacuation at Dunkirk on 1
June 1941.

Trent's rugby team attacked the 1933–4 season with only Button
absent among the backs, as he had left the school, but with only
Sedgwick remaining from the previous year's forwards.

By the season's end, they had 34 wins, one draw and two losses,
with a brilliant unbeaten run of 31 games spanning almost two years
that fell to Worksop College by a try to nil (3–0) in November: the
other loss was to Leicester Thursday in February 1934. The team
scored 984 points and conceded 85, and Harrison was the captain
until Alex took over for the two Lent-term matches against Leicester
Thursday and King Edward's.

Alex's tries 'helped pull them [Trent] out of the fire' in close wins
over Corsairs, Nottingham A and Nottingham University. He scored
two against each of Tulloch's XV, Nottingham and Nottingham
University, three each against Broughton Park, Cranwell, Stoneygate,
Ilkeston and Derby, five against Denstone College and six in a 61–3
trouncing of the Old Tridents, when Harrison at centre added two
tries and eight goals.

In later accounts, for all the success, the recollection of the loss
at Worksop College on Saturday 18 November was always prominent.

Canon Frederick Shirley, the hosts' headmaster, led the cheer-
leading, and the time-honoured elements of English public-school

sport were in play: a local rivalry with the schools 45 miles apart and harsh weather, a record to be shot at and a star player who brought the best out in his opponents.

Alex was head of his house and fresh from a hat-trick of tries in a 30–0 rout of Ilkeston. His school had just had the fun of incinerating 'Hitler's Hades', and Trent had thrashed Worksop 33–0 the previous season, when Alex scored four times. On this damp, blustery afternoon, the players in their Cotton Oxford boots shuffled hunch-shouldered out of the changing rooms for the rematch.

Worksop pressed hard for most of the first half and almost worked their captain J.B. Wentworth Smith over, then Alex – who was referred to as 'Obo' in the *Observer* the next day – made a couple of dangerous runs ended by splendid tackles from his opposite number. A few minutes into the second half, Trent conceded the only score: a try by the centre F.T. Hopkinson.

Penned between their goal line and 25-yard line, Trent's boys unleashed their best handling, with Harrison and Button in string mittens at full stretch to manipulate the 'antelope-like' Alex into space on the wing. The home full back Bob Rennie dived to fling Alex into the corner flag and deny an equalising score. It was another lesson for an aspiring wing to learn: the pivotal consequence of being caught by a defender.

That night, at Trent, the corridors were quiet and in the dorms only hushed whispers were heard.

Alex gained his school certificate with the Oxford and Cambridge Examining Board in 1931 and his Higher Certificate in summer 1933, and during his final year he was a pillar of the school, sharing the senior prefects' study with Alec Goodrich, the head boy, and Peter Blix.

In April 1934, on the school's sports day watched by the Right Reverend J. Theodore Inskip – the Bishop of Barking and Trent's chairman of governors – Alex won four events, including a long jump of 20 feet 5½ inches to break the school record. He also took the 100 yards in 10.6 seconds, the quarter-mile in 55.4 seconds and the shot put – or 'putting the weight' – with a distance of 34 feet 4½ inches.

In his final summer of cricket, Alex was 'much above the average' as a wicketkeeper, '[but] his batting has been at times disappointing, since he should be a more consistent scorer; there is a suspicion of a "flourish".'[1] As captain of a first XI with only two wins, Alex made 122 runs in 10 innings, with a top score of 45.

His rugby was much more notable and earned national recognition. Alex was first reserve for the English Public Schools against their Scottish counterparts at Richmond on 1 January 1934, and in April he represented the North's Public Schools in a 19–6 win over the South at Waterloo, though he did not score.

Alex also played senior club rugby before he left Trent College. Assisted by his connection to Notts Rugby Club via Lilian Carlin, he turned out three times for the first XV, all in away matches, against Saracens (one try in an 11–6 win on 31 March 1934, which was Easter Saturday), Derby and Waterloo.

In the December 1933 issue of *Trident*, Wright House had extended a 'hearty welcome' to 'Obolensky II', 14-year-old Teddy, who would eventually follow his brother into the rugby team, without making the same impact. Teddy also played six times for Nottinghamshire from February 1936 to December 1938, and for the Rosslyn Park club.

The siblings played together briefly for Wright House in Trent's inter-house matches of 1934, as Wright won that mini-tournament for the first time. With Bonas at full back, Alex was 'too strong a runner for either of the other Houses to cope with', and he put seven tries and two goals past his pal Bishop and Hanbury House.[2]

Typical of all English public schools, Trent was committed to preparing pupils to serve king and country. The Officer Training Corps (OTC) comprised 150 boys and Alex was promoted from lieutenant-corporal to sergeant in the pre-Christmas term of 1933, along with Harrison, Bishop and Reggie Blix. All four were in the rugby team. Goodrich was the company sergeant major, and M.A. Tulloch was the officer cadet in charge.

On Armistice Day, the corps marched the three-quarters of a mile from the school to Market Place in Long Eaton for the annual memorial ceremony. Trent had a military band in a smart uniform with caps, and Goodrich and his lieutenant corporals played the 'Last Post' and 'Reveille' as Alex and his pals listened to the haunting brass notes and reflected on a war that had ended when they were toddlers, but never left the consciousness of the generation that preceded them. Two weeks later there was an eight-mile march to Castle Donington.

Alex was a good all-round rifle shot, the best at Trent, and he practised on a range next to the lower field. He top-scored for his school in the Bisley Shoot of 1934, leading them to 38th place out of 81 in the National Rifle Association's Ashburton Shield for public schools. There, he rubbed shoulders with boys from Eton, Harrow and Rugby.

Alex considered his promotion to sergeant of the OTC as reaching the 'giddy heights', and he loved wearing a uniform and carrying a rifle. But he soon decided the corps was not a particularly militaristic institution. One afternoon the boys formed a platoon on the cricket field, and Alex looked round and thought 'this is a sloppy bunch of twerps', although he excepted John Harrison.

A ruddy-faced sergeant major bawled: 'Get in step there, you bloody bastards. The Corps is here to teach you how to walk!' Alex wrote later: 'This was practically all it would teach us, as far as modern warfare is concerned. Still, it was a means for the War Office to use up old uniforms and rifles.' He believed OTCs should include 'gas-mask instruction, the art of making gas attacks and all the other useful horrors' in their curriculum.[3]

On every Remembrance Day, the names of Trent's war dead were read aloud on the outdoor terrace. Eighty-three names would be added during the Second World War, and inscribed on a huge stone plaque on the wall of the chapel. It can be seen today and it bears the dedication: 'See that ye hold fast the heritage we leave you.'

Within the school's main building, there is a less obvious memento. At the far corner of the wood-panelled Fenn Room is a bench between the window and a fireplace beneath a pair of photographs of the Reverend Thomas Ford Fenn, the first headmaster, and Mrs Fenn.

In Alex's day this was the 'quiet reading room' and one afternoon he slid onto the bench, fished a knife from his satchel – every boy in the OTC possessed one – and set to work on the window.

His blue eyes narrowed as he drew the point of the blade across the glass in short, screechy scratches. First an 'A', then an 'O', a 'b' and an 'o'... The 'E' and the 'N' were in capitals and, although it was awkward to fashion a proper signature, it was legible when it was finished. 'A Obolensky' had been added to the small cluster of names already on the pane.

Was it a nod to tradition or an act of rebellion? Whatever the case, this was one of many ways in which Alexander Sergeevich Obolensky left his mark on Trent College.

The engraving on the window can still be seen, if the light is right and you know where to look.

CHAPTER 8

UP TO OXFORD

A POPULAR VISION OF Alexander Obolensky was of a wealthy party animal who led the life of Riley while playing dazzling rugby, but there was barely a penny of spare cash in Alex's baggy-trousered pockets as he shoved open the heavy wooden door at the enormous arch-shaped entrance to Brasenose College on his first day at Oxford University in October 1934. A lack of ready money would dominate his everyday existence as an undergraduate, but if your ambition in the 1930s was to play rugby for England, this was a great place to start.

Oxford and Cambridge were the most productive nurseries for the England rugby team at this time, and for several decades before and after. The powerful selectors from the Rugby Football Union watched the universities' matches and picked young men from them directly into the national team. The universities played against top club sides from the start of term up to the Varsity Match, played between Oxford and Cambridge at Twickenham in December, which was an unofficial national trial. Based on that game and two or three trial fixtures of 'Probables' versus 'Possibles', involving 40 or 50 players, the England XV would be picked for the annual International Championship involving matches with Wales in January, Scotland in February and Ireland in March. In certain seasons England had the extra and extremely glamorous challenge of a Test match against a touring side from New Zealand or South Africa.

Brasenose, known colloquially as 'BNC', was constructed of the honey-coloured Cotswold stone that predominated in Oxford's centrally located colleges. As the writer J.B. Priestley noted, even when the sun is obscured and the light is cold, the walls are 'still faintly warm and luminous'. Anyone familiar with the TV series *Inspector Morse* would recognise the scene, as Brasenose was renamed 'Lonsdale' to double as the eponymous detective's former college.

Alex's acceptance there had been a lengthy business. His rugby prowess counted in his favour, as Oxford placed a high premium on sporting talent, and he tried first for St Edmund's Hall, only to fail the standard for a modern-languages exhibition or scholarship. He switched to Brasenose, another college that would value his rugby prowess, and where his uncle Vadim Narishkin – half-brother to Alex's mother – was a lecturer in French. A little nepotism was useful, whether you were in Russia or England.

Vadim had been a captain in the Russian army and he had persevered in his war-torn country for four years after the revolution before he emigrated. He matriculated at Oxford in 1925 and now had a nice house in Church Street in Headington, where he let a studio to Cyril Arapoff, a Russian emigré photographer whose mother was a governess to Vadim's children.

In March 1934, Vadim contacted Charles Sampson, the principal of Brasenose, about a college grant for Alex, laying out the family's distinguished genealogy and parlous circumstances: 'A. Obolensky is the second child of a family of six, all dependent on their father, Prince Serge Obolensky, late of the Imperial Guards, who is now a representative in France of an English engineering firm, Green & Son, Wakefield.

'Prince Serge has in addition to his family an old invalid mother dependent on him. His income is insufficient to meet the expenses of sending his son to Oxford.'

Geoffrey Bell from Trent College supplied testimonials of Alex's conduct. 'I can speak highly of the boy,' Bell wrote. 'He has good intellectual powers, and gained his Higher Certificate last year. He is Head of his house, and has performed his duties to our satisfaction. He is also rather an exceptional Rugby football player, and good at other games.'

Someone needed to pay the annual fees for tuition and lodgings of £230 [the equivalent of £15,000 today], plus living expenses, and as Bell wrote: 'It is so much a case of finance – practically speaking, he has no funds from which to draw.'

Alex tried and failed to obtain a county scholarship worth £100. Bell tried and failed to raise money from a company in the city of London. Then Uncle Vadim found a sponsor in Henry Spalding, who had a family fortune from the manufacture of sports equipment. Spalding was a patron of the Brasenose Boat Club and a former colleague of William Stallybrass, the vice principal of Brasenose, at the Ministry of Munitions. A trust set up by Spalding and his wife Nellie in Oxford promoted 'understanding between the great cultures of the world [through] the study of their religious principles'.

Spalding put up £30 a year to add to any grant the college was prepared to make to Alex. On 9 September, Bell wrote to Sampson: 'There has been a good deal of delay . . . but at last a certain friend who has been very good to the Obolensky's [sic] and employs his father, has promised 130 £ per annum to the boy.'

Once again, Frank Green had come to the rescue, and now just the 'caution money' – a security deposit in case of non-payment of bills – remained. Bell told Alex to ask his family and, after another fortnight's delay, Serge wrote to Sampson from his home in Lyon: 'I will see that it [the Caution Money] is deposited before the term begins. I appoint my brother-in-law, Capt. Narishkine, to act as guardian to my son, Prince Alec Obolensky, while he is at Oxford.' Green had covered this sum too and, at somewhere close to the 11th hour, Alex was enrolled in a degree course in Philosophy, Politics and Economics. It was due to take nine terms over three years. In fact, he would be at Oxford for 12 terms, until the summer of 1938.

One step inside Brasenose's main entrance took Alex into the Gate Lodge, where wooden pigeonholes held the students' incoming mail. Straight ahead was the main quadrangle, the 'Old Quad', a pretty square of neatly mown grass edged by a flagstone pavement. The dormers and little windows of the rooms above were a tableau unchanged from the mid-17th century. The place smacked of privilege, even to a man with a princely background.

Latchkey in hand, Alex climbed the stairs to room 'VII 4' on the second floor, and stepped into the snug quarters that would be his home for most of the next eight months. The main room contained an iron single bed and a fireplace, a chest of drawers, a bookcase with an in-built cupboard and a writing desk with a leather inlay. A tiny ante-room had a small white basin; that would do for his rugby kit and boots.

Three short strides took Alex from the main door to the windows, which had a pair of openers to the left and right, each divided into eight oblong lights. He levered a window ajar and gazed over the quintessential 'Oxbridge' scene. Below was Deer Park, the middle of Brasenose's three quads; straight ahead was the chapel with its stained-glass windows. The Old Cloisters were huddled to the left, and, partly visible beyond the chapel to the right, was the New Quad. The passageway to the chapel had round windows resembling the portholes of a ship. Just as at Trent, the chapel was a centrepiece: a mix of the Gothic and Baroque, with a 200-year-old eagle lectern at its heart.

Alex lit a cigarette and unpacked his suitcase: a couple of pairs of baggy slacks, three cotton shirts, a tweed jacket and a black tie from Trent. He pondered the yellow-painted walls and curtains of plain cherry-red. A decade earlier, these rooms were occupied by Edward Atiyah, a Christian Lebanese student who repapered the walls and spread a leopard skin over the bookcase, topped off by a bust of Dante imported from Florence.

The adornments were long gone, and Alex would not be redecorating. His rooms at £8 per term were the cheapest Brasenose could offer. The most expensive were occupied by a darkly suave individual who carried a little pot of hair oil to the shower block to smooth his receding locks. John Profumo, son of the 4th Baron Profumo, had arrived from Harrow School to read Law the year before, but he quickly switched to Agriculture and Political Economy. He would become an MP at the age of 25, a brigadier at 30, and Secretary of State for War aged 45, before a scandalous resignation amid the Christine Keeler affair of 1963. In this Michaelmas term, Profumo was paying £21 for Room 4 on Staircase V.

Alex knew his room would be cosy enough once the fire was going. He clattered back down the staircase, past the hall where he would take his communal meals. The musty wood was a familiar scent, but the surroundings were more majestic than Trent. Immediately outside was Radcliffe Square, dominated by one of the world-famous sights of Oxford, the Radcliffe Camera, a library with a spectacular dome-shaped cupola covered in silvery-grey lead. It was common for a Brasenose student to regard a blue in sport as a more realistic goal than first-class honours in his studies. Sir Charles Holmes, the director of the National Gallery from 1916 to 1928, and a Brasenose graduate who became an Honorary Fellow in 1931, said: 'As Balliol enlisted clever heads, so BNC enlisted stout arms and legs.'[1]

This is not to say there was an absence of academic rigour. Ian Peebles, a cricketer who went up to Brasenose in 1929, and took 80 wickets to set a record for an Oxford season, was ejected for his exam performance. 'You obtained one per cent on one paper,' he was told by his tutor, 'and were not so successful in the other.'

Brasenose College in the 1930s was shaped not by Sampson, its principal and a devoted churchman, but by 'sozzled dons' such as W.T.S. Stallybrass, the 51-year-old barrister and teacher of Roman Law who was principal-elect when Alex arrived.[2]

Stallybrass was known as 'Sonners' by every student and don. During the Great War, he and his Moravian-Jewish father had altered their surname from Sonnenschein to the English-sounding Stallybrass, but it was the German name that endured.

'Sonners' was Brasenose, and Brasenose was Sonners, from his arrival as an undergraduate in 1906, through his service as vice principal from 1914 to 1936, senior proctor in 1925–6, and as principal from 1936 until his death in 1948, when he fell off a train, returning from a legal dinner in London, having mistaken a carriage door for the lavatory.

A convert to Christianity, Sonners read the lessons in chapel but he was far from pious. Two years before Alex's arrival, he had helped abandon compulsory attendance at morning chapel. Sonners had French Huguenot ancestry on his mother's side, and he disliked social barriers. Brasenose's scholars (who were funded on the basis of academic merit) and commoners (generally those who paid for their own tuition) mixed together, whereas at other colleges they dined on separate tables. Sonners' quarters on Staircase IV were the college's 'engine room . . . fuelled by alcohol and fired by a powerful sense of collegiate pride'.[3]

Anyone fearing an institution of sober scholasticism was disabused by dinners with Sonners, which were actually mammoth drinking sessions. A fellow student made this rough count of liquid consumption at two in the morning: a glass of champagne, two glasses of port, two glasses of brandy, half a glass of chartreuse and three pints of beer.

Still, Sonners would be up for breakfast, barrelling across the quads in his dressing gown and slippers, while the 'scouts' – who were servants employed by the college – brought hot water to the rooms to shave with, and removed chamber pots if necessary. Sonners insisted the scouts, porters, shoeblacks and bedmakers worked hard, but the start to their day was sweetened by a gallon of beer. He once bet a bottle of port that he could state the initials of more than 90 per cent of the members of the college; by tripping up over 44 names, he managed a mere 80 per cent and duly paid up. If Alex gained a fondness in life for pushing every social occasion to the limit, Sonners was partly responsible.

Sonners revelled in Brasenose's rugby stars – men such as Ian 'the Flying Scotsman' Smith and Norman Strong, who played on the wing and at scrum half respectively in arguably the strongest Oxford XV of the inter-war period, in 1923 and 1924. Smith of Scotland scored a record eight tries in the International Championship in 1925, and 24 in 34 Tests from 1924 to 1933, assuring his place in the pantheon of wings.

There had been five Oxford rugby blues in the Brasenose team of 1931–2, and in cricket there were seven Brasenose men in the Oxford team who met Cambridge at Lord's in 1934–5. BNC's new chaplain, Reverend R.H. Owen, had rowed for Oxford in 1910. And the stroke to the Brasenose rowing eight at this time was John Gorton, who would go on to be prime minister of Australia in the 1960s. Asked what he had studied at BNC in the 1930s, Gorton replied: 'Rowing, mainly.'

Other BNC alumni include Colin Cowdrey, the England cricket captain of the early 1960s and, in the 1820s, an Anglican clergyman named William Webb Ellis, who has a much debated place in rugby folklore as the supposed inventor of the game when he was at the school of the same name.

'Sport is a school of courage,' Sonners said. 'It is virtuous and disciplined and free.' He loved cricket and ran various touring teams: the Brasenose Wanderers, the Authentics and the Limpsfield Strollers. A favourite challenge when taking a team to the coast was a race along the seafront in which Sonners ran 50 yards backwards quicker than many could run 100 yards forwards.

Lectures were conducted around the colleges with a tutor for each subject. Alex was supposed to spend an hour a week with each tutor, reading an essay on the book or subject he'd been given to study. One tutor was Jimmy McKie, a twinkly-eyed Liverpudlian who had coxed the Brasenose eight in 1922. Garrulous and kind and prone to confused thinking, McKie was partly responsible for the college's lamentable performance in PPE, with two Firsts between 1926 and 1955. There again, it was a comparatively new subject with fewer candidates than most others. Alex's first public examination, which he would pass in 1935, comprised Latin, French, political economy, and constitutional law and history – the latter dating back to the Magna Carta.

It is fair to say Alex wasn't naturally suited to working 'with his sleeves down', as a Russian might put it, or to 'sporting his oak' – the old Oxbridge term for shutting an external door to concentrate on work or a tutorial. He did not feel hopelessly out of place, intellectually, but he knew where his major talent lay.

CHAPTER 9

MAKING WAVES AT HISTORIC IFFLEY ROAD

OXFORD'S RUGBY PLAYERS were granted a grand theatre to parade their talent: Iffley Road, home ground of the university's rugby club, and a name made famous around the sporting world as the place where Roger Bannister ran the first sub-four-minute-mile on the neighbouring athletics track in May 1954.

Alex's first taste of Iffley Road was in October 1934, for the traditional freshmen's rugby trial on the first Tuesday of term. In the pavilion at the corner of the pitch, the walls beneath the vaulted ceiling were covered with photographs of past university XVs, and some of the world's most celebrated rugby players stared out from the sepia prints, the great England wing Ronnie Poulton-Palmer among them. An open coal fire stood ready for colder days, and spectators milled at the bar, having a drink and a smoke.

In the changing room, Alex made a last adjustment of his laces – tight enough so his new boots would not rub the soft skin on his feet into painful blisters; not so tight as to hamper his running. Someone had suggested a quick sherry would put fire in his belly, so maybe he had the faint taste of the drink on his breath. He pulled on the plain white jersey of Oxford's second-string team, ready to face the first-string and naturally more fancied 'Colours', playing in blue. There were five Brasenose men among the 'Whites' and three in the Colours.

Emerging from the pavilion, with its dainty clock set into the pitched roof, Alex clip-clopped down the brick-built steps, then through the gate in the white, slatted fence. He took a lungful of autumnal oxygen, and broke into a sprint past a couple of teammates

less fussed with showing their paces. A low, covered terrace of spectators' benches stood along the touchline to his left, and the green
spire and square Norman tower of the Greyfriars monastery loomed
beyond the corner flag. The main grandstand stood sentry on the
halfway line to the right, narrow but with a high roof. The pitch
had a slight slope, touchline to touchline.

Alex was accustomed to playing against stronger and older men
from his matches with Trent College and Notts RFC. On some days
the ball would come easily to him, and on others he had to be
patient. On this day, the fledgling students kicked aimlessly until at
last he was lobbed a pass and half a dozen opponents closed in, like
hunting dogs catching the scent of a fox.

Pace and an instant change of direction were givens in Alex's game
by now, and he had developed a firm hand-off. To swerve while
running was barely a conscious decision. As the Colours tacklers
approached, Alex transferred his weight instantly from his right foot
to the left, then pushed hard off that foot to leave the pursuers
grasping a patch of empty air where his torso had been, and get
away for a try.

Noel McGrath, who had propped for Ireland against Wales earlier
in the year, and had five seasons with Headingley and Yorkshire
behind him, had a good match for the Whites, as they lost by a
creditable 15–13. But most of the team were fresh out of school,
and included a tall, sturdy second-row forward with thick, dark hair
and bushy eyebrows, who swooped on a ball squirting out of a rush
of forwards for a good try. 'Well played, Paddy,' someone shouted.

Patrick Canning Wemyss Disney was a celebrated player at
Cheltenham College who had just won a scholarship to Brasenose.
He was a personable chap from classic, English middle-class stock,
a studious thinker on the subjects of religion and politics, and one
of the military-sporty types who were prominent throughout Alex's
life. 'A man's man,' Alex liked to say, while undergrads asked Paddy,
ad nauseam: 'Any relation?' – even though he had only a distant
familial link to Walt Disney, who was finding fame with his Mickey
Mouse movie features at the time.

Paddy was the eldest of four sons of Lieutenant-Colonel Henry Anthony Patrick Disney, who at a young age had served as a pilot in the Royal Flying Corps on the Western Front. All four boys would become officers. The second son, Hugh, was a football blue for three years, and he learnt to fly with the Oxford University Air Squadron before being commissioned into the RAF Volunteer Reserve in March 1938.

Paddy and Alex had been born three weeks apart – Disney in Hertfordshire in January 1916; Obo in St Petersburg on 17 February – and they were to forge such a deep and lasting bond that when the eldest of Paddy's four children was born in London on 15 June 1941, he was named Alexander.

It's worth a brief pause here to revisit the patterns of play in mid-1930s rugby, and how they affected the likes of Alex on the wing.

The offside law stated only that the opposition had to stay behind the ball so, at a scrum, the wing forwards (the flankers of today) often disengaged as soon as they knew possession was not coming out on their side, and could be on top of the scrum half or fly half as soon as he received the ball.

Players kicked to touch from anywhere, without losing ground, and play was restarted either by a lineout or a scrum ten yards in from touch, the side not kicking the ball out having the choice. Such stoppages might number more than a hundred across the 80 minutes of play. Teams tended to kick off to the left, because it invited the defending side to return the ball to the nearest touchline, which gave the kicking-off team a chance to take a scrum near their left touchline. This in turn gave their scrum half feeding the ball into the scrum on the left-hand, 'loosehead' side a chance to set off on a run or make a quick pass when – with a bit of luck – it emerged cleanly out of the rear of the pack. That chance was reduced if all the above took place on a team's right-hand wing, with the scrum half's back to the open field.

There might be up to 50 scrums a match, and if one was wheeled as the team feeding into it wanted, the ball could be held in their pack before any one of the five forwards behind the three in the front row broke off and hacked it on with their feet. This 'dribbling' was highly valued as a rush downfield, closely supported by team-mates, and demanding bravery from any of the defending backs who fell on the ball to kill it in the face of those marauders. Dribbling was more likely to be seen if a pack was set up in the comparatively 'narrow' 3-2-3 formation, rather than the 'wider' 3-4-1 – the difference here being the positioning of two side-row forwards who could pack down in the scrum on either side of the second row with a lock forward behind them to hold the whole thing together (3-4-1), or on either side of the lock (eventually to be known as the No. 8) so as to make a back row in the 3-2-3 set-up.

A quick heel by the hooker out of the scrum could enable a quick transfer of the ball to the three-quarters (the two centres and two wings). Still, precision was demanded of the fly half and centres to take and give a pass in the space of a stride or two as defenders engaged them.

The day after the trial match, *The Times* picked out Micky Walford, the Colours' fly half who had come up from Rugby School, and among the 'other good outsides' was the name of 'A. Obolenski', bracketed with W.N. Renwick, M.D.P. Magill and W.J. Tyson.

Alex snipped the report for a scrapbook he had purchased at Woolworths, and kept another article from the same page that described 'Mr J.D. Profumo (Harrow and BNC)' as 'one of the more famous members of the Oxford University Dramatic Society – he specialises in imitations of Douglas Byng'. Byng was a gay singer and songwriter in West End theatre, 'bawdy but British', and famous for songs full of sexual innuendo and double entendres.

Rugby at Oxford was simultaneously serious and amateurish. The first XV was as strong as any of those of the leading clubs – Richmond, Harlequins, Leicester, Northampton and Sale – or of the teams attached to the London hospitals such as St Mary's and St Bartholomew's, where Harold Geoffrey 'Tuppy' Owen-Smith and Peter Candler, England's full back and soon-to-be capped fly half respectively, were studying medicine.

Student rugby players were fit by the standards of the time, with two or three matches each week and training on other afternoons, and they were encouraged to think up fresh tactics and methods of play. Yet Oxford had no school of physical education or up-to-date gymnasium.[1] The boxing club hired a small privately owned building and the swimming club was in the public baths.

The rugby players had seven crowded weeks to prepare for the glittering goal of the Varsity Match, and Oxford and Cambridge were staples on the fixture list of the famous touring teams; distant travellers with an almost god-like aura – South African Springboks or New Zealand's All Blacks.

Alex scored again in the second Oxford trial, then he popped back to Derbyshire to play for his county team, Notts, Lincs & Derbyshire, in a heavy loss to Warwickshire at Chesterfield. A packed diary of fixtures set the underlying rhythm of his first two terms, but it was rare for a freshman at Oxford to be picked for a blue, although Peter Cranmer, the chap everyone in the rugby club looked up to, had achieved it in the season before this. Cranmer was England's most precocious talent for many a year, a lean, ebullient three-quarter with clever defence.

Cranmer had played in the 1933 Varsity Match and made his debut for England against Wales aged 19 in January 1934, five months after leaving St Edward's School in Oxford – where he was a choral scholar and a leading light in the city cathedral's choir – and five years after his first rugby match. He helped England win the Triple Crown, by beating Wales, Scotland and Ireland, for the first time in six years.

Alex played for Brasenose against the Greyhounds, who were past and present members of the university, and then he was picked for the Greyhounds' annual meeting with the first XV, and made his mark with a tackle on his opposite number, Anthony Lawley 'Tim'

Warr, a fellow Brasenose man. After this match, he introduced himself to the fair-haired Cranmer in the Iffley Road bar.

Cranmer had broken a number of athletics records at his school – he ran the 100 yards in 10.6 seconds, and also won the hurdles, the high hurdles, the long jump and the high jump. 'You mustn't listen when people say you are just a sprinter,' he said. 'Did you play football at school?' Alex replied, yes, he had done at Ashe. Cranmer believed boys should play football until they were 14. 'It teaches you balance and the angles for passing. It can be a bad thing teaching kids of six to pass and fall on the ball and tackle and scrummage and kick; they can easily lose heart. When I got to St Edward's, the rugby players had to practise dribbling with the oval ball whereas I found it fairly easy. Of course I was told not to swank!'

Cranmer remembered his first Varsity Match, when Tuppy Owen-Smith – who had a boxing blue – threatened to punch his nose if he didn't get over his nerves. They ended up winning 5–3 in a game in which Tuppy excelled.

Alex flitted between student and county matches, attracting national attention. He scored for the Greyhounds on the great club grounds of Llanelli and Gloucester. Twelve days before the 1934 Varsity Match he played for Oxford's first XV for the first time, wearing the famous dark-blue jersey with a white crown on the left breast. It was due to an injury to Warr, who duly recovered to face Cambridge at Twickenham, but Oxford might have been better off with Alex, as they were trounced 29–4 by 'the other place'. By January 1935, the *Daily Sketch* column 'Echoes of the Town' noted: 'Prince A. Obolensky . . . is considered by many unlucky not to have already gained a "blue".'

In the Hilary term, after Christmas, the onus was on formulating the first XV line-up for the following season, and Alex impressed in a run of home games in Oxford's first team, scoring three tries in six matches against London Scottish, Edinburgh University, Richmond, the Royal Air Force, Bristol and Harlequins.

He was also having tremendous fun. The form after a match at Iffley Road was a beer or two in the pavilion followed by a short cycle ride or 20-minute walk back into town, while the opposing team made the journey on their bus.

Sometimes the destination was Vincent's, the exclusive social club with a subsidised bar handily placed in King Edward Street, a side road off the High, opposite Brasenose. Accomplished sportsmen and those who liked to keep their company had gathered at Vincent's since Victorian times. It was founded by Walter Bradford 'Guts' Woodgate, a larger-than-life figure who once stepped out of a pub in London and walked non-stop to Oxford to win a bet. Woodgate was a champion rower who loathed the Oxford Union, so he established his own club above a small printer's named J.H. Vincent. The members selected annually required 'all-round qualities; social, physical and intellectual', and they ranged from Olympians, Test cricket captains and rugby union internationals to senior civil servants, cabinet ministers, leading industrialists and kings, including Harold Macmillan, the future prime minister not noted for his talent at games. To this day, about 150 students, male only, are elected to the club each year.

In his room on Staircase VII, Alex pasted dozens of match reports and other articles into his scrapbook. It had blue covers and on the inside front page he had glued a cartoon of himself, wearing the Oxford University Greyhounds rugby blazer, drawn by his old guardian Charles Carlin. Next to it was 'A. Obolensky' written in pale blue ink in his curvy handwriting. Alex confided to Paddy Disney how he wanted to complete an English education and become a typical Englishman, without sacrificing everything that was best in the Russian aristocracy. Paddy would write later that Alex had the 'perfect charm of manner' and 'dignified presence' that stamped him as an aristocrat, though this was not to say his friend was without flaws.

Alex's pigeonhole filled with intriguing invitations, and he made touch with Oxford's 'Russian Society', but the letter from the October Club, whose students preached Communist ideas, went straight into the waste bin. The Great Depression had hammered most of the world's major economies, Joseph Stalin had come to power in the Soviet Union after Lenin's death in 1924, and the idea of a restoration of Russian royalty was further away than ever.

CHAPTER 10

NEW AUDIENCES IN LONDON AND LEICESTER

TWO OF THE best-known rugby clubs in England wanted a piece of the Obolensky action during Alex's freshman term, and the first of them, Rosslyn Park in south-west London, made use of their links with Trent College.

Alex's Trent teammates John Harrison and Errol Button had joined the club known simply as 'Park', who had a committee member deputed to tap up players from the public schools. Alex dutifully followed the trail laid by Harrison, his former captain, and he was given a discounted Varsity membership and soon whizzing on the train from Oxford to the capital. His brother Teddy would join on a full membership in 1936.

D.K. Huxley, a fine all-round forward and place-kicker, was another new name in the Rosslyn Park squad of 1934–5, and he and Harrison, Button and Micky Walford had all been in the same English Public Schools team. They joined Ernie Nicholson, the Oxford blue who would be England's hooker this season, and Ernest James 'Jim' Unwin, a commissioned officer in the Middlesex Regiment, a triple sporting blue at Sandhurst in rugby, cricket and hockey, and a wing with strong claims to be picked by his country.

In foggy weather near the end of November, Alex pulled on Rosslyn Park's jersey of red-and-white hoops for the first time in a 10–3 win over London Irish at Old Deer Park, the beautiful green space next to Kew Gardens that was the club's home until it moved to Roehampton in 1956, and is today occupied by London Welsh.

Alex also played for Rosslyn Park against Oxford before he swapped back to the university team's Christmas tour to Ireland for a 10–9 win over North of Ireland, playing alongside two international wings, Tim Warr of England and Geoffrey Rees-Jones of Wales, although Warr switched to fly half. Then with Peter Cranmer at centre, fresh from an England trial, there was a 3–0 loss to Dublin University, aka Trinity College.

During the trip, Alex was interviewed for the *Irish Times*. Under a tagline of 'A Princely Footballer', the 'Irishman's Diary' columnist wrote: 'The young Prince, who is now eighteen, tells me that he was born in St Petersburg in 1916, the year before the Revolution broke out. When that historic cataclysm occurred in Russia, the Oblensky [sic] family escaped to Riga [and] they were brought to England on a British minesweeper battleship.'

Another piece in the *Morning Post* described Alex as 'a rare forager', while the *Daily Sketch* had him as 'A. Oblansky . . . about the most enterprising of the Oxford backs'.

Alex's second invitation to thrill new audiences was not far behind. He made his first appearance for the Leicester Tigers on Boxing Day, 1934. While one of Alex's sisters was at school with the daughter of J.G. Grahame, a Leicester committee member, the direct invitation was made by Tom Crumbie, the club secretary. In those days of amateur rugby, players were not tied by registration to one club, and turning out for more than one during a season was commonplace; the Tigers ran the kernel of a regular squad while inviting prominent players to make occasional appearances.

Leicester's Welford Road ground was one of the grandest in English club rugby, and reminiscent of a football stadium or a smaller-scale Twickenham, with large banks of terraces and seats, and high roofs over the spectators' heads. Alex had played there in November in the Notts, Lincs & Derbyshire team that surprisingly beat Leicestershire in the County Championship. Now Leicester made a late call for him to play against Birkenhead Park when William Sheppard, the right wing, withdrew.

Alex found the tiny changing room under the main stand and the first person to shake his hand was a tall man with short, dark hair swept back from his forehead. He had a welcoming smile but there was steel in his narrow eyes. Alex recognised him as Bernard Gadney, scrum half for England in seven matches across the past three seasons, including as captain for the Triple Crown victory over Scotland the previous March. And he was wearing a suit. 'Saving myself for the Barbarians tomorrow,' Gadney said. 'We're expecting big things of you at Tigers, Obo. And put that cigarette out, would you? Plays havoc with my asthma.'

Gadney was seven years older than Alex and he had a reputation as an aggressive player. Rumour had it he had once killed a man with his reverse pass, though not intentionally.

Alex was an instant hit, scoring two tries in front of a crowd of 6,000, and although there were no tries against Manchester two days later, when he spent most of the afternoon hacking the ball out of the mud, that was one of only two of his nine appearances in his first two seasons with the Tigers in which he failed to score.

On New Year's Eve at Old Deer Park, Alex suffered his first major rugby setback, playing for Rosslyn Park against Fettesian-Lorettonians with three Trent College boys in the back division – Harrison at full back, Alex on the wing and Button at centre – and the three-quarter line completed by the Unwin brothers, Jim and Frederick.

Alex scored a try racing down the left touchline, but soon after-wards he was clattered into touch by the opposing full back. Bumps and bruises were par for the course, soothed between matches by a drink and a cigarette and the adrenaline generated by the next kick-off, but this was different. *The Times* reported that Alex was badly shaken and had to leave the field, which was always done with reluctance as there were no substitutions.

He didn't play again for almost a month, but there were other ways to have fun. Alex had a pal, Michael Berresford, at Wadham College and they took drives to London in Berresford's Standard Special. 'It's a marvellous new car; it does 90 miles per hour,' Alex wrote in what he called a 'lengthy epistle' to Irena, his sister. Berresford would become a captain in the Royal Corps of Signals and, after the Second World War, the chairman of his local Liberal party in Chesterfield.

Alex could not afford a car, so he cadged lifts or used a bicycle he had bought for a pound and tried not to envy Berresford or Profumo, who had acquired a Vanden Plus Continental Tourer and, not much later, a £3 speeding ticket.

In January 1935, Alex was in London again for the marriage of Frank Green's great nephew, Simon Green, to Gladys Ranicar at St Peter's Church in Eaton Square. Simon was the younger son of Lieutenant Colonel E.A. Lycett Green of Ken Hill in Norfolk and Madame de Alvarez of Lisbon.

The wedding made the newspapers for a curious incident involving a shouting onlooker, as the bride was accompanied by her brother George Ranicar, holding up her velvet train. The Ranicar connection to the Obolenskys grew from here. Frank was guardian to Gladys Ranicar after the death of her father, and Alex's sister Maria would marry Gladys's brother Sydney, a sea captain, in 1943. This union was against the wishes of Alex's parents, but Maria moved with her maid to Sydney's impressive home near Wigan, where the couple kept beehives and sent honey to Saudi Arabia to be used on horses with breathing ailments. A lodger of Ranicar's described Maria as an ethereal princess: 'She sometimes came down to the shop, walking about in a gown that touched the floor. She never said very much but I remember she was always smiling.'

There is contrasting testimony of Maria's later life and it revolves sadly around depression. Alexandra Hulse, née Obolensky, the daughter of Alex's brother Michael and the latter's first wife Anne Helbronner, remembers visiting her grandparents in the late 1950s. Serge and Lubov's flat in Iverna Court, west London, was shared by Maria, who occupied a tiny bedroom. 'I was about six or seven years old and as a shy, withdrawn child, I did not make much conversation,' Alexandra told the author. 'However, I do remember seeing this rather lost and depressed figure that was "Masha". Even at my young age the melancholy in that flat was palpable.'

CHAPTER 11

VADIM AND VODKA AND FRANZI AND GEORGE

VADIM NARISHKIN'S PRESENCE at Oxford was a constant reassurance to Alex. His uncle was a handsome man, with a balding pate, a slightly bulbous nose and a thin black moustache that matched his eyebrows. He and his wife Elli had three children – Vadim, Maria and Theodore – and a lodger, a plump girl named Ariadne Moutarieff. Years later, when Elli passed away, Vadim married Ariadne, having been seduced by her during Alex's Oxford days.

There was a pub called The Black Boy opposite Vadim's home in Headington, and after a few drinks there on a Sunday evening, the Narishkins kept a booming, noisy, musical open house. Vadim smoked a cigarette in a mouthpiece he called a 'mundstuck', and played Russian tunes on a balalaika, plucking the heartstrings of his guests as he plucked the three strings on the triangular wooden instrument. Elli played along, oompah-oompah style, on a guitar.

Alex and other Russians studying at Oxford took up the choruses, swaying and singing and clapping rhythmically, as Vadim brought out bottles of vodka and grumbled about Russia and Stalin and the bastard Communists, and Alex listened to his uncle declaiming how the revolutions would never have happened if the Great War had not happened first.

When Alex found it easy to accept drink after drink at a party, he was living up to a long-accepted custom of Russian hospitality. The close affinity of Russians with vodka, and drinking in general, dated back almost as far as Rurik, through epic imbibers from Peter the Great to Joseph Stalin. Another prince and fellow reveller at the balalaika-playing evenings was George Vladimirovich Galitzine, the son of Prince Vladimir Emmanuelovich Galitzine and Countess Catherine Gräfin von Carlow – Alex's father Serge had laboured briefly on Vladimir's pig-and-poultry farm in Surrey in the early 1920s.

George had an open, attractive face with pale, smiling eyes, and wavy hair fighting a battle between brilliantine and unkemptness. He matriculated at Brasenose a year after Alex, with a Hulme exhibition in Modern History from St Paul's School, and grants through the Thomas Wall Trust, Surrey County Council and Sir Richard Stapley Educational Trust that just about covered the £230 for tuition and lodgings.

As Vadim refilled everyone's glasses, he recalled how he did not join up with the White Army, and helped instead to build the new territorial army, until it was obvious he was wasting his time.

'You were just a kid, Alexander Sergeevich, living in a foreign land,' Vadim said. 'I stuck it out until 1921. I thought the revolution would unravel, and the good parts of liberalisation might survive. The typical peasant was shrewd and pleasant, with a strain of lofty idealism. But life had become dirty and nerve-racking. Yes, the old regime might not have been ideal. But any regime established by revolution is usually worse than the one it has overthrown.'

Some things were better left unsaid, and they never discussed the fact that both Alex's mother and Vadim were illegitimate. Alex could not read or write Russian, but he understood it fairly well. He was attached to and defensive of his Obolensky name, while also respectful towards Vadim.

Other exotic nobles at Oxford included a Hungarian son of an Austrian princess. His name was Prince Franz Hohenlohe or, to quote it fully, Franz Joseph Maximilian Rudolph Weriand Stephan Anton zu Hohenlohe Waldenburg Schillingsfürst. 'Actually, it may be the other way round: "Anton Stephan",' he liked to say. 'I chose them at my confirmation in Magdalen College and frankly I can't remember which order they were in.'

'Franzi', as everyone knew him, was born in Vienna in December 1914 to Stéphanie Richter, the illegitimate daughter of a Jewish woman from Prague and a moneylender. Stéphanie married Prince Friedrich Franz von Hohenlohe Waldenburg Schillingsfürst in Westminster in May 1914, but Franzi's father was the Archduke Franz Salvator, a son-in-law of Emperor Franz Joseph I of Austria. The delicate matter was covered up through Stéphanie's marriage to the accommodating Hohenlohe.

Franzi went to boarding school in Switzerland and northern France, he passed his baccalaureate at the Sorbonne in Paris and he'd had his name down for Magdalen College almost since birth. He had a wicked sense of humour, and he was on pocket money of $30,000 [about £6,000] a year, paid into his account at Coutts. He did not smoke or drink alcohol, but – true to a 1930s fad – he swallowed vitamins from a shiny little pillbox in what he called 'quasi-industrial quantities'.

If anyone named a sport, Franzi had tried it. 'Let me see now,' he said at a sherry party. 'When I was at school, or in the holidays, I was made to sail, paddle, fence, surf, ride, drive, waterski, box, skate, ski, luge, toboggan, curl, bowl, skin-dive, cycle, shoot, fish, run, jump, long-jump, pole-vault, throw the javelin, tennis, football, volleyball, squash, ping-pong and basketball. I have added golf and rowing at Oxford, and gained a blue for swimming.' Only rugby was absent, and still Franzi had an answer: 'Our headmaster in Normandy played rugby for France.'

Franzi's baby face – described later in life as a cross between the sleek roundedness of a Brâncuși with the rugged primitive of an Epstein sculpture – had counted against him when he was thrown out of a brothel in Rouen at the age of 13. In another misadventure, at 14, a family friend arranged an assignation with a Polish woman in Paris that got no further than her scrubbing Franzi's private parts with a wet flannel.

Franzi had a grandmother, Ludmilla Kuranda, who was a human battleship in petticoats. 'She is always reluctant to draw her bedroom curtains at night, due to a mild case of claustrophobia,' Franzi said.

'We remonstrate with her that the people across the street may see her undressing, and "Mil" simply points out: "Nothing is to prevent them from looking the other way."'

Franzi's friendship with Alex would eventually draw another of the Obolenskys into a perilous escape from Berchtesgaden in the days before the Second World War.

Another student who intersected with this cosmopolitan group was Yvonne Gaunt, later Yvonne Allen Fox. When the author met her at her home in Salisbury, she described Alex's character in these formative years. 'Of course he was of interest to the university because he was a great rugger player. The Oxford and Cambridge match was always a great excitement and everybody made an effort to get to it.

'But if you asked him about his rugby, he'd say: "It is a gift and I get on with it, and I have other things to do as well." He was very pleasant and he had none of the boastfulness that might have gone with his situation. At that age he was more of a discreet person than, say, Franzi Hohenlohe, who was the centre of a crowd in Magdalen.'

One evening Alex and Vadim took a train to London to watch a bill of all-in wrestling. They might have watched it in Oxford, but it was banned by the city council.

The protagonists – 18-stone men with bare bodies, save for their outsized underpants - cleverly crafted the impression of inflicting terrible pain and occasionally chucked an opponent out of the ring to add to the effect. Alex, who had boxed a little at Trent College, roared his encouragement at the choreographed entertainment, shouting to Vadim over the cheers of the audience: 'I can see what they mean by "all-in" – hitting, kicking, punching and biting! It's bringing out my barbaric instincts!'

When Alex mentioned the wrestling in a letter to Irena, it wasn't clear whether he quite comprehended the artifice of the event. 'They twist each other's feet, arms, and noses; they try to open out each other's ribs and to split each other by pulling the legs apart.

It is dreadful to see two huge monsters howling with pain like babies. Of course any normal man would be killed by this sport. There were some very thrilling contests, and the champions of England, Holland, Italy, France and Ireland were performing. What amazed me was the number of women who go to see these atrocities.' He also mentioned a trip to the theatre to see the movie actors Owen Nares and Ursula Jeans in Philip Johnson's *Lovers' Leap* – a comedy on the merits and pitfalls of marriage. Alex thought it was 'excellent'.

Irena, who signed herself 'Rinshka', had written to Alex from Lyon with news of acquaintances they had made the previous summer. Alex responded with unselfconscious badinage about the opposite sex.

'Am glad to hear you frequently see François d'Avancourt,' Alex wrote. 'She seems to be a very good sort. You may tell her that I am flattered to hear she still remembers me and thank her for her love. You may also give her my love and anything else that she would like. I am v. interested to hear about all your "boy-friends". It is a pity that Rochetaillé is such a complete "washout". As a matter of fact I have a very poor opinion of the French masculine sex. I hope you will be able to come over to Oxford some time, and then I shall be able to introduce you to some really fine fellows.'

At Easter 1935, Alex went on Leicester Tigers' tour of England's West Country, where he got to know Gadney better and scored a try at Bristol on the Saturday and another at Plymouth Albion on the holiday Monday. Then rugby took a break for the Trinity term, and Alex played cricket for the BNC Hornets and his wicket keeping led one newspaper to speculate he might earn a blue. He ran the 100 yards for the Oxford Centipedes (the university's second team) against the South London Harriers at Iffley Road. He watched Eights Week on the River Cherwell and ogled debutantes up from London in their billowy summer dresses and large straw hats. While Franzi was rowing for Magdalen, he enlisted Alex to entertain Prince Chichibu, younger brother of Japan's Emperor Hirohito, and keep him supplied with tea and cakes.

On 6 May, most Britons paused for the celebrations of the silver jubilee of King George V. At Brasenose, the undergraduates and servants gathered in the Hall of Fellows, at half-past noon, to drink to the monarch's health. Charles Sampson, the principal, proposed the toast, followed by a full-throated singing of 'God Save the King' by 200 men and one Mrs Sampson.

After dark, the High and many buildings in Oxford were floodlit, and Alex and his pals went out to Youlbury House on Boar's Hill to see the lighting of a beacon and gaze down on the illuminated city. There was no hint of the impending slump in the fortunes of the royals. A typical remark from the king was: 'I am going out for a drive . . . to the little streets, the small mean streets, to be among my people, and to thank them for their warm-hearted loyalty.'

CHAPTER 12

SEX AND THE
SINGLE ALEX

A LEX'S LETTERS TO his sister Irena demonstrate a one-track mind in favour of the opposite sex, and one of the few cuttings in his university scrapbook that mentions anything other than sport is a photograph of an unnamed young woman whose curly hair is being blown by the wind. She is dressed in shorts, ankle socks and what appear to be hockey boots, a woollen sweater empha-sising her feminine curves, and a collar carelessly half tucked in.

In the autumn of 1935 Alex moved from Staircase VII to share adjoining rooms four and five with Paddy Disney in St Mary's Entry, an alleyway adjacent to Radcliffe Square. With a crane of the neck you could see the Radcliffe Camera through the bedroom window, and Paddy and Alex funded the 20 pounds per term between them. Only 4 per cent of Oxford's undergraduates were reckoned to be rich, and Alex was at the opposite end of that scale.

The daily routine was familiar by now. Once the 100 or so Brasenose residents had risen at 8 a.m. and strolled round the quad (never across the grass) to sign the list in the lecture room, there was a voluntary visit to chapel for prayers. Any lazy or hungover undergrads removed the flannels they had slipped over their pyjamas and returned to a still-warm bed. It took until 1974 for women to be in residence.

Some of the students trod the boards with the dramatic society, whose guest directors and actors included John Gielgud, Peggy Ashcroft and Edith Evans. Others busied themselves debating at the Oxford Union; two future prime ministers, Harold Wilson and Ted

Heath, had just come up to Jesus College and Balliol respectively. Others preferred a little light reading followed by a game of shove ha'penny in the pub or, in the summer, tennis or golf or a jaunt to London. And in the evening, trips to the theatre or the cinemas round Oxford: the Majestic and the Headington, the Ritz and Electra and Super and Scala.

Alex had embarked on his second year at university with a reputation as an enthusiastic mixer, and a cartoon entitled 'The Fresher's Progress', in the *Isis* of October 1935, could have been drawn with him in mind. A young man is tripping over a rug as he slumps against his mantelpiece and stares at his bleary-eyed self in the mirror. He has an empty bottle of alcohol in his hand, another discarded on the floor and a third next to a pipe and corkscrew and box of tobacco on the table.

There was no indication Alex was promiscuous, at this time, but it was customary for his pals to prattle on about 'free love' and the reliability of various contraceptives. It was regarded as wrong for a 'nice girl' to go to bed with a man before marriage, but some of the 'undergraduettes' went ahead and did so, just the same. Given Alex's good looks and rugby talent and noble back story, you could understand why a girl might set her cap at him and lay down a deposit on a possible husband, however mistaken the dream of money and privilege might be.

The 800 female students at Oxford were hugely outnumbered by just under 5,000 men. Most of their parents had lived through the Great War, supposedly treating each bout of sex as if it might be the last.

Sherry parties were popular, before which the male host might receive handy instruction from a scout. Entertaining the girls from Oxford's four female-only colleges – Lady Margaret Hall, St Hilda's, St Hugh's and Somerville – was more convivial with the fortified wine as oil in the conversational wheel.

An even more benign-sounding tea or cocoa party might metamorphose into a sherry party as someone slipped a 35-shilling American jazz record by Cab Calloway or Louis Armstrong onto the gramophone, and the sitting room was cleared for dancing with soapflakes spread on the floor to make it slippery. The party might go further if there were maybe half a dozen attendees of each sex, and more potent brews alongside the sherry decanters, and a bedroom festooned in cushions next door, which is not to say it was always used.

The one advantage in being a female at Oxford was freedom from the proctors, the university officers who kept male students to the rules with the help of quasi-policemen known as bulldogs, or 'bullers'. Dressed in top hats and tail-coats, they watched out for prostitutes, whisking them to the train station as soon as they arrived. Undergrads could stay out until midnight, but after 10 p.m. 'gate money' had to be paid. Anyone late beyond midnight had to shin over the wall of his college or face being nabbed. Students residing in out-of-college 'digs' still ran the gauntlet of landladies who reported them if they were home late.

A joke in a forthcoming edition of the *Isis* would be: 'There is absolutely no truth in the rumour that Prince Obolensky has been signed on, on a three years' contract, by the Proctors' Marshal. So you can all breathe again.' In other words: try slipping away from a misdemeanour when you have the nation's fastest rugby player on your tail.

One circle of Alex and Paddy Disney's friends was half a dozen girls known as 'The Family', who supported each other through every essay crisis and romantic entanglement. They included Sheila Lesser, a student at St Hilda's who went on to become a news sub-editor at the BBC. Sheila wrote a note home in autumn 1935: "If this letter is very illegible you can put it down to shandy at a very mad lunch & darts party at BNC with Paddy, Alec & Co!'

Alex had an influential friend who took a dim view of the amount of sex between students at Oxford. Keith Briant was a wordsmith with a cutting wit and a distinctive appearance; he wore dark double-breasted suits, and had receding hair and a slightly crooked smile. In 1937 he published a book, *Oxford Limited*, for which he interviewed dons, undergraduates, female students and scouts.

'Promiscuity as a fashionable pastime is dated,' Briant wrote. 'But if two people feel that they have a deeper feeling for each other than physical attraction, in seven cases out of ten they give expression to it.'

No such risqué subject made it into the *Isis*, the student magazine subtitled 'A Social View of Oxford Life', edited by Briant and based on reports from the junior and middle common rooms within each college (the middle being for graduates) and the university's many clubs and societies. The *Isis* carried book, theatre and cinema reviews, news of all the sports teams, and poetry and short stories. Articles ranged from the skittish or determinedly irreverent to the politically polemic.

Briant reckoned sex fell into four categories: masturbation, homosexuality, lesbianism and 'normal' – and he described the first of these as 'a depressing idea, a depressing practice, and depressing in its effects'. Alex said: 'We barely saw a girl when I was at Trent.' Briant sympathised with any boy from a public school who had spent five or more years only in the company of dozens of males.

A variation on the theme was written by Tom Harrisson, an alumnus of Harrow School and both Cambridge and Oxford, in 1933: 'Ox is a quagmire of sex muddle and self-abuse . . .' and 'everyone ought to get drunk once every three months – there is nothing like drunkenness to lower the barriers.'

In early December 1935, five days before his first Varsity Match, Alex sent a letter to his school friend Gerald Charles Nepean Bishop, who had just been made a second lieutenant in the Royal Marines.

'Life is grand, Bish old boy,' Alex wrote. 'For the first time in my life I have fallen in love. She inspires me to score tries and to work.'

We cannot be certain of the object of Alex's affections, but some of the available clues point to a lady who was destined to be the love of his short life.

The previous February, this lady had received gushing praise in the university magazine as the 'Isis Idol' for Valentine's Day: 'We have chosen our Idol for no communal, cultural or athletic prowess, though she may have all these. We have chosen her for attributes that we feel will be far more acceptable to St Valentine – namely, an attractive face and an attractive personality.'

This piece appeared when Alex was barely six months out of school and the woman it described might easily have fulfilled in physical form the romantic and intellectual imaginings of a man of his limited experience. A review in the *Isis* described her 'grace and mystery' in her role in Jean Cocteau's *Orphée*, staged by the university's French Club. She had alabaster skin, baleful eyes and strikingly high cheek-bones, her name was Countess Tatiana Vorontsov-Dachkov and she had arrived at the all-female St Hilda's College in Oxford in 1933, with a degree in English from the Sorbonne in Paris.

Tania, as she was known, was 23; Alex had just turned 19. As he left no diary and no note of the first time his blue eyes were trans-fixed by her cool gaze, all we have to go on are his letters to his sister Irena, and testimony and artefacts gleaned from family and friends. Certainly, the two young Russian exiles in Oxford began socialising during the winter of 1935 into 1936.

Some time in December or January, the university's Russian Society organised an 'entertainment' of ballet starring the eminent dancers Alicia Markova and Anton Dolin at Oxford's Masonic Hall. The Markova-Dolin company had wowed the New Theatre in the city during a provincial tour.

The Russian Society had been founded by the man who, in 1909, signed the register of University College, Oxford, as 'Felix comes Soumarokoff Elston filius natu quartus Felicis principis Youssoupoff de urbe S. Petersborgii'. This was Prince Felix Felixovich Youssoupoff, who in December 1916 supposedly fed cakes containing potassium cyanide to Rasputin and subsequently shot him in the chest and beat him over the head before the corpse was tossed into the River Neva. Youssoupoff had studied Forestry and English at the college, before returning to St Petersburg in 1914, and he helped establish a tradition by inviting the famous ballerina Anna Pavlova to dance in Oxford.

The Markova-Dolin company were led by two faux foreigners –
Markova was born Lilian Alicia Marks in Finsbury Park, north
London, and Dolin as Patrick Kay in Slinfold in West Sussex –
whereas Tania and Alex, of course, were the real thing. After the
show, in which Dolin's 'David', the slayer of Goliath, was, according
to one critic, 'mild, cool and rarely passionate', the company and
their mainly Russian-descended hosts gathered for sherry and cocktails, and a photograph of them appeared in *Tatler* in March 1936.
Alex kept it in his scrapbook and George Galitzine, who wrote the
visit up for the *Isis*, kept a couple of prints too.

Tania and Alex stood side by side – she in a coat with a wide fur
collar and gold pendant earrings, he dressed plainly in a suit, with
a cigarette in hand. Alex was laughing his head off alongside the
dancers in their flamboyant costumes and thick stage make-up. The
performers included dancers Travis Kemp, an understudy to Dolin
from Nottingham, and Molly Lake.

On these social occasions and others, Alex discovered Tania's
story and the connections between them, which included a
mixed-up start in life. Tania had been born illegitimately in St
Petersburg in May 1912. Her mother, Ludmila Schollar, was a
ballerina, born in St Petersburg in 1888. Her father, Count
Alexander Illarionovich Vorontsov-Dachkov, was a second cousin
of Alex's, a 31-year-old hussar in the Life Guards and an aide-de-
camp and tennis partner to Tsar Nicholas II. Tania's mother had
studied at the Imperial Ballet School and graduated into the
Mariinsky Theatre, where her 'delicate beauty and musical technique' was spotted by Sergei Diaghilev, founder of the Ballets
Russes, the influential and revolutionary dance company.

Ludmila joined the Ballets Russes in 1909 and danced in a stellar
cast with Pavlova, Tamara Karsavina and Vaslav Nijinsky in *Les
Sylphides*, and with Nijinsky and Karsavina in *Jeux*, which dealt with
a *ménage à trois*. Ludmila returned from this hectic life to St Petersburg
to nurse with the Red Cross during the Great War, before she danced
again at the Mariinsky from 1917, and resumed travelling. Her
toddler daughter Tania was looked after by a guardian in the south

of France, and later attended the Lycée in Paris. As for Count Alexander, his ancestors were devastated economically in the war of 1812 and lost their estate named Troitskoe to the revolution and civil war. A story circulated in 1916 that he had been assassinated in Russia, but in reality he had fled to San Francisco.

In 1921, Ludmila married Anatole Vilzak, a Lithuanian *premier danseur* at the Mariinsky, and they toured with the Ballets Russes until 1925. Then there was a labour dispute, Ludmila was dismissed for sympathising with striking dancers, and the couple left for Argentina's Teatro Colón. By August 1936, Tania was travelling with Anatole and Ludmila on the SS *Champlain* from Le Havre to New York, and noted as 'step-daughter' to Anatole on the passenger manifest.

When Tania was 21, her birth father recognised her status and settled money on her. This confirmed her as a countess, and she was recorded as such on her documents at the Sorbonne. But that was the end of the contact between father and daughter.

CHAPTER 13

FIRST ENCOUNTERS WITH THE ALL BLACKS AND A CLASSIC TACKLE

OXFORD'S RUGBY FIXTURE list in the Michaelmas term of 1935 contained two red-letter days: the Varsity Match, played as always on the second Tuesday in December, and this season's star attraction of the Dark Blues hosting New Zealand at Iffley Road on 7 November. Alex was a certainty to play in both, barring any aberration by Ken Jackson, the Oxford captain, fly half and chief selector.

The third All Blacks – so named as they had visited the UK in the 1905–6 and 1924–5 seasons – had been picked from a series of 10 trial matches involving 188 players in May and June. They would play international Test matches against Scotland, Ireland, Wales and England, interspersed with games against clubs and representative sides: 28 fixtures in all, plus two in Canada on their way home.

The date with England fell three and a half weeks after the Varsity Match, which was regarded as the equivalent of a national trial, and established players such as Gadney at Leicester were vying for selection with young hopefuls like Alex in a range of university and club games topped off by the formal national trial matches at Moseley and Twickenham on 7 and 21 December. Then the team would be picked to face New Zealand at Twickenham on 4 January, in England's most prestigious and glamorous match since the visit of South Africa four years previously.

Alex began his season at Leicester, scoring a try in the 30–11 win over Bedford on 7 September, in a Tigers squad boasting 10 international players, including Gadney. Another try in a big win over Penarth readied Alex for the first of what would turn out to be three monumental jousts with the All Blacks, as he played for the Midland Counties (a combination of Warwickshire, North Midlands and Notts, Lincs & Derbyshire) at Coventry RFC on 19 September, four weeks before the start of term at Oxford.

It was the second match of the All Blacks' tour and five days earlier they had beaten Devon & Cornwall 35–6 in Devonport. In between times they visited Rugby School, Shakespeare's birthplace in Stratford and the Humber-Hillman motor works for tea with the chairman of directors.

There was a crowd of 15,000 at Coundon Road and much conjecture over the tourists' forwards, who packed down in a 3-4 formation at first and used the eighth man, Cyril Pepper, as an extra scrum half, which attracted offside decisions against him from the referee. In the second half, Pepper switched to playing as a New Zealand-style wing forward in a 3-4-1 formation, which was to say he could pack down on either flank or between the two second rows, in the manner of a modern-day No. 8. This tactical debate was a running sore for the New Zealanders throughout their tour.

Alex did not score but he showed the All Blacks his pace with a surging run along the right-hand touchline. The Midlands' second-row pair of Allan Clarke and the captain Philip 'Pop' Dunkley laid down a marker for England selection in a good all-round forward effort.

In the clubhouse after the All Blacks' 9–3 win, Alex chatted with the visitors, who had spent five weeks on the RMS *Rangitiki* from Wellington to London. There was Pat Caughey, the second five-eighth (the New Zealand version of the British left or inside centre) who would be the top try-scorer on the trip: a wealthy company director destined to be knighted in 1972. Jack Hore, the prop, was a butcher, and among the 27 other players there were four farmers, a plasterer and a gold miner. The full back Mike Gilbert was a telegraph linesman by trade and similar to Alex in build – 13 stone 3 pounds, just over six foot – although lacking his pace.[1] Like Alex, Gilbert was playing in a different country to the one of his birth – the Christian names Graham Duncan McMillan were a clue. He had been born in Rothesay and his family had emigrated from Scotland when he was two.

Howitzer goal-kicking was Gilbert's specialty, and he would play in all but three matches on the tour, for which he was selected ahead of the great George Nepia. He was a square-shouldered warrior with a cheerful disposition, happy to pat the back of an opponent who had just knocked him off his feet. He amused spectators in the later match at Newport when he tossed clods of mud at a dog that invaded the pitch.

Alex resumed his try-scoring for Leicester at home to Waterloo and away to Coventry, where 4,000 spectators saw an interception score from his own half. He switched to Rosslyn Park for a try from the halfway line in a loss to London Scottish.

Now the Oxford term began. As a first-choice player in his second year, Alex's role in the trials was reversed. He played for the senior 'Colours' versus the 'Whites' in October, scoring one try in the first trial and three in the second. *The Times* reported: 'Prince Obolensky was outstanding, and he continually beat the opposing defence with his speed and determination.' Button and Paddy Disney were also praised.

Oxford had a low-scoring loss at Old Merchant Taylors in Teddington, then two tries for Alex in a home win over Newport (12–0), and another mention in *The Times*: 'Prince Obolensky ran brilliantly, and his tackling was better than usual. [For the first try] he swerved past three men to score in the corner.' The *Evening News* described Alex as 'going all out for the line instead of looking round for someone to pass to'. But they also had him as 'a Georgian prince, who is a naturalised Englishman', neither of which was true – and these subjects would soon make banner headlines and split public opinion.

Oxford were shaping up well, with nine old Blues and little need to risk freshmen. After a 24–0 win over United Services, a team photo appeared in *Tatler*, and Alex and his family collected it, together with almost every cutting that mentioned him.

After Oxford had won the annual match with the Greyhounds 26–5 and beaten Richmond 20–9, Alex's try tally was six in the university's four matches. Howard Marshall wrote in the *Daily Telegraph*: 'Obolensky on the right wing . . . is an uncommonly fast and clever attacking player, full of dash and determination. He will need to tighten up his defence, which at present is very poor, though here a little instruction would doubtless put him right.' The Reverend P.C. Matthews might have nodded in agreement.

On 7 November 1935, Oxford University met New Zealand, at Iffley Road; the 16th match of the All Blacks' tour and the one that catapulted Alexander Sergeevich Obolensky to a new level of national acclaim. The *Daily Express* billed it as 'a British Empire gathering . . . [the] Dark Blues will be under Malcolm McG. Cooper, himself a New Zealander, with Australia, South Africa, England, Scotland, Wales and Ireland contributing players to his team.' There was no mention of Russia; not yet.

Sheila Lesser and a friend named Michael Gilbertson met for the Thursday afternoon kick-off. The weather was ugly: dark clouds over Oxford's dreaming spires tipped torrents of rain onto Iffley Road, but Sheila didn't have far to walk: St Hilda's College was just next door. Michael said Paddy Disney had ricked his back and was not playing. 'I hope he's well enough for the Varsity Match,' Michael added. The Oxford team had already been hit by the withdrawal of Jackson, the captain, with a pulled muscle. The crowd on the open terraces was going to get soaked, and the straw hats of the spectating schoolboys turned more pulpy with every minute, but the excitement would be worth it. All the tickets had been snapped up within two hours of going on sale.[2]

Jackson's stand-in as captain was 'Mac' Cooper, Oxford's honorary secretary, who would win two caps for Scotland in 1936 despite being born in Napier, New Zealand. Similarly Charlie Grieve, the Oxford fly half in his third year reading history at Christ Church, was born in the Philippines to Scottish parents. Grieve had been knocked out playing for Scotland against Wales the previous spring and was only just playing again after nine months' convalescence.

The All Blacks had continued their sightseeing at Windsor Castle, Smithfield Meat Market, Harrods and Eton. At Buckingham Palace they watched King George V and Queen Mary wave from the balcony alongside the just-married Duke of Gloucester and Lady Alice Montague Scott. The day after the Oxford match the tourists were hosted by Edward, the Prince of Wales, at York House.

The weather prohibited the kind of spectacular display the teams had given at Iffley Road in 1924, when the All Blacks won 33–15, but the tourists paid Oxford the compliment of picking almost their strongest available XV.

Oxford set off defending the goal line at the pavilion end. Alex did his bit as the Dark Blues were made to tackle, tackle and tackle again. Grieve, small, stocky and nimble, played wet-weather rugby, leathering the ball 30 or 40 yards into touch.

Gilbert missed a long penalty shot at goal, then Alex's sudden pick-up and run took him 40 yards along the right wing, half-rounding Gilbert before the full back made the tackle. Gilbert and Cooper each missed difficult penalty kicks, then Gilbert fumbled in front of the All Blacks' posts and from the scrum, with steam rising off the forwards' backs, Grieve dropped a goal for Oxford to lead 4–0.

Ten minutes before half-time, New Zealand's second-row forward Roderick McKenzie scored a try converted by Gilbert, and the tourists were 5–4 up. The teams eschewed the customary half-time chat on the field to take shelter in the pavilion. After the resumption, Alex concentrated hard while wiping drips from his eyebrows. He didn't want to lose focus and be caught 'counting the crows', as his father would say.

Then came Alex's moment: a surprise break as scrum half Jan McShane, the Australian Rhodes scholar, Mervyn Hughes, the Welsh wing forward, and centre Micky Walford made the play, and Walford's pass to Alex brushed an opponent. Alex raced straight on, head back and untouched from the 25-yard line as he curved behind the posts to make the conversion simple for John Brett. It was 9–5 to Oxford and the crowd went potty.

The All Blacks raged later that Alex had run 'two yards' outside the touchline, and their first five-eighth Jack Griffiths, centre Charlie Oliver and left-wing Nelson 'Kelly' Ball had let him go. Yet neither referee R.B. Hunt, from the Eastern Counties union, nor the touch judge spotted anything amiss. None of the next day's newspapers mentioned any unfairness.

The All Blacks were not finished. Their tiny scrum half Joey Sadler scored a try through a wall of dark blue jerseys, with three minutes to play, leaving Gilbert with a monstrous conversion kick to win the match. The crowd hushed as he placed the sodden ball in a muddy spot near the touchline, stepped back, eyed up the posts and began his run. Such was the gloom, it was not until the ball landed and the touch judges' flags were raised that a sound was heard – and, then, bedlam: 10–9 to the All Blacks and the third time on the tour they had prevailed by the narrowest margin.

The players showered and shared a drink in the clubhouse. Alex regretted a half-chance missed near the end when he took his eye off the ball – but he pumped Gilbert's hand in congratulation. The full back said: 'We won't forget your try in a hurry.'

'We are going to beat Cambridge,' Sheila Lesser said, looking forward to the Varsity Match with conviction, and already planning a sherry party in Alex and Paddy's honour. Bernard Gadney was a spectator, too, and he had noted, with the England match in mind, that Gilbert was not the quickest or most mobile last line of defence.

The next day's newspapers gushed with praise for Alex, and now they highlighted his background. 'Prince Obolensky, the Oxford wing three-quarter, ran like a borzoi from his native Russia.'

The highlights kept coming. Nine days later, Alex's first appearance at Twickenham was spectacular: a hat-trick of tries in Oxford's 21–6 win over Harlequins. His first try finished a handling move, the second was a scoop-up of a loose ball and the third was a clever interception. *The Times* reported that Walford, his centre, 'played just the type of game to make the most of his partner's speed'.

Meanwhile the *Mail* said that such was the extent of his speed for one of the tries, 'the crowd laughed before they cheered'.

All things considered, early December was not the time to see Eastbourne at its best. 'This is the place elderly people come to when they know they are due to die,' said Alex, as he pulled up the collar of his tweed jacket. Paddy Disney laughed and said: 'Come on, Obo, the press photographer's waiting. He wants us to dance down the esplanade.'

This was the 1930s version of warm-weather training: a long weekend by the sea in Sussex for the Oxford players preparing to face Cambridge at Twickenham. They trained at Eastbourne College, practising scrums and lineouts and quick passes to the wings, and played golf at the Eastbourne club. And they went to the esplanade and Alex and Paddy and six teammates did as they were asked, linking arms and skipping along the front.

Alex would look at the photograph later and remember the mood. All the chaps had turn-ups in their baggy trousers, apart from Paddy, super-dapper in his golfer's plus fours and carrying a newspaper. There was Noel McGrath: stocky and with a wide grin; Charlie Grieve with a little quiff at the end of his fringe, Charles 'Bloggers' Bloxham, about to win the second of four rugby blues; Mervyn Hughes, the quick wing forward who would be ordained as a priest in 1938 and become a stalwart of Gloucester rugby club; Jan Pienaar, the prop from Stellenbosch University in South Africa, and the unluckily injured captain, Ken Jackson, holding a camera of his own.

Alex himself was pictured with a slight grimace, maybe worried at the state of his scuffed shoes or the thought of the hotel bill. The players were expected to pay for themselves; nevertheless, they had chosen a nice hotel, the Cavendish, and each day before breakfast they ran to the top of Beachy Head. 'I have never felt better in my life,' Alex wrote to Irena in Lyon, two days before the match, enclosing a press cutting headlined 'Prince of the Blue'. 'Tuesday is the day-of-days, I do hope you will think a little about me – it may bring me luck!' And he implored his sister to visit Oxford the following summer. 'You could stay with Uncle Vadim & I would get you invitations to parties, dances etc. Must end now. Will write again when we have beaten Cambridge. With lots & lots of love, Yrs, Alex.'

The players went to a concert given by Richard Tauber, an Austrian tenor, and gatecrashed a wedding reception, dancing with the bridesmaids. Alex laughingly told Paddy: 'If or when I get married it will have to be far, far away from the Oxford University Rugby Football Club.'

After the excitement of the one-point loss to the All Blacks, Alex's next three matches for Oxford had brought him two tries in wet conditions against Leicester, followed by the Twickenham hat-trick.

On 18 November 1935, Jackson awarded Alex his blue. Alex was the third Trent man to be selected for a Varsity Match (Errol Button would become the fourth – and to date the last – in 1936), and it was a double celebration as his brother Teddy scored in a win for Trent College over Oakham the same day.

When Alex scored again at London Scottish on 23 November it was his 13th try in 10 appearances for Oxford. The newspapers were raving over the Dark Blue centres R.F. Harding and Walford making the most of Obolensky and Geoffrey Rees-Jones on the wings. *Punch* wrote of Alex, somewhat superfluously: 'He is certainly the finest wing three-quarter Russia has ever sent us.' The *Field* said: 'Obolensky . . . has not only exceptional pace but football brains.'

The last warm-up for the Varsity Match was a meeting with Major R.V. Stanley's XV at Iffley Road, and Alex did well in front of John Daniell, the chairman of the England selectors. Roy Leyland, who had been England's left wing the previous season, was alongside Peter Cranmer and Tuppy Owen-Smith in the Stanley's back division, as well as Harry Sedgwick 'Hal' Sever, the wing from the Sale club expected by many to make his England debut in place of Leyland against New Zealand. The incumbent England right wing from the previous season was Lewis Booth, a Yorkshireman who had scored three tries in his seven Tests since 1933, and would later lose his life as a bomber pilot officer in the Second World War.

Alex took a bang on the leg in the first half and he hobbled off for a few minutes, but he came back on and scored a try that grabbed Daniell's attention with the attacking devilry of its execution. Cranmer threw out a wild pass but Alex, coming into the centre, gathered the ball and ran towards the space guarded only by Owen-Smith.

Alex had beaten countless schoolboys and club defenders in these situations, but now he was faced by the great 'Tuppy', England's full back. Owen-Smith was one of the finest all-round sportsmen of the inter-war years, a doctor from Cape Town playing rugby for St Mary's Hospital, who came to Britain with the South African cricket side in 1929; his batting and fielding made him one of Wisden's five Cricketers of the Year. The following year he returned to study Medicine at Oxford on a Rhodes Scholarship, earning blues in athletics, boxing and rugby.

Owen-Smith had made his rugby debut for England in 1933; he knew his way around Iffley Road, and he was an expert in shuffling wings into touch, either single-handedly or with delaying tactics while his centres and wing forwards came to cover.

'Hold, hold,' Alex said to himself. Then 'go!' and with a jerk of the hips he swerved past one of the world's great defenders on a 40-yard sprint to the line. The result was a 23–15 loss for Oxford but Alex showed he had defensive quality, too, by keeping Sever from scoring. In the changing room Jackson spoke the magic words to confirm the Varsity Match line-up: 'Gentlemen, I should like you all to play at Twickenham!' Cue a round of delighted 'hoorays' – and a rush to the bar.

Film of the 1935 Varsity Match survives in the British Movietone archives, and much of the action is familiar: hefty collisions on and off the ball, and a sharp contest for possession after the tackle is made. The notable difference in this contest is the use of the feet – rucking – and not the hands as is common in today's 'jackalling' to steal the ball from the tackled player or 'clearing out' of the opponents getting in the way.

The equipment and pitches were generally of a shoddier standard, and Alex addressed the former with a visit to a shop in Wimbledon, south London.

'I don't wish to be a nuisance, Mr Law,' he said, knowing he was being exactly that. 'But I need them to be lighter and I need them to be stronger. Can you do it?'

George Law turned the boots over on the counter and stroked his chin. The leather was thinner than standard rugby footwear, and one of the boots was split down the side where the strain of the Obolensky sidestep had been too much for the stitching and glue. George called to his son in the storeroom: 'Sandy? Call the suppliers, would you? Tell them our favourite Russian has another request.'

These were the days before sports shoes were mass-produced and the stars of professional teams struck lucrative sponsorship deals. Alex wanted a pair of boots to make him faster across the field – and it made him a pioneer in rugby.

G.T. Law & Son knew their stuff. Their kangaroo leather was double the price but half the weight of the more common calf leather, and it would be used by Jack Lovelock when the elegant New Zealander ran to a gold medal and world record in the 1,500 metres at the Berlin Olympic Games in 1936, and by Roger Bannister when he ran the first sub-four-minute mile at Iffley Road in May 1954.

George traced the outlines of Alex's feet and promised the boots would be ready for the Varsity Match. When Alex left the shop, George told his son: 'That man is something you'll never be – a real prince.' And he charged Alex a knockdown price, which was handy as the famous customer was hard up as usual.

The Oxford team returned from Eastbourne to a hotel in Weybridge, from where they drove to Twickenham for the Varsity Match in Rolls-Royce cars decked with dark-blue streamers. Cooper, the captain, and five others had played against Cambridge the year before. For Alex, this was a first.

The national selectors from England, Wales and Scotland were present and tries were expected, with 456 points scored by the teams in their 28 preparatory matches. Oxford had 27 wins to Cambridge's 22 in the historic fixture first played in February 1872, 11 months after the world's inaugural international match, between the Scots and the English.

The *News Chronicle* beforehand had a photo of Alex in full flight, while 'Scrum Half' in the *Daily Mirror* predicted a 'Rugby Rhapsody in Blue – Oxford's Flying Winger as the Reply to All-Star Cantab Three-Quarter Line'. Henry Blythe Thornhill 'Teddy' Wakelam, the BBC commentator and former Harlequins captain, wrote in the *Morning Post*: 'Cambridge will be wise to die with the ball rather than sling it about wildly when Obolensky is anywhere around.'

Another preview said of Alex: 'A Russian prince as a Rugger Blue is an entertaining novelty, but if he were plain John Smith he would be quite as interesting on the football field by reason of his phenomenal speed. I should place him with [Scotland's] Ian Smith and J.C. Gibbs [the England wing of the mid-1920s] among the three fastest of post-war Rugby footballers, and I am inclined to believe he is the fastest of the three.' This reputation of Alex's as England's quickest wing had become a recurring theme.

The *Manchester Guardian* painted an intriguing portrait of Alex: 'In appearance he is somewhat melancholy, with straight straw-coloured hair falling over his forehead and a slightly stooping carriage . . . In the dull moments of a wing three-quarter's day he is not exciting, but when something is doing he is a formidable figure. He has a remarkable power of acceleration, as well as a high top speed. In a few yards he can beat the wing three-quarter against him and the touchline and then beat the full back and the touchline . . . When he swoops on an opponent's dropped pass he is off from the stooped position with the rush of a sprinter coming out of his holes.'

Ken Fyfe had scored for Scotland against the All Blacks at Murrayfield the previous month, and he also ran in three of Cambridge's six tries against Oxford in 1934. The 1935 match, the 60th of its kind, would be very different. In a wooden cubicle inside the East Stand at Twickenham, E.A. Montague of the *Guardian* dictated his report down the telephone to Manchester, trusting his words to convey the excitement the copy-taker might not have been expecting after a 0–0 draw.

'Suddenly Wooler . . . *that's W, double O, double L, E, R* . . . got the ball in his own half and broke away diagonally towards the right . . . *comma* . . . beating man after man. McShane got him on the Oxford twenty-five . . . *comma* . . . but the ball was in Rawlence's hands and Rawlence . . . *yes, L, E, N, C, E* . . . was in full stride for the line . . . *full point.* He seemed certain to score when suddenly a dark blue thunderbolt hit him amidships . . .'

As the Reverend P.C. Matthews at Trent had been first to address, tackling did not come naturally to Alex, and Montague's report described several efforts as 'recklessly courageous, crude and uncertain'. But the thrilling cover tackle on John Rawlence transformed these perceptions.

The headline-making moment, midway through the first half, is visible on the surviving news film in excellent detail. The tall slim centre Wooler provides the impetus, gliding through a gap before giving a beautiful pass as McShane brings him down. When Rawlence receives the ball he has the momentum to surge outside Stuart-Watson, the Oxford full back.

Now we see Alex, racing diagonally across the Twickenham pitch, in a chase he has begun on the Cambridge 10-yard line. He spreads his arms into the shape of a clamp before wrapping them round Rawlence and bundling him over the touchline four yards short of the corner flag.

The tackle and the pace at which Alex arrived exhilarated the 40,000-strong crowd. Those with long memories recalled Oxford's H.B. Tristram tackling the 'unstoppable' three-quarter W.E. Macalgan, at full gallop, almost 50 years before.[3] While it appeared Rawlence had fallen unwittingly into Alex's trap, the Cambridge man had probably underestimated his opponent's foot speed. Oxford's defence continued to defy Fyfe, Cliff Jones and the wonderful Wooler, who was six Tests into his 18-cap career for Wales.

Once the first Varsity Match without a point since 1892 was over, the Oxford team were treated to champagne, then it was off to the theatre in London for a traditional barracking of those on stage, before they joined their Cambridge counterparts at the Park Lane hotel.

The next morning, Alex felt a kind of numbness. The build-up had been so intensive and it went back to the initial whispers of Oxford while he was at Trent. The reporters were making a great deal of the tackle on Rawlence, and Alex wouldn't have persuaded them otherwise. Still, he knew it was pace that had got him picked, and to have failed to collar his opponent would have been a dereliction of duty.

Every rugby enthusiast knew a good Varsity Match would lead to Alex playing in the national team's trial on the weekend before Christmas. Selection for England against New Zealand was edging closer.

CHAPTER 14

THAT'S OBOLENSKY
WITH A 'Y'

AN EDITION OF the *Sketch* just before the 1935 Varsity
Match captured the attention surrounding England's exciting
new prospect: 'I hear that Prince Alexander Obolenski . . . has been
more photographed since he got his Blue than any man in Oxford.'

For one press photo on the pitch at Iffley Road, Alex wore his
rugby kit of jersey, shorts, socks and boots, topped off by his white
OURFC jumper, dark-blue scarf looped round his neck, left hand
nonchalantly stuck in his shorts pocket, right hand holding a rugby
ball – and the collar turned up on his much-prized, recently gained
blue's blazer.

At another session, the photography was more formal. Two days
after the Varsity Match, he went to the Bassano Studios in Dover
Street, London, where those in the news were given a free sitting,
on the proviso the press might use the pictures for fees. Viscount
and Nancy Astor were there in the previous week.

Last time Alex had done this, it was with his mother and he
had worn a kiddies' sailor outfit; now he was the dapper man
about town, dressed in a sharp suit and tie with his hair flattened
by brilliantine and parted marginally off-centre. His moody expression was reminiscent of Rudolph Valentino or some other matinee
idol.

The spelling of Alex's name with a final 'i', as seen in the *Sketch*,
could be explained by the varying transliterations from the Russian
Cyrillic. It allowed Alex a joke when Michael Peacock, a friend at
Brasenose, spotted an issue of *Punch* from 1903: 'In Russia people

have been trying to assassinate Prince Obolenski on the paltry ground that he had thirty-five peasants whipped to death.' Alex replied: 'Now you know why I prefer to spell my name with a "y"!'

While this was a bit of fun, Alex was a live candidate to play for his adopted country, and it raised the serious subjects of nationalism and nationality. No one of Russian birth had represented England in any sport, and no one could have contemplated the comparatively conservative game of rugby union setting the trend.

Political sentiment towards Russia in Britain was a jumble of memories of historical friendship and suspicion, of cooperation in the Great War and Communism's subsequent advance. Russian culture was popular through the written works of Pushkin, Turgenev, Dostoevsky, Chekhov and Tolstoy, the classical music by Tchaikovksy, Mussorgsky, Rachmaninov and Rimsky-Korsakov, and the dancers Pavlova, Nijinsky and the Ballets Russes.

In rugby union, the question of nationality had been a muddle throughout the 65-year history of international matches. Deciding a team based on national borders raised an inevitable question, literally and figuratively: which side were you on? Should you qualify for a country only through your birthplace, or also by the birthplace of one of your parents or grandparents? How about if you had lived in a country for a certain length of time, or married into it, or fought for its army? There were no easy answers.

Geopolitically speaking, Alex and his family were stateless. In December 1921, Lenin revoked Russian citizenship from expatriates who had fled the country. In March 1922, the new Nansen Passport allowed a refugee to travel between countries under protection from deportation, to find work or family members. International rugby was largely confined to the British Empire, and players swapped countries within it – the likes of Mike Gilbert and Tuppy Owen-Smith.

Today, World Rugby, the sport's global governing body, has written lengthy stipulations on nationality into its 'Regulation 9'. If it had existed in 1935, Alex would have been cleared to play for England as a resident for more than five years and having represented no other country. But the regulation did not exist in 1935 and opinion on an always emotive issue was inevitably divided.

In November 1935, Alex, still a minor at the age of 19, applied to be naturalised as British. He revealed to a reporter from the *Daily Mail* that he was thinking of applying to join the civil service, but it was also pertinent to his eligibility to play for England. The reporter noted: 'The prince has a personality and a style which have made him already much of a hero with Rugby football enthusiasts here . . . When I called on him at Brasenose College I found that to everyone in the university he is "Mr Obolensky". He is, as one might expect, in perfect training. With fair hair and complexion, he looks a typical English public-school boy, and there is nothing of the popular notion of a Russian prince about his appearance.'

The *Daily Express* spotted the implication and also a problem of timing, as naturalisation would not be immediate. Under a headline 'Prince Obolensky Wants To Be British' it reported that, 'One of the most spectacular players in Rugby football is applying to become a naturalised Englishman . . . If he becomes naturalised the objection [to being an England player] vanishes.' The *Daily Mirror* added: 'The only player who walks into the [England] side is Cranmer, with Gadney and Unwin definite first choices . . . Obolensky might be the other wing – by courtesy of the Home Office.'

The *Sunday Post* the same week quoted an unnamed England selector: 'Though there is no precedent, once Obolensky is natural-ised there will be no bar, provided he is thought good enough.' The reporter added: 'Good enough! From what I have seen and heard, Alex, with his speed and fine physique, looks like the answer to a selector's prayer.'

On the day of the Varsity Match, the *Express* had changed its interpretation: 'Obolensky has lived 19 years of his young life in England, which is a residential clause strong enough to satisfy anyone.' The *West African News* had another variation: 'The Nawab of Pataudi and Duleep Sinji played cricket for England. Any member of the

Empire – be he Indian, African or Seychelle Islander – who has a *bona fide* residential stake in the United Kingdom is qualified. Similarly, Obolenski, by virtue of his membership of Oxford University, being bound by its laws, is entitled to its privileges. You can't force him into a cap and gown and refuse him a "cap".'

Some reporters attempted to clarify the rules and regulations – or the lack of them. An agency piece on 20 November stated: 'There is nothing laid down regarding the rules of qualification for national [rugby] teams. The question has been discussed for many years in all the playing countries without anything definite being done. The case of Obolenski, it is understood, would be considered in the light of its individual circumstances'.

In other words, the selectors and the Rugby Football Union were obliged to make it up as they went along.

J.B. Hughes, a Welsh writer in the *News Chronicle*, was sympathetic to Alex: 'I imagine the All Blacks care not who wears the English white jersey, providing, of course, we do not go to extremes. Personally I wish Obolenski were a Welshman . . .

'Those who saw him in the Varsity Match – and who will forget that tackle! – saw what novelists call a "clean-limbed young Englishman" . . . With his wonderful speed, his fair hair and blue eyes, he reminds one indeed of that "typical" English athlete, Lord Burghley [who would be portrayed by Nigel Havers in the Oscar-winning 1981 film *Chariots of Fire*].'

An article in the *Field* gave the most informed view, noting that eligibility to play had always been a tricky subject. So far it had been left up to individual countries, which had led to anomalies, including James Marsh playing for Scotland in 1889 and for England in 1892.

'At first sight a qualification of birth or parentage would seem to be ideal. But let us first decide precisely what is the character of a team chosen to represent a country . . . Is it not desirable that teams should be representative of the full strength of the game as played in the respective countries – in other words, that the players should be products of the game in the different countries and not just players chosen by birth who may or may not be actually playing in their native country? . . . It is indisputable that Prince Obolensky is a genuine product of English Rugby – even more so than H.G. Owen-Smith, who learned his Rugby in South Africa, though by residence in England he has become equally as part of the English game.'

While the papers rehearsed arguments on both sides, the issue was upsetting to Alex. He was young and he had no press or public relations adviser to lend support. The answers he gave to reporters were formulated himself or chewed over with confidants such as Sonners and Paddy Disney.

In the 'dear Bish' letter, Alex revealed his fury at being in the eye of the storm, wrapped up in an apology to his old cricket teammate from school for not making contact sooner. 'Have had a hectic period dealing with press reporters,' Alex wrote. 'At first I told them to go to hell, with the result that they made up my life story. I was dubbed as a Pole, a Georgian, etc & the Obolensky pride revolted! They stated I was being naturalised solely for the purpose of playing for England. This is libel as I put in my application long before there was any talk of an international cap! I am qualified for England by residence – if they want to play me they can do so.'

CHAPTER 15

THE BIG FIVE AND A PIVOTAL VOTE

THE TALE OF how a formal proposal went before the Rugby Football Union to deny Alexander Obolensky his England debut in the big match with the All Blacks, which would have changed sporting history, has stayed hidden in a book of minutes stored in the World Rugby Museum at Twickenham, until the research for this book.

The initial decision rested with the 'big five' selectors – men vested with immense power over both the players and public opinion. They were envied and often heavily criticised but no one could say they were an inexperienced bunch. Between them John Daniell, the chairman of the panel, Harry Coverdale, Bob Oakes, Doug Prentice and Cyril 'Kit' Lowe had 55 caps for England and the Lions.

Daniell had been a selector since 1913, and did the same in Test cricket from 1921 to 1924. A 58-year-old former schoolmaster and tea planter in India, he had been a forward for Cambridge University, Clifton, Richmond, Middlesex, Somerset and the Barbarians. He had a nickname, 'The Prophet', coined during his university days.

Lowe had been a talented fighter pilot, awarded a Military Cross and Distinguished Flying Cross in the Great War, and he was now a wing commander and chief instructor of the Oxford University Air Squadron. He was also one of rugby's most brilliant wings, who had scored a then record 18 tries in 25 internationals, and won four Grand Slams, in the six seasons played between 1912 and 1923. Though he sometimes modestly decried his ability to spot talent, he saw in Alex the speed of a track sprinter and balance of a dancer; qualities Lowe had possessed in his own game.

Daniell and Prentice knew the vagaries of taking a punt. When the British Lions touring squad of 1930 assembled, the intended captain, Wavell Wakefield, was injured. Daniell said to Prentice: 'Look here, Doug, I reckon you'd better skipper this outfit. After all, you're by far the eldest.' Prentice was 31, he did not play well and took the unusual step of dropping himself for three of the four Tests in New Zealand.

Daniell believed he and his colleagues had a tougher job than their Welsh, Scottish and Irish counterparts, as there were so many English clubs and he felt there were 'so many good players, and so few outstanding ones who pick themselves and – what would be still more comforting to the selector – continue to pick themselves for several years'.

The selectors picked Alex for the second and final England trial at Twickenham on 21 December 1935. He and the other Oxford and Cambridge players had automatically missed the first one, in which the Probables beat the Possibles 21–8 at Moseley on 7 December. The Probables' wings were Jimmy Unwin of Rosslyn Park and Hal Sever of Sale, opposed by Lewis Booth of Headingley and Leicester's John Charles, and the only wing to score was Sever.

On the weekend of 14 December, Alex was with Oxford for a four-day tour to Scotland and matches against Glasgow Academicals and Edinburgh Academicals. During the trip the club decided Mac Cooper would be captain and Paddy Disney would be secretary for the 1936–7 season. Playing in the second fixture, Alex did not over-extend himself, although one run brought an Oxford try.

Alex was saving his energy for the pivotal trial, playing for 'England' versus 'The Rest'. Unwin was moved to the left wing to accommodate his occasional clubmate on the right. Leo Munro in the *Express* wrote: 'Public hero Number 1 in English Rugby football this season is Russian Prince Alexander Obolensky. The "fans" have taken the dashing young three-quarter to their hearts . . . Let us hope he succeeds. England must counter speed with speed to have a chance of beating the All Blacks.' And on Alex's right to a cap, Munro had altered his opinion: 'Bother the international qualification bogey! That's a "switch-over" on my part . . . But what's the use of being a stickler? There are no hard-and-fast laws on qualification. The international authorities do not seem to worry. So good luck to Obolensky . . . he has lived in this country ever since he was a baby.'

Alex had a magnificent trial, his team won 26–12 and he scored a hat-trick of tries.

Nicholson for 'England' outhooked Doug 'Joe' Kendrew in the scrums, while Pop Dunkley and Allen Clarke were prominent from lineouts. Gadney dominated play at scrum half and the Bath centre Ronald 'Gerry' Gerrard made a punt ahead that Alex chased and gathered for his first try.

The second came from a fine round of passing involving Dunkley, Candler and Cranmer, and it was 20–5 at half-time. Then Gadney and Candler engineered a clever try for Alex, and Unwin beat three men in a burst for the corner. Micky Walford was playing for The Rest and he dropped a goal, but his England chance would have to wait. Meanwhile, in Cardiff, New Zealand were losing a tight match to Wales, 13–12.

By any standards, and certainly remarkably for a teenager, Alex had produced a wondrous rush of form for his clubs and Oxford and now in the great trial, thrilling crowds around the country and accumulating 22 tries in 20 senior appearances. Nevertheless, it flushed out a number of objectors.

Trevor Wignall in the *Daily Express* noted '[Frederick] Hovde, an American, operated on the wing [for Oxford] in 1931 – but it will be strange if Obolensky is given an opportunity of distinguishing himself in a rose-bedecked jersey against Wales and Scotland and Ireland.'

The *Devon and Exeter Gazette* of 28 December responded under a headline 'No Nazi Rugger' that 'surely no intelligent sportsman wants the Rugby Union to go Nazi and insist on a pure Nordic strain in our Rugger. Though Russian by birth, "Obo" is British by adoption and naturalisation. Why should he be ostracised in the free and open sporting arena?'

The England team to meet New Zealand was selected on the day after the final trial and published in the Monday newspapers. There were to be three new caps: Alex, Hal Sever and Edward Hamilton-Hill, the wing forward from Harlequins. Not yet 20 years old, Alex was set to be the third youngest England wing at that time – 120 days older than W.M. Lowry when he played against France in 1920; 21 days older than A.C. Harrison against Ireland in 1931. He made a short call to his parents in Paris, where Serge was working for Frank Green's company, and they gave their congratulations.

Alex was staying with friends in Warwickshire, so his invitation sent by the Rugby Football Union was redirected from Brasenose. The envelope had the red-rose emblem of the RFU embossed on the back. Inside was a pro forma with the blanks filled in, in the immaculate handwriting of Alfred Wright, the diligent clerk at Twickenham.

'Dear Sir, you have been selected to play for England v. New Zealand at Twickenham on Saturday, 4 January 1936 . . . Jerseys will be supplied to players and must be returned to me in the dressing room directly after the game.' There was detail about being available to play and travelling expenses. 'Yours faithfully S.F. Coopper, Engineer Commander RN, secretary, Rugby Football Union.' And, underneath in Sydney Coopper's own handwriting: 'Congratulations, SFC.'

Alex read it and reread it. Then he turned to the newspapers, which were already looking ahead.

The *Yorkshire Post* said: 'Obolensky may have to do a great deal of foraging, for Cranmer is notoriously an individualistic centre, but Cranmer is a great player for all that and he may very easily find the same path through the New Zealand defences that Wooller trod so thrillingly [in Wales's win] on Saturday.'

'Lysander', writing in a northern newspaper about an England team dominated by players from the south, forecast a 'pretty severe hammering at headquarters next Saturday'.

Cranmer came in for particular criticism. 'His mistakes in defence are apparently forgotten when he brings off the devastating tackle of which he is capable . . . Though Obolenksy scored three tries against the Rest, Cranmer had no part at all in two of them and in the second half he quite ignored his quick-running partner.'

On nationality again, a reader wrote to the *Daily Telegraph*: 'We have Scots and South Africans in the team, why not this fellow?' And in the *Daily Mail*: 'A Russian aristocrat is to upset all our notions of Russian aristocrats by playing Rugby – and for England. Rugby crowds will soon learn new cries: "Come on, Prince!" "Played, Obbles!"'

Most controversially, dissent from within the RFU was coming to light. The *Lancashire Daily Post* of 28 December stirred the pot. Despite acknowledging that Obolensky had grown up and always played rugby in England, the reporter did not agree he was eligible for the national team: 'A member of the Rugby Union talked to me with regret on this subject last Saturday [after the final trial] . . . I am at one with the distinguished Rugby Union authority. I would rather see an England team of fifteen Englishmen beaten than see an England victory won by the aid of players of foreign birth and nationality.'

The hint of trouble emanating from 'the distinguished Rugby Union authority' was true. Alex's right to play for England had been debated by the full committee of the Rugby Football Union on the day before the final trial. A proposal was made not to pick him until he was naturalised – which would have been after the New Zealand match.

The committee who met at the Metropole Hotel, at 2.15 p.m. on Friday 20 December 1935, were dyed-in-the-wool rugby men; long-serving administrators who saw the England team as the RFU's property – which, in a sense, it was, though of course it was meant to be representative of the nation at large.

The relevant item in the minutes was headed 'International Player's qualifications' and it stated: 'Mr Minahan moved that Prince A. Obolensky, who had been selected to play for England against The Rest, was not qualified to play for England. This was seconded by Air Commodore Warrington Morris. Mr Milnes, seconded by Mr

Oakes, moved an amendment that he be not qualified until he is a naturalised British subject.'

James Milnes had been the captain of the Manchester club in 1905, before representing Lancashire on the RFU. At this time, he was the national body's immediate past president.

Robert Frederick 'Bob' Oakes was not only a selector but had also been president of the RFU the year before Milnes, in 1933–4. Now aged 62, he had earned his eight caps for England in the 19th century. He was secretary of the Yorkshire union for 40 years and represented that vast county on the RFU from 1920 to 1945.

Oakes was a rigorous defender of the sport's amateur principles – not that this view put him at odds with the RFU committee, among whom the code was a sine qua non. It was another 50 years before rugby union went 'open' and, even then, most of the RFU had to be dragged kicking and screaming into accepting it.

J.B. 'Jimmy' Minahan was the honorary secretary of the East Midlands union up to the 1933–4 season, then the president, and their representative on the RFU committee for many years. Originally from Gloucestershire, the 69-year-old had white hair, bags under his eyes and a thinning moustache. Minahan had missed just one RFU meeting in the previous 15 years. A genial soul, he was synonymous with the Northampton club for over 30 years.

Air-Commodore Alfred Drummond Warrington-Morris was a founder member of the RAF rugby union in January 1920, and served on its committee until his death 42 years later, when he collapsed and died on the way home from the RAF v. Army match at Twickenham in 1962. Warrington-Morris had played rugby for England at the age of 17 in 1909. He represented the RAF on the RFU from 1923 to 1925 and then from 1927 through to 1945.

While no detail survives of the committee's debate, we can imagine the voices raised and fists banging the table, as dogma and long-rooted opinions were aired. Some of these men were steeped in military service and all were faithful to 'king and country' and rugby union's amateur ideology. The implications of a Russian playing for England would have been contested with the utmost seriousness.

The minutes relate: 'The amendment was put to the vote and lost. The original motion was then voted on and lost.'

Alex was a unique case – and he won the day. He could get on with preparing to face the All Blacks, who were proceeding solidly on their tour, giving Ron Bush, Arthur Collins, Herb Lilburne, Tonk Mahoney and Tori Reid debut caps in an 18–8 win over Scotland on 23 November, when Bill Hadley's hooking and the lineout play had impressed. On 7 December 1935, in Dublin, they beat Ireland 17–9, with Doug Dalton at prop, replacing Hore who had broken a bone in his hand against the Scots. Two weeks later, in the loss to Wales in Cardiff, Caughey was unavailable, so Oliver moved to second five-eighth and Neville 'Brushy' Mitchell from wing to centre. Nelson 'Kelly' Ball on the wing scored two tries.

The squad spent Christmas Day watching four fellow New Zealanders, including George Nepia, playing rugby league for Streatham & Mitcham; on Boxing Day they met London Counties for a second time and Merv Corner and Eric 'Snowy' Tindill played themselves into the team to face England nine days later. Jack Griffiths was dropped in favour of Tindill for what would be the latter's only Test. Normally a half-back, Tindill had been picked as a first five-eighth for this tour; he also played cricket for his country. Ball was considered lucky to keep his place ahead of George Hart, with Mitchell restored to the other wing.

On 27 December 1935, Alex played for Leicester in a 0–0 draw with the Barbarians at Welford Road. His scrum half was Bernard Gadney. For the captain of England and the dashing Russian prince, it was the last match before the big one.

CHAPTER 16

THE MATCH

ROWS OF FACES bathed in the light of the cinema screen are obscured by a grey mist of cigarette smoke as they gaze at a mighty road bridge under construction over the Firth of Forth. The message from Scotland is clear: 'Britain is building!' The pictures fade and darkness briefly floods the space before the next segment of film rolls with the chatter of unseen sprockets. Brisk and brassy music strikes up, accompanying titles in white letters on a black background: 'Rugby International, England v. New Zealand at Twickenham, Pathé Gazette.'

A wide view of a vast rugby stadium appears. Thousands of spectators can be seen packed into the terraces and stands. Then, in close-up, 15 men in all-white kit trot onto the playing field through a gap between piles of straw and form themselves into two rows for a team photograph. The commentary is in high-pitched King's English: 'At Twickenham for 70,000 rugger fans it's the high spot of the season, when England come out for their first international match, against the All Blacks. England is playing in white and standing in the middle is Obolensky, destined to play such a great part in this match. Many at first thought the All Blacks unbeatable, but their recent whacking by Wales had given England new hope. And today, if they don't put up a good show, His Royal Highness the Prince of Wales and 70,000 others will want to know the reason why.'

The themes of the match are succinctly established: Empire and invincibility; solemn duty to king and country, and the promise of a breath of exotic fresh air. The first All Blacks, aka the 'Originals', had beaten England 15–0 at Crystal Palace in December 1905; the second All Blacks won 17–11 at Twickenham in January 1925. Across three trips from New Zealand to the mother country spanning 31 years, they have yet to lose on English soil. On this visit they have been beaten by Wales and Swansea, while winning 24 games and drawing the other on a rain-ruined afternoon in Ulster.

The headline acts are a pair of princes on differing paths: Edward, the Prince of Wales, a super-celebrity; handsome, informal, beautifully dressed and popular with the public, who at this time know little of his philandering with the American divorcée Wallis Simpson. And Alexander Sergeevich Obolensky, the teenaged debutant sprinkled in stardust.

The cinema audience have paid a penny each for an hour's worth of news and cartoons. They sit in rapt attention as the spectacular action unfolds.

On the day of the match, the first spectator to arrive at Twickenham, at nine o'clock in the morning, fully three hours before the turnstiles clanked into life, was a Shropshire lad. John Henry Farnell, the 17-year-old son of a master builder and undertaker, had begun the 180-mile journey from his home in Whitchurch at 10.30 p.m. the night before. 'I have never seen a big match before and I just had to see this one,' John told a reporter seeking colourful copy for the Saturday-evening newspapers, which would carry the result to a waiting nation within minutes of the final whistle. The first editions would go to print even sooner, with only a report of the first half included.

Two 'older youths' identified as J. Featherby and R.A. Knowler had left Sutton in Surrey at 6 a.m. and now they sat on boxes next to John. Just before 10 a.m., along came Commander Reginald Lawrence – winner of a DSO in submarines in the Great War – with his wife Theresa and their 12-year-old son, Peter, up from Hampshire. 'It is a habit of mine to be first at big matches,' said Theresa. 'I find it exhilarating, even if I do not know the players.'

Inside the stadium, four groundsmen inspected the pitch.

PRINCE OBOLENSKY

Alex, the Flying Prince, in Oxford University kit in the Wills
cigarette card set 'British Sporting Personalities', 1937.

Alex's mother, Lubov Alexandrovna Narishkin, aged about 18.

His father, Prince Sergei Alexandrovich Obolensky, a mounted captain in the Imperial Horse Guard.

The last known photo of the Obolenskys on Russian soil, summer 1918. *Left to right*: Alex, an unknown friend or relation, Maria and Lubov holding Irena.

Lubov Obolensky with her four eldest children, in 1920. *Left to right*: Irena, Teddy, Maria and Alexander.

Alex in his uniform at Ashe School in Derbyshire, aged about 10, *c*.1926.

The record-breaking Trent College first XV of 1932–33; Alex, aged 16, seated on the far left.

Alex in full Oxford University rugby garb, including the prized 'Blues' blazer, 1935.

Alex drawn by his some-time guardian Charles Carlin in an Oxford Greyhounds blazer, 1934.

In Eastbourne preparing for the 1935 Varsity Match. *Left to right*: Noel McGrath, Charlie Grieve, Alex, Ken Jackson, Paddy Disney, Charles Bloxham, Jan Pienaar, Mervyn Hughes.

Vadim Alexandrovich Narishkin: Alex's uncle, his mother's half-brother.

Tania Vorontsov-Dachkov, aged about 20.

Alex and Tania, far left in back row, with friends George Galitzine (fifth from right) and Franzi Hohenlohe (third from right), and the Markova-Dolin ballet group, winter 1935–36.

FROM THE NEWSREEL . . .

1. Fly half Candler flicks the ball to Alex.

2. Alex breaks his stride; history seems to stand still.

3. He instinctively steps inside.

4. Alex heads straight for the left corner.

5. Picking up speed across the 25-yard line.

6. He barely sees his teammates as he sprints onwards.

7. Head back, he's at full throttle now.

8. Mitchell races across to intercept.

9. All Alex sees is the goal line.

10. Mitchell makes his despairing dive.

11. He scarcely touches the Flying Prince.

12. Over the line, Alex cuts in towards the posts to score – and Twickenham erupts.

England v New Zealand, 1936 – the second try.

Alex reviews the big match with New Zealand's George Hart at London's Metropole Hotel.

In between playing rugby for England, Alex running the 100 yards for Brasenose College at Iffley Road, February 1936.

The England team v New Zealand at Twickenham, 4 January 1936. *Back*: Peter Candler, Ernie Nicholson, Ronald Gerrard, Edward Hamilton-Hill, Allan Clarke, Alex, Hal Sever, Pop Dunkley, Tuppy Owen-Smith, Wilf Faull (referee). *Front*: Peter Cranmer, Ray Longland, Joe Kendrew, Bernard Gadney (captain), Charles Webb, Bill Weston.

Tom Webster's cartoon of the England v New Zealand match, in the *Daily Mail*.

Opened in 1909, Twickenham was well established by now as the monolithic headquarters of English rugby union, with a vast open terrace at the south end and roofed grandstands along the full length of the other three sides. A seat in the North Stand behind the posts, or in the East Lower along the touchline, cost 10 shillings. (And you could still stand on the North or South Terrace for 50p when England met the All Blacks in 1973. By 1979, a North Stand seat was £5; in 2018 the best seat cost £170.)

The match programme costing tuppence had a part-colour front cover with the red rose of the Rugby Football Union above the words ENGLAND v. NEW ZEALAND picked out in red, the date of SATURDAY 4th JANUARY, 1936 in black, and a photo of the stadium that also served as a map. Fields and woods predominated where today there is a maze of residential streets and retail estates.

More than 30 special trains ran from Waterloo to Twickenham station, a 15-minute walk from the ground. A new section of the nearby Chertsey Road had opened in December 1933, to reduce the old two-mile traffic jam. Turnstile operators accepted cash for the South Terrace; there were standing areas at the front of the East and West Stands too.[1]

It was the kind of English winter's day when any yellowish light of the sun at midday would be gone by mid-afternoon, leaving a quintessential sporting scene tinged an almost monochrome blue-grey. The recent rain had left enough moisture on and below the surface of the pitch to leave muddy smears on knees and elbows and backsides when the players slid on the turf.

In the west car park, Geoffrey Archer sank his teeth into the yielding white bread of picnic sandwiches and chatted excitedly with his father, who had driven them the short distance from Epsom in the family Vauxhall.[2]

Geoffrey was a schoolboy who – entirely coincidentally – would later lodge with Serge and Lubov Obolensky in London. His father preferred golf and boxing to rugby, but he was good to Geoffrey, who had two older brothers, and took him to one or two internationals at Twickenham every season.

Geoffrey's father had obtained 'four very nice seats' in the West Stand, at seven shillings and sixpence each. The car park was where all their friends went, and it was, Geoffrey told the author decades later: 'A tremendous pleasure just to have that, in comfort. It was enormous fun, going to an international.'

Elsewhere in the West Stand, in a box adjoining the scoreboard in the centre of the upper tier, sat the owner of an inch-wide moustache and the best-known voice in rugby. Henry Blythe Thornhill 'Teddy' Wakelam was broadcasting for BBC Radio, and he had been doing this job since England's match with Wales in 1927 – the first live running commentary of any sports event in Britain. Multitasking, as the rugby correspondent of the *Morning Post* from 1928 and the writer of well-received books, Wakelam was a major chronicler of the game, and a former player for Marlborough School, Harlequins, Cambridge University and the Barbarians.

The BBC coverage on the 'national' channel was billed in the *Radio Times* of 27 December 1935 as 'England v. New Zealand, a running commentary on the rugby union football match by Captain H.B.T. Wakelam, relayed from Twickenham, by courtesy of the Rugby Football Union'. It went on air at 2.05 p.m., through to 3.45 p.m., and was a break from the rest of the radio schedule, which was made up almost entirely of music.

Sport on the air was very rare – in the next six weeks, the rugby-union home internationals were relayed live and in full but, apart from that, there was the second half of the England v. Wales football match from Wolverhampton and of Bradford Northern v. Wakefield in rugby league, a boxing title fight, and half an ice hockey semi-final from the Winter Olympic Games in Garmisch.

Standing to Wakelam's left, Leslie Murray was on duty for British Movietone News, operating a camera on a long-legged tripod, looking down slightly to one side of the halfway line. Murray had a good 'feel' for rugby, a sport that thrilled him. It would be his role later to remind the editor to include his shots of the Twickenham scoreboard, showing an astonishing result. 'There are many things of an incidental nature which, carefully edited, help to tell the story,' Murray said. 'Particularly if it shows England winning against New Zealand.'[3]

Wakelam knew the ground like the back of his hand, as he had played there for Harlequins and worked as a steward at internationals and Varsity Matches. His aim was to anticipate play by a split-second and enable the listener to mentally trace the path of the ball. There was extra guidance in the use of grid references that corresponded to a diagram of the pitch divided into eight sections and printed in the *Radio Times*, which sold almost three million copies.

Wakelam's microphone and another one outside to pick up crowd noise were connected to an engineers' van in the car park, and the blended result was sent by landline to a central station. Radio was a worldwide medium, of which the dying king was considered a master. Jack Manchester, the All Blacks' captain, had spoken a Christmas greeting to New Zealand over Wakelam's BBC microphone a few minutes after the match against Wales. 'A winning greeting would have perhaps suited them and me better,' Manchester had said wryly.

One thing Wakelam knew he needed to blot from his mind was the notorious 'Twickenham knock'. Immediately behind his wooden hut were the spectators' seats, and no matter how much soundproof boarding and sheets of rubber the BBC put up, a moment of excitement produced a banging and stamping of feet heard clearly over the airwaves.

An hour before kick-off, Alex and his teammates came onto the pitch. They had walked the 15 minutes from the Cole Court Hotel, and as they mooched across the turf, people on the terraces who had brought picnics while they sat on hired cushions were being jostled to a standing position. Alex dug in a heel, and found it was fairly easy to make an indentation in the earth beneath the grass. Still, it was likely his footing would hold when he made a sprint or sharp change of direction.

Above the spectators' heads, seagulls fluttered and squawked, and aeroplanes flew past, trailing advertisements. A noticeboard was carried round at pitch level: 'Still missing: Mr Rees Davies of West Herts Rugby Club. Please report to any steward if seen.' Beyond the car parks outside, a few penny-pinchers climbed leafless trees to gain a limited view.

This was England's 44th match at Twickenham, and there had been 153 tries scored in internationals at the ground. A try was worth three points, not today's five, whereas conversions and penalties were the same at two and three points respectively. A dropped goal brought four points, making it a handy weapon in the arsenal, although England had scored only four of them here to date.

Up in his eyrie, Wakelam opened his programme with the teams listed as follows on the centre spread, and diligently set out with line spaces to show the different formations of the respective back divisions: for England, a full back, four three-quarters (two wings, two centres), and two half backs; for New Zealand, a full back, two wings and a centre, two five eighths and one half back. The teams were, in full:

England
15   Tuppy Owen-Smith;
14   Prince Alexander Obolensky
13   Ronald Gerrard
12   Peter Cranmer
11   Hal Sever;
10   Peter Candler
9   Bernard Gadney (captain);
1   Ray Longland
2   Ernie Nicholson
3   Joe Kendrew
4   Allan Clarke
5   Charles Webb
6   William Weston
7   Pop Dunkley
8   Edward Hamilton-Hill

New Zealand

1 Mike Gilbert;
5 Nelson 'Kelly' Ball
3 Charlie Oliver
7 Neville 'Brushy' Mitchell;
4 Pat Caughey
9 Eric Tindill;
13 Merv Corner;
15 Artie Lambourn
14 Bill Hadley
17 Jack Hore
20 Tori Reid
21 Ron King
25 Jack Manchester (captain)
26 Hugh McLean
29 Athol 'Tonk' Mahoney.

Among England's mix of new and old faces, Wakelam knew Owen-Smith was always game for a run, while Candler was coming up to his 22nd birthday and his second England cap; he was garrulous and outgoing, with a side-parting as wide as a B-road.

Both sides had decided to pack down in the scrums in the 3-4-1 formation. Weston and Hamilton-Hill were England's wing forwards and Dunkley was the lock, wearing number 7 though today he would be the No. 8. His job in the scrum was to push his weight and bind the second row together.

The tallest players, the second-row forwards Webb and Allan Clarke, a marine, weighed in at a combined 31 stone, 17 of them belonging to Clarke. At the training session the day before, Gadney had drawn set plays in lines, crosses and arrows on a blackboard. 'We have a heavy pack,' he said, 'let's make sure we use it.' He nodded to Webb and the 22-year-old man-mountain Clarke, whose face during a match was as red as a harvest moon. 'You two shove in the first few scrummages like you've never shoved before.'

Ernie Nicholson, the hooker who had played four Varsity Matches, winning three, had chipped in to advocate the Oxford ploy of choosing a scrum instead of a lineout, whenever England had the chance on the left-hand side of the field.

The stoical lumps liable to be muttering witty *bons mots* under their breaths were the prop forwards, Douglas Anthony 'Joe' Kendrew and Ray Longland. The latter's game was based on tough scrummaging. Kendrew, a regular Army captain, had toured New Zealand with the 1930 British Isles team without playing a Test. He was a leader with inexhaustible stamina. But he had lost three times to these All Blacks, including 6–5 with the Combined Services, when he had Webb alongside.

Another loss had come when Kendrew captained London Counties against the tourists, with Candler at fly half: match number 15. In the rematch on Boxing Day, the pair were joined by Hamilton-Hill, a fast breaker from the open side of the scrum who played as a No. 8, too, and was now the third of England's debutants.

Gadney had faced the All Blacks for Leicestershire & the East Midlands and he watched them at Oxford. He admired their 'shadowing' to cover gaps in defence, but he was confident he and Cranmer could make breaks through the line. The forwards would do the heavy lifting in scrums and mauls, then it would be up to the new wings Alex and Hal Sever to do the rest. Sever had put a lovely try past the All Blacks in match seven, for Lancashire & Cheshire, while Gadney, Longland, Nicholson and Northampton flanker Bill Weston had all played for Leicestershire & the East Midlands in match 19 at Welford Road.

Jimmy Unwin was on hand as one of England's two non-playing reserves. He was excited for his friend Alex's breakthrough, but for his own part he knew he would stay a spectator unless someone from the starting XV went lame before kick-off.

Overall, this was a young England team: only Webb, at 33, and the 31-year-old Bill Weston and Pop Dunkley were out of their 20s. Longland and the right centre, 'Gerry' Gerrard, were each making their sixth England appearances at Twickenham, the most in the team. Only Gerrard had played in England's most recent meeting with a touring team, the 7–0 loss to South Africa in 1932, which was his debut. He was sturdy and difficult to stop when he got going, and the All Blacks were impressed by his handling in their sixth fixture, against Gloucestershire & Somerset. Wakelam wondered whether the powerful running of Gadney, a big man for a scrum half at 6 foot 1 inch, would tie in New Zealand's back row; some said Gadney was getting too slow. And how about Cranmer, perceived by some as inconsistent (though he would never be dropped across 16 appearances for England from 1934 to 1938 until injury intervened).

Opposite Wakelam, in the press box in the East Stand, Leo Munro of the *Daily Express* regarded Dunkley as a 'veteran . . . but young in stamina and liveliness and always in the right place'. A colleague remarked disparagingly about the dire state of wing three-quarter play in international rugby; in their minds' eyes, the standard-bearers were Cyril Lowe, Carston Catcheside, J.C. Gibbs and Ian Smith.

When the England players had changed and come out for the team photograph, Alex stood in the back row and heaved in a deep breath. Clarke on his right gave a confident smile. Sever to his left had his hands in his pockets and turned his head impatiently before answering the photographer's shout to look to the front. On the end at the back was Wilf Faull, the Welshman about to referee his first international; later in life he would be president of the Welsh Rugby Union. Cranmer and Weston, seated at either end of the front row, rubbed their knees for warmth. Gadney, in the middle, rotated the ball so the manufacturer's slogan 'Match' could be clearly seen.

'This mass of people,' Sever was thinking to himself, 'how wonderful it is.'[4] Alex would leave no written account of his experiences, more's the pity.

The group broke away back to the changing room and left the pitch to the band of the Grenadier Guards, marching in their scarlet and gold uniforms, and playing old favourites such as 'I Do Like to be Beside the Seaside' and 'Pack up Your Troubles in Your Old Kitbag'. The man from the *Observer* jotted a sniffy note: 'A Twickenham crowd is a marvel of self-repression. A monster-parade of the middle class and it will not have anything flashy – no rosettes, no ribbons, no singing.'

It was now that Alex had his famous exchange with the Prince of Wales, and John Daniell reiterated his instruction to Cranmer to play as England's left centre. Cranmer and Gerrard were used to interchanging, and Gerrard was apt to run straight, with a fearsome hand-off and juddering power in the tackle. A quiet and modest chap who had played for Bath and his county while still at Taunton School, he was destined to be killed in action in Libya in the Second World War, having won a DSO for leading his men through a minefield in Alamein.

Jack Manchester – a man 'built like a giant oak' – won the toss of the coin for ends and chose to play with the light breeze behind his team. England would defend the goal line at the south end. The reporter from the *News of the World* checked his watch and reckoned the referee's first whistle came three minutes early.

More than 70,000 pairs of eyes are trained on 'Gerry' Gerrard as he kicks off for England, long towards the north end of Twickenham, where Pat Caughey, the second five-eighth for New Zealand, catches the ball and wallops it into touch.

England take a scrum, not particularly steadily, but Nicholson hooks the ball back to Gadney, who sets off on a run. He is tackled and waits for the All Blacks' boots to run over him, but no trampling comes. For the home captain and scrum half it is an immediate hint that the mighty tourists, never beaten in England in 57 matches on three tours (23 in 1905–06, 21 in 1924–5, 13 in 1935–6), might be a notch below their best.

New Zealand move into the England 25; McLean makes a run and Oliver kicks ahead. Owen-Smith fumbles the ball and hurriedly kicks it into touch. The New Zealand tackling contains England's early attacks – and then Alex makes his first intervention. He uses his boot to trap a cross-kick from Candler and kicks to the New Zealand 25-yard line. With the adrenaline rush of his first run, air rasping into his lungs, Alex chases hard as the ball rolls a foot inside the touchline, until the All Blacks' full back Mike Gilbert nudges it out of play.

In these early minutes of parry and thrust, England lose ground as Cranmer has a break but Sever muffs a pass. Then Gadney finds a long touch to the All Blacks' 25, but the position is lost to a free kick against England for 'foot-up' in a scrum – the hooker dangling a boot towards the ball before it has been fed in. Owen-Smith answers those who doubt his poise by sending a finely judged penalty kick to halfway, after an offside by New Zealand's scrum half Merv Corner.

Hamilton-Hill and Candler each have a good run, then Hamilton-Hill stops a New Zealand pass away from a wheeling scrum, churning the turf beneath the forwards' feet. A New Zealand passing movement ends with Alex diligently tracking 'Kelly' Ball, his direct opponent on the All Blacks' left wing, and flinging himself into a tackle to bring his man down. The *Observer* reporter notes: 'Those who said that Prince Obolensky was uncertain in defence can forget their words.'

With 15 minutes played, Gilbert initiates the first really dangerous movement: a catch of Gerrard's punt and a counter-attack through four opponents. New Zealand are known for brilliant scores from such positions, but Tori Reid is well tackled.

The All Blacks press hard and Caughey, the scorer of three tries against Scotland in Edinburgh six weeks earlier, attempts a burst but Candler cuts him down. 'Grassed him!' says the *News of the World*.

Alex's first significant run sees him caught by Ball in a passage of play largely in the England half. King is nearly in for a try from a forward rush, then Caughey tries again to crash through on his own. Five rows from the front of the West Stand, young Geoffrey Archer is entranced with the 'wonderful view'.

With about 25 minutes played – though some accounts say 28 or 29 – England have gained a good idea of the strength of their opponents, and are ready to show their own hand: using their hands and passing and pace to move the ball instead of kicking predictably for position.

England put in to a scrum in midfield in their half, the forwards heel the ball smartly, and Gadney slings it to Candler for the fly half to get his backs moving. Candler passes to Cranmer, who passes to Gerrard, just before he is hit by Caughey. In a flash the ball is with Alex on the right wing, 15 yards infield and on the England 10-yard line.

Running parallel with the touchline, he races outside Oliver, who is unable to change direction in time, then swerves off his right foot inside Ball, who manages no more than a slap on his opponent's thigh. Unbalanced briefly as he crosses the halfway line – Wakelam in Monday's *Morning Post* will report, 'He went down on one knee, to spring up again' – Alex balances himself with his arms spread like a tightrope walker's and regains momentum.

There is no time or necessity to think what to do next. Alex lengthens his stride, and his head tilts back as he runs. Reaching top pace, he sees a familiar figure approaching: Mike Gilbert, the last line of New Zealand defence. Alex veers towards the touchline, on the trajectory of a classic outside break. The spectators in the nearby East Stand are rising to their feet, and the ones on the terraces are shouting and waving their arms and hats and programmes. With Alex now 30 yards from the goal line, Gilbert realises he is not going to make it; he lunges forward to attempt an ankle tap with his left hand, but misses.

There will be no All Black moans of a foot in touch this time. Alex is a yard infield, and the New Zealand 25 stretches before him as a beautiful space amid the amphitheatre's din. He makes a slight turn towards the goalposts to improve the angle of the conversion, but Merv Corner is covering faithfully, and at the last second Alex decides discretion is the better part of valour, and grounds the ball midway between the touchline and the posts. He slides onto his backside, left arm shooting upwards in an almost apologetic reflex, as if he had indeed contemplated jinking round Corner for a final flourish.

The grounding of the ball is not entirely safe, and a broad smudge of mud appears on Alex's white shorts, but the crowd is ecstatic. There is 'the most deafening cheer ever raised at Twickenham', as the *Daily Express* had it, or a 'bull-throated roar', according to the *Sunday Graphic*. The sound is almost primeval; a primal scream of delight from somewhere deep in the soul at bearing witness to the battle-ground of rugby elevated to a rare plane of beauty. The Prince of Wales leans forward, smiling, his knuckles showing white on clasped hands. At home, his ailing father, the 70-year-old king, is 16 days from death. The nation needs a lift and Alex has provided it.

The skill of the try is perhaps best appreciated from the rear, on the slope of the South Terrace. The slight move inwards on receipt of the pass from Gerrard, making Ball attempt his tackle lower than intended; the little jump that nearly became a stumble; the recovery of balance and the sudden beautifully timed acceleration to fox Gilbert, who came across with the unhurried air of a man certain his prey will not escape. The banter to Gilbert later is bound to be: 'You showed him the outside – and he took it!'

The reporters jab each other with their elbows as they scribble and type, while Gadney lies prone to steady the ball for Dunkley's attempted conversion, but the kick falls on the crossbar and drops on the wrong side, so England's lead is three points when it might have been five. Gadney's heart sinks just a little, as he knows the All Blacks need only a converted try or a drop goal to be in front.

The action resumes, with the All Blacks roused into retaliation. Tindill and Caughey are tackled close to the line, then a score from a scrum appears certain until McLean is bundled into touch by Owen-Smith. From the lineout, England's workhorse Hamilton-Hill stays squarely on Caughey, and the danger is cleared.

Another New Zealand attack has Oliver going outside and kicking inwards, and Wakelam in his commentary box is telling his listeners Dunkley's missed kick might have been costly. Oliver sends Mitchell away in a long dribble but Sever covers smartly.

In Gadney's mind, the realisation is dawning of how magnificently his midfield three of Candler, Cranmer and Gerrard are tackling. The captain can feel the New Zealanders being driven cross-field, and England are playing above the form the tourists had expected. Could this be the day the long record is broken?

*

It is said of the battlefield that there is always a moment of absolute calm before the bombardment and the chaos. England's second try begins with an innocuous piece of possession but it presages a passage of play that will be retold and reshown for decades to come.

Again, England demonstrate the will to attack that is the hallmark of the day. Cranmer is just inside his half as he spots a gap to run into, straight up the middle, and shifts his feet to leave Reid sprawling on the halfway line. Alex knows his job as the openside wing is to run in support of his centre. Cranmer, his friend and mentor, strides confidently with the ball in two hands, but he needs reinforcements. He appears not to see Alex on his right shoulder and, only later, when he watches the replay, does he realise an All Black, 'Kelly' Ball, was in between them.

Cranmer half-dummies a pass, then gives the ball inside to his left to Candler on the New Zealand 10-yard line, as Gilbert arrives with an ineffectual, head-down, two-handed shove. Years later, Cranmer will describe this pass modestly to a BBC audience as a glorious error; a kind of serendipity. At this point Alex, still tracking the play, pauses to avoid over-running Candler.

Above Wakelam's head in the West Stand, the 'Twickenham knock' is beginning to be heard, testing the best efforts of the sound engineer to blend the commentator's voice with background sound. Leslie Murray pans his camera right to left with the move and he is beginning to breathe a sigh of relief at his choice of a six-inch lens. A two-inch lens would have given too general a view, making the players' bodies too small on the screen. A 12-inch lens might have caught Alex in greater close-up, but the sweep and vivacity of his attack would be missed.

Alex is perfectly placed to keep the move going. Candler flicks his hands to pass sharply left to right, and Alex takes the ball square on the chest and clutches it in both arms. This breaks his stride again briefly, setting him back on his heels, and rotating his body a few crucial inches to the left. He makes a skip from one foot to the other and, in this split-second pause, history seems to stand still with him. The orthodox option is to veer to the right, towards the touchline, as Alex had done for his first try. Even if a covering opponent came across, useful ground would still have been gained. His eyes flicker and scan, his lungs take in oxygen, the muscles in his legs tense for action.

Alex's body is facing away from that orthodox option, and his mind and heart and soul are happy to follow. Moving with apparent certainty and purpose, diagonally towards the left corner, he gets away from Ball, who halts his defensive run and glances behind himself in shock. In his seat, Geoffrey Archer is watching in wide-eyed disbelief. His impression is that England's brave new wing has moved backwards in the instant of the skip. 'What is the chap doing? He's not going to score.'

Alex is committed to his unconventional path. All the worries and joys of his life are out of his mind and yet bound up in this moment. He picks up speed across the 25-yard line, and Corner, like Ball, is left in swivelling, flat-footed limbo. Hamilton-Hill is there to help but Alex barely sees his teammate as he sprints onwards. Faull, the referee, has to check his stride to allow Alex to run unimpeded.

Mitchell races across and makes a dive, utterly in vain, scarcely touching England's flying prince. Nicholson and the scrum-capped Weston and Sever are also on hand, but Alex doesn't need them. He stretches his arms again for balance as he cuts inside to ground the ball nearer the posts. Jack Haigh-Smith, the portly touch judge dressed in jacket and plus fours, follows him round. Sever watches Alex drop to the ground then turns away, hands on hips, a non-speaking extra to the lead actor commanding the grand stage. Is Sever peeved at not being passed to on 'his' left wing? He hinted at it, years later, albeit light-heartedly: 'As Obo reached the left wing I thought he was about to pass to me, a few yards short of the line, but anticipating that I would probably drop the ball in the excitement, he confounded friend and foe by nonchalantly running round my opposing wing to score near my corner-flag, to the most tumultuous roar I ever remember hearing.'[5]

With this second try, incredibly more fabulous than the first, England lead 6–0. Dai Gent, the Welsh-born fly half who won five caps wearing the red rose, the first of them against the 1905 All Blacks, dictates his running copy to the *Sunday Times*: 'In a flash he saw that the way to the line on that [right] side was closed. But, glancing left, he thought he saw a "tunnel" there. Away he went, to the added confusion of the defence.' In the *Sunday Express*: 'How, in those moments, Obolensky got from his wing to Candler's side is a mystery. But there he was, taking a short pass and streaking diagonally like greased lightning . . . Amazing anticipation and a truly wonderful try.'

Alex walks back to his position, heaving in deep breaths while giving the appearance of calm, probably comprehending no more than the simple fact of what he has done. Gadney reckons the huge and sustained roar from the crowd could be worth an extra five points. All around, there is the scintillating sense that something epoch-making has occurred. The try has blasted apart conventional thinking.

The All Blacks hardly bother to charge the conversion attempt, taken by Candler, but it is a poor effort and England lead 6–0 instead of by 10–0 (in modern scoring values, 14–0) if both kicks had gone over. No matter; it is a two-score advantage, and Twickenham is agog and humming, save perhaps for a large group of New Zealanders congregated in the lower West Stand.

Murray the newsreel cameraman will be asked often how he kept the players in focus, as he has 'perpetuated every detail of those crowded seconds'.[6] His camera was about 100 feet from the near, left-hand touchline. With focus set at infinity, and exposure at f8, everything beyond 112 feet distant was sharp.

Pathé have a camera in the north-west corner of the ground, recording what many a modern eye would regard as the top shot: Alex head-on and racing in for his try. Though his body is slightly out of focus, the blurring of the background throws him into sharp relief.

The half-time whistle is blown, and the teams stay on the pitch, with a visit to England from Haigh-Smith, wearing a delighted grin beneath a wide centre parting. The 51-year-old is a former front-row forward of Blackheath and Hampshire, and in his 11th year of 30 as honorary secretary of the Barbarians.

The *Leicester Mercury* man is sending over the first-half copy that is all the evening paper can accommodate before its deadline. He mentions the Leicester players Gadney, Obolensky, Kendrew and Nicholson, and that the 'interest of women in the match [was] particularly noticeable'. His *News of the World* counterpart reckons 'at least 25 per cent of [the crowd were] women and girls'.

Commander Coopper pops into Wakelam's box to give the crowd figure and other titbits of information. 'Well begun is half done,' someone says.

Alex's feelings of pride and happiness can be easily imagined as the second half kicks off, with a good return by Candler from Gilbert's kick. But the match still needed to be won, against opponents Alex knows will not give up.

In the second half, England's defence is cast iron, and while Gadney sees the swinging of the scrums as troublesome, he is content to wait for them to straighten.

Every second is important; any loss of concentration could be crucial. In a typical exchange at a lineout, Mitchell throws in for the All Blacks, Weston marks Hore at the front, Longland is matched with Lambourn, and there is a flailing of arms aimed at grasping the ball or, failing that, palming it to a teammate. New Zealand catch it, and Hadley and Manchester protect it, but Clarke and Webb come in from the tail to drive destructively into the resulting maul.

New Zealand make a terrific rush, and the forwards dribble the ball over the line, but lose control of it into touch. Mitchell makes a run vaguely reminiscent of Alex's second try, but he lacks support. Tindill attempts a drop at goal, unsuccessfully, followed in kind by Gilbert, whose kick drifts wide after he has collected a clearance from a hard-pressed Sever.

With another six minutes played, there is a scrum, and Candler shoots the ball out to Cranmer. He fancies trying for a break, but when he shrugs off one tackle he is caught by Caughey, who holds on to his left leg. 'Fair enough, I can drop a goal from here,' Cranmer decides, and does so with his right foot. 'Ooh, lovely kick,' says Gadney, with a surge of relief that this has 'put paid to everything'. England are 10–0 up.

Cranmer keeps New Zealand on the defensive, with clever kicks to touch. Gadney slips away from a scrum and the dashing Hamilton-Hill, then Weston, steer England close to a third try. The All Blacks are rattled, as first Owen-Smith, then Sever, use the touchline well to press the opposition into their 25. Cranmer thinks to himself: 'I don't need to look behind to see what is happening. Old Tuppy can get himself out of any mess.'

Reid responds by setting Tindill away, only for the fly half to be collared by three Englishmen simultaneously. Gilbert comes up to halfway, but in spite of good backing-up by Reid, another assault fizzles out.

Now it is time for Sever to have his moment. Hamilton-Hill attacks from a loose scrum, and the home backs are off again: Candler to Cranmer, who glides free and approaches Gilbert before firing a pass with a whip of his body to Sever. The pass is awkward, at head height and a little behind England's left wing, but Sever, with barely a trace of slackening speed, swerves round Gilbert and leaves Reid trailing with a 35-yard sprint to score near the posts. 'Cranmer's . . . burly yet streamlined figure seemed to be all over the place, always doing the right thing,' noted the *Observer*.

A third missed conversion, the second from Dunkley, leaves England 13–0 ahead, when it might have been 19–0 – but with less than a quarter of the match to play, it is a huge advantage, unprecedented for them against southern hemisphere opposition.

The tiring England pack begins to yield almost every scrum; they shout instructions and encouragement to keep each other going, around the field. Muscles strain and ache, while the falling temperature of the late afternoon lends a chilly tingle to the sweat on their brows. Jaws clench as they drive into tackles with the thud of bone on angular New Zealander bone, grunting with the effort. Or, as the *Observer* puts it: 'The darting black figures were felled by flashes of white lightning.' A raid by Oliver and Mitchell is checked by Sever forcing Mitchell into touch.

A clever pick-up by Owen-Smith stops a dangerous dribble, Candler has a kick charged down, and Ron King for New Zealand chases a bouncing ball down the touchline to within a few yards of the England goal line. Gadney chases and grabs his prey, falling on top of him. Gadney is flipped over and King is injured. The news-reel shows a gust of misty breath expelled from the All Black's mouth as he lies on his back, and he is forced to go off for two or three minutes.

Alex is constantly on alert. New Zealand get the ball out to the left wing twice more, but Ball makes no headway. He hands Alex off once, but Alex comes at him again to make a sound tackle.

Gilbert takes two penalty shots at goal, for offside offences, and misses with both. In between, Reid and Mahoney join forces, but Mitchell is pushed into touch near the goal line. England close out the match in a state of steely, strong defence that emphasises the clear-cut scoreline. When the final whistle blows, they have driven the All Blacks back to where it all started on the halfway line, a tumultuous hour and a half before.

CHAPTER 17

THE AFTERMATH

WHEN FAULL BLEW the final whistle, the Englishmen had barely moved a muscle before Jack Manchester and his All Blacks were among them to shake hands. Alex would tell reporters: 'There are no congratulations I appreciate more than those which have come from the All Blacks themselves.' No one swapped jerseys, but the respect was mutual and heartfelt.

Gadney led his victorious players to the changing rooms, where a row of ceramic baths and a throng of gentlemen in bowler hats were waiting. The RFU's committee men, some of whom had not wanted Alex to play, were out of their seats in double-quick time to bask in the glory.

Alex took a swig from a champagne bottle as he hauled off his kit, and scraped mud from the studs of his boots, before climbing into the soothing warm water of the bath. It was impossible to take in what had happened, beyond the simple understanding that it could not have gone better. He had enjoyed every minute and he must have felt an elemental mixture of relief and elation at having been able to demonstrate his gifts. It was a fine match, an ambition fulfilled, and there were no regrets – what more could any sportsperson wish for?

Within a few minutes, John Daniell made it clear there would be no changes for England's next match, against Wales in Swansea in two weeks' time.

Towelled down, and with his hair slicked back, Alex put on the dinner suit he had brought with him and went upstairs to mingle among the two teams, who had all done the same. He wore a black bow tie with white wing collar and a white handkerchief poking from his top pocket. Gadney was in a corner, giving quotes to Sunday-newspaper reporters. 'Obolensky played a marvellous game,' the captain said. 'I'm sure he is the fastest man in England. But the side as a whole played exceptionally well, and I am very proud of them.' The reporters turned to Hugh 'Mac' McLean for an All-Black verdict. 'Obolensky is grand. What a boy! We needed a shotgun to catch him. England should win the home championship easily.'

As the crowd outside dispersed, Geoffrey Archer returned home to Epsom. Years later, he recalled: 'All Obolensky's movements happened right in front of us and I remember it distinctly. When you think about it, it was fantastic.'

Alex had Geoffrey Bell, Alec Goodrich and several old friends from Trent College to clink glasses with – they had been to a reunion of Old Tridents at the Connaught Rooms near Covent Garden the night before. Bell fished a copy of *Trident* from his pocket, the December 1935 issue that mentioned Alex: 'Whenever he plays – for Oxford, Leicester, or Rosslyn Park – many of the reports are eulogies.'

They laughed and Alex asked after Reverend Matthews and M.A. Tulloch and said he would never forget where he had been taught to play. Looking around the bar after another beer, Alex realised that the other England players had already left, boarding a bus for central London, where the formal celebration was a dinner for the teams at the Metropole Hotel.

Luckily, another of the stragglers was John Greenwood, who was in his second year as president of the RFU. Greenwood was an Oxford man from his days at King's College, and an England international either side of the Great War. He had revived the Varsity Match in the dark days of 1919, going up to Cambridge for a fifth year to help get the fixture running again. He had brought his wife and son to this match, and now they hitched a lift to the station in an open police car. 'Jump in with us, Obo!'

They fell into conversation about Teddy Wakelam, who had missed a blue for Cambridge when they had six international forwards to choose from, much to the regret of the captain of the time – which was Greenwood.

At the Metropole Hotel, Alex arrived as the teams were sitting down to dinner, having missed the pre-dinner drinks reception. The wine was still flowing, though, and Alex sat next to Tori Reid as the world and his wife offered their congratulations.

Gadney could not stop smiling. He felt England had produced a magnificent team performance, sharp in attack and terrific in defence; Bill Weston had played particularly well – no one had got past him on the blind side. Jack Manchester stood up to speak and admitted he had never felt such pressure in the scrum. The England players described Gadney as a great organiser and captain. Candler quietly fretted he had sometimes overplayed his hand, but no one was having that.

Jimmy Unwin strolled from table to table with a menu to collect signatures. 'Here's looking at you Jim!' wrote Pat Caughey – seven years before the remark was made popular by Humphrey Bogart's character Rick in the movie *Casablanca*.

Near the bottom of the front page, above the signature of Tuppy Owen-Smith, were the words 'May your shadow never grow less', popularly used to wish a friend good health or prosperity.

Alex took Unwin's pencil and, not for the first time on this day, he spotted a gap – left by Owen-Smith between his name and message at the left-hand corner. Alex wrote: 'A. Obolensky' – the A formed in part by a long sword-slash of a line; the 'O' of Obolensky incomplete as it met the edge of the card. The pencil must have left a mark on the cotton tablecloth beneath it. Later, someone – probably Unwin – added the word 'Prince' to the menu, above the 'A', just as the match programme had 'Prince A. Obolensky' in the team list next to the number 14.

A reporter had made it to the dinner, and Alex gave some quotes that within a few hours were in the later editions rolling off the presses of Fleet Street, two miles away: 'I played for England as a Russian because my naturalisation papers are not through yet. But my heart was with England. I was proud to be a member of the team. Somehow I cannot think of myself as a Russian and I intend to settle down in England and, if possible, to enter the British civil service – if they will have me.'

The quotes in the *Sunday Express* appeared under the introduction: 'Last night a slender, fair-haired Russian prince was the hero of English sporting folk.' There was a photo of Alex with Reid, and another in the *Sunday Times* of Alex in his dinner suit, his right fist clenched, discussing some aspect of the match with the equally animated George Hart and Merv Corner. The headline in the *Sunday Graphic* referred to England's two previous losses to the All Blacks: 'Victory to England in the third battle of the Thirty Years War.' The *New Zealand Free Lance* hazarded a less popular view: 'Hart could have brought down Obolensky.'

Alex's unique backstory, and the bravado and unorthodoxy of his tries, lit up all the newspaper copy. The *News of the World* predicted he would become 'just such an idol with English Rugby crowds' as Ronnie Poulton, the prolific try-scorer and captain of England who had died in the Great War.

The *Sunday Express* carried a long report by Frank Shaw, embellished by three excellent photos of the forwards and a graphic showing the provenance of Alex's second try. Shaw wrote: 'Twickenham has never known such a day . . . The much-discussed match of the century – seventy-three thousand fervid spectators, including the Prince of Wales, kept on tenterhooks for nearly ninety minutes – tries to remember while life lasts – England's day of glory.'

At the *People*, they drew a box to summarise the scoring: 'Obolensky scored try after 28 min., Obolensky scored try after 36 min., Cranmer dropped goal after 45 min., Sever scored try after 61 min.' And there was a subheading with another new abbreviation of Alex's name: 'Prince "Obby" shows his heels.'

Gent told the readers of the *Sunday Times*: 'This Prince Obolensky is armed at all points.' In the *Sunday Referee*, 'Obolensky proved that the highest grade of football does not throw him out of gear. With his phenomenal speed and quick football brain he should be destined to do great things for the country of his adoption.'

The first try, which on another day would have been quite the story in itself, was given its due. 'No other player living could have scored it,' said the *Sunday Express*, while Kenneth McMillan of the *Daily Herald* penned a delightful interpretation of Alex's body language: 'To give Obolensky the ball is to turn him into a human bullet. As Obolensky walked back to his place with the grace of a Russian ballet dancer, I almost thought he was going to bow, so pleased he looked.'

After a long evening of celebration, Alex retired to bed. The following day, the reporters chased his next move. 'It was impossible to keep up with him. He has vanished,' wrote the *Express*, speculating that Alex had gone to visit his parents in Paris.

Others waited in the lobby of the Metropole, and Alex laughed when one of them called him 'Obbles'. The quotes attributed to him continued on a theme: 'As I want to settle down in England and go into the civil service, I must become nationalised. I don't even feel like a Russian; I can't. Think of my position. I was born in Petrograd nineteen years ago. Two years later my family came to England. I have been here now for seventeen years constantly, except for occasional trips to Paris to see my parents, who live there. I enjoyed every minute of the game yesterday. It was a fine sporting game and one of my greatest ambitions was fulfilled when I was chosen to play in it.'

And with a few shakes of the hand, he made his excuses and left – but not to Paris. Having received an invitation from an old acquaintance in Britain's minor aristocracy, Prince Alexander Sergeevich Obolensky spent the Monday morning after the match as the honoured guest of an eye hospital.

The great Wales full back Vivian Jenkins wrote of Alex: 'He was a lovely bloke and great fun, a real White Russian Parisian type who loved to celebrate – truly one of the lads.'[1]

It was a description that demands some decoding. Alex's denotion as a prince in the press and the Twickenham programme stood for something, surely, but his place on the British social ladder would have been unclear to most of his new fans. To those in the know, he was a rung or three below the king, and more on a par with the minor aristocrats whose births, deaths and marriages, and holidays and parties, filled the 'Court and Personal' columns, and features in *Tatler*. One such acquaintance was the vivacious Lady Grace Weigall.

Alex and his sister Maria had still been at school when they were introduced to her in 1927, at Petwood House, a lavish bungalow built by Lady Weigall and her second husband, Sir Archibald, as a country seat at Woodhall Spa in Lincolnshire.

Lady Weigall was well connected and a serial adulteress. Her first marriage had been to Baron Hermann von Eckardstein, a diplomat of the German Embassy in London. They divorced, and along came Lieutenant Colonel Sir Archibald Weigall, former MP for Horncastle in Lincolnshire and former governor of South Australia. He was a handsome, old-fashioned dandy: 'tall, charming, good-looking, pink-faced and vague'.

The Weigalls had another residence, Delamere, at Skegness, and Grace's friend Princess Marie Louise was there in May 1927 when she opened a convalescent home, accompanied by Neville Chamberlain, then the Minister of Health.[2] In 1933 the Weigalls sold Petwood and moved to Englemere House near Ascot; its elegant edifice ranged over three storeys in the Georgian style, with a portico of four columns. The mansion was famous for its grand summer soirées, where orchestras played on floodlit lawns and costumed waiters served exotic fruits.

Grace was three months pregnant with a daughter by an unknown man when she married Sir Archibald in 1910, during his successful campaign to be elected an MP. The daughter, Heather Tovey, wrote a moving memoir of her childhood and subsequent search for Grace; she had been whisked away, and her true identity hidden, to avoid embarrassment to her birth mother.

Grace was manipulative but she was also sedulous in looking after those less fortunate than herself – and those more fortunate. Princess Marie Louise would take a flat on the top floor of Englemere early in the Second World War. 'She was generous, warm-hearted to a degree . . . and she could have made her fortune as an interior decorator,' Marie Louise wrote. 'She was [also], may I say with all affection, rather spoilt, as no doubt the only child of a multi-millionaire is apt to be.'

On the afternoon after the New Zealand match, Alex pitched up at the Weigalls' London home on Porchester Terrace. In the hallway he met the plump lady of the house, who was wearing a double string of large white pearls and a blonde wig with a blue bow to match her eyes, and approaching at pace in a motorised wheelchair. 'Alex, darling,' Grace said. 'Come inside and take the weight off those gorgeous limbs.'

The wheelchair had come about after Grace's daughter Kit, by her first husband, died under anaesthetic. When Grace subsequently slipped a cartilage in her knee, she was too frightened to take chloroform to enable the proper treatment, and became chained to her chair, bringing out a gilt version on special occasions. She had two resident doctors: a youngish male social secretary and a mysterious old gentleman called C.J., who read *Horse & Hound* all day and was rumoured to have been another boyfriend.

Over tea, Grace made a suggestion for Alex's sister, Irena. 'I have a wealthy American friend who does a lot of travelling and needs a private secretary. I ask but one thing in return. Archie and I have just donated £200,000 to the Royal Eye Hospital. Would you be an angel and pay a visit? It's in Southwark near the Thames; we'll arrange a car. Now you are England's most famous rugger whatsit, they would be thrilled to see you.'

Alex almost choked on his Darjeeling. It was the type of engagement British royals undertook as a matter of course. Princess Marie Louise had recently been seen on a newsreel, opening a ward at a London hospital, bestowing her gracious presence on awestruck children. He mentioned the Oxford rugby club's plan to visit the United States over Easter. 'Well, if you go, you must look up David Niven,' Grace said. 'It was Priscilla who told him to be a movie actor.'

Priscilla was the Weigalls' daughter and a one-time debutante of the year, a flashing brunette with a delicious sense of humour. She had just been married off to Viscount Curzon, otherwise Alex might have been a suitor.

The next morning, Alex dutifully pitched up at the eye hospital in St George's Circus on the corner of Blackfriars Road. 'A promise is a promise,' he said, as he greeted the chief consultant with a slight bow. An elderly, bespectacled outpatient removed his hat as they shook hands. 'We had the rugger on the wireless. Splendid effort, sir, splendid.' There were congratulations from patients and staff who had read or heard about Alex's tries.

The day after that was Russian Christmas, and Alex accompanied his Uncle Vadim to the Russian Church of St Philip in Buckingham Palace Road. Later he left London to join friends at Kinwarton House near Evesham in Warwickshire, where there was a hunt ball in the evening and hunting the following day.

He wrote to Irena with Lady Weigall's secretaryship suggestion, mentioning he had posted his mother a Bassano print as a late Christmas present: 'It was the cheapest thing I could send because now that I am famous the London court photographers are only too pleased to photograph me for nothing!'

The letter mentioned his rugby, but as not much more than dates in the diary, including an admission he had failed to send anything to his older sister Maria for her 21st birthday, apparently as it coincided with the New Zealand match. Alex promised or at least hoped to buy 'a little present' when he returned to Oxford, and he continued to Irena: 'I am sure when you come to England and meet English society, you will marry some nice wealthy Englishman. You girls are lucky – you don't have to wait till you can afford marriage! If the family do not come over in May then you, Irene, must come to Oxford in June. I will arrange with Uncle Vadim for you to stay at Headington. I will also introduce you to my friends – arrange for you to go to all the dances, etc. (But probably my friends will relieve me of this privilege.)'

And Alex inserted a jaunty PS: 'Excuse vile writing but have such a huge correspondence that my hand aches with writing. Would you like to be my secretary?'

CHAPTER 18

THE ROLE OF THE MEDIA

ENGLAND'S WIN BY 13 points to nil was their first victory over New Zealand, and there were another 31 meetings and 25 losses for England before they posted a greater winning margin against the same opponents, in a 38–21 success at Twickenham in December 2012. The 1936 match also stood as the only defeat of an All Blacks touring team in Britain and Ireland, outside of Wales, until 1972.

These records and Alex's tries guaranteed his contribution would never be forgotten, but his lasting fame was undoubtedly assisted by the newsreel film adding to the radio coverage and reports in newspapers that sold in the millions.

The coronation of Tsar Nicholas II in 1894 was one of the earliest world events committed to documentary film, and it was a wonder to the audiences of the day, but it was scratchy and vague and one-paced compared with the vivid depiction of Alex's feats. In Pathé's pictures of the second try, you can pick out individual strands of straw on the grass.

The newsreel cinema was an American phenomenon imported to Britain in 1931. Tiny halls – sometimes conversions of struggling picture houses – offered an hour-long show in city centres, often at railway stations, to amuse waiting passengers or shoppers or business folk taking a break.

The three main British companies – Pathé, Gaumont and Movietone – were competitive, and each had a camera crew covering the match. Versions were released countrywide on the Monday for showing between features and in news segments.[1]

The cumbersome equipment was on show the day the All Blacks arrived at Tilbury Dock in September 1935: three bulky two-reel cameras each mounted on a tripod on a rack on top of a car, an arc light and boom microphone shared by the crews, and a reporter with a notebook standing next to a photographer with a box camera. The press conference was stage-managed and stilted by today's standards, but it made the players more human and relatable.

Each of the films of Alex's tries contains its special moments. For the first score, a surreptitious splice brings together a long shot of a different scrum with the closer-in pictures of Alex taking Gerrard's pass. For the second, there is brilliant work by the Gaumont cameraman at Twickenham's north-west corner, filming head-on. It made some in the cinema flinch as they felt Alex might run right over them.

Wakelam, the BBC radio commentator, dubbed on the staccato commentary post-match, and used the present tense to add excitement. Here is Pathé on Alex's first try: 'For the first half-hour it's a lightning to-and-fro struggle in midfield. And then Obolensky steps right into the picture with a magnificent demonstration. From a scrum the ball goes out to the three-quarters, Obolensky takes it from Gerrard, going like a racehorse, he sweeps round and touches down 10 yards from the posts.' The low angle from behind the posts, tracking smoothly with the running wing, gives a great sense of speed and of Mike Gilbert's unsuccessful tap-tackle.

For British Movietone, Wakelam conveyed the exhilaration in a high-pitched voice. 'Cranmer is soon at it again, going through brilliantly with Sever up to take the final pass and race away from Reid for the last try . . . King gets hurt.' The clip concludes with the pre-match photoshoot: 'And here is the victorious England team.'

Deeper analysis arrived with the newspapers on the Monday and Tuesday. The busy Wakelam wrote in the *Morning Post*: 'Runners we have seen before, but since the days of C.N. Lowe — at the moment, no doubt, a very, very proud selector — never such a runner with such an innate idea of where to go and how to get there.'

The *News Chronicle* noted: 'The margin of victory has only been beaten three times before, by the All Blacks, who scored 15 points to nil against both England and Ireland in 1905, and 19 points to nil against Wales on the last tour . . . England obtained more tries than in all their [three] international games last winter.' Their correspondent 'Astral' added: 'England confounded all the critics and the prophets and I gleefully kiss the rod of correction.'

Leo Munro wrote in the *Daily Express*: 'The All Blacks were blacked out at Twickenham. A triumph . . . grandly earned by superb teamwork, brilliant attack, and grim defence by thirteen home-bred Englishmen, one hair-raisingly heroic South African, and a flying young "wizard" from Russia. And the Russian was the man who rammed home the vital blows – Prince Alexander Obolensky – "Obo" for short – fair-haired, craggy-nosed right wing three-quarter . . . The Rugby genius who . . . set England "tails up" on the victory road.'

The newspapers' cartoonists echoed the exoticism. Harold Gittins in London's *Evening News* described Alex and Owen-Smith as 'our allies', with a pointed caption of 'three rousing cheers for the first ever English thirteen to beat the All Blacks'. Of Alex, he riffed: 'His first try was greatski – he tookovitch the ballski hereovitch . . . But his second was absolutely itski! It wasn't so much a try as a fairy tale!' Gittins had England working on a '10-year plan', as a reference to Soviet economics, and scrummaging to the song of the 'Volga Boatmen': 'Yo-o, heave-ho!'

Tom Webster's cartoon in the *Daily Mail* similarly hailed 'The Russian prince . . . built better than any five-year plan', and added: 'Not since the war have we seen 14 Englishmen and one Russian prince throw themselves so valiantly into the fray.' He drew the rugby posts at Twickenham topped by the onion domes of a Moscow cathedral.

A *Daily Mail* column on the Tuesday skilfully blended all the available media: 'So many of us who should have been at Twickenham to see it all, instead of listening-in to it, or reading about it, from first thrill of result in Stop Press to last deep-digested theory of the

Monday morning critics, went last night to see the news-film views of the man who has pushed Mussolini, and [racehorse] Golden Miller, and Mrs Fred Perry and all, out of the headlines to make room for his own long Russian name.

'We have known them all – those football geniuses. 'Member Jerry Shea? And A.L. Gracie? And W.J.A. of undying memory? 'Member Herbert Waddell and the dropped goal that beat England in the match that opened Murrayfield? Is Obolensky to join that immortal gallery? The news films say "Yes" . . .

'It is the second try that lifts you out of your tip-up ease . . . Obolensky comes galloping straight at you, bigger and bigger and bigger, till every instinct in you cries to you to tackle him yourself – except that if you tried it he'd probably beat you just as he beat the others.'

The report bracketed Alex with rugby greats: 'Jaureguy, the Frenchman, he of the dead-white face and the high knees that made him so impossible to tackle' and 'Eric Liddell, the Edinburgh student who became a missionary and who broke evens on the track', as well as Ian Smith and Rowe Harding. 'Each, in turn, the "best wing three-quarter in the four countries". Will Obolensky rank with them? Or even higher, the "greatest Roman of them all"?'

The newsreel enabled the sports fans of 1936 to layer their personal interpretation onto the words crafted by the reporters. City workers checked viewing times in advance, arrived in groups to pay their shilling each, and left satisfied after seeing the rugby. A man called Fred Mellor wrote in 2007: 'I was 16 at the time of the Obolensky try. Wonderful. I remember borrowing money from Matron to go to the cinema and see it all over again three times. He also came to Wakefield to play; we couldn't get near him for girls!'

Another who viewed the newsreel was Catherine Campbell, writing a gossip column as Princess Galitzine, her maiden name, in the *Sunday Mail*. She was excited to see Alex at the Russian Church three days after the match. 'He remains oblivious of all his glory,' she wrote in *Topical Talk*, 'oblivious of the fact that, wherever one goes now one hears "Obolensky" or "that Russian chap" discussed.

'The rugger hero is quite the most modest and the most retiring creature imaginable . . . He stood beside his uncle, his young face so earnest, so serious, it seemed almost incredible that was the same man I saw as "a flash" in the cinema or the one described as "the fastest thing on earth".'

E.W. Swanton, for the following Saturday's *Evening Standard*, described Alex as 'the man who had restored the value of speed', referencing Ian Smith and Cyril Lowe, in keeping with an era of fanatical interest in the breaking of records on land, water and in the air. Howard Marshall wrote in the *Daily Telegraph*: 'I shall never forget how Gilbert raised a hand helplessly, with a look of almost comical resignation on his face as Obolensky lengthened his stride and raced around him.

'Obolensky has a genius for the game, or I am much mistaken. The instinct which took him inwards from the right wing to run diagonally across the field and score his second try in the left corner showed the real player. Here is no mere sprinter, but a footballer who uses the weapon of exceptional speed with intelligence and precision. Obolensky has the most deceptive change of pace. He fades past opponents like a ghost, and how refreshing it is to see a wing three-quarter in full cry for the line!'

In a long, reflective piece, Marshall extolled the ability of 'only great individual players' to raise rugby, the epitome of a team sport, above the ordinary. And he pondered how a combined team of the home countries might look at this moment: 'Personalities are returning to the game. Another golden era may lie before us . . . Jenkins or Owen-Smith at full back; Obolensky and Rees-Jones, or Fyfe or Sever, on the wings; Cranmer and Wooller in the centre; Cliff Jones or Shaw at stand-off half; Gadney or Morgan or Logan at scrum half, and a bewildering choice of forwards.'

And as the flood of praise continued, it would take many forms. The *Manchester Guardian* was remarkably prescient to predict Alex would be remembered by future generations, as they could not know the tries would survive on videotapes and DVDs and YouTube. 'Which of the great moments between England and New Zealand will be mentioned most in the conversations of old men in the chimney-corners about 1970?' the *Guardian* wondered. 'The soaring exultation of seeing Obolensky clear of Gilbert's straining finger-tips and flying for the line will certainly be hard to forget, and there will be some who hold that the second try was an even finer sight.' A War Office film in mid-1944 included the tries, offering them as a message of hope to a beleaguered nation, and segueing into images of gutsy, well-organised cross-Channel swimmers. If Hitler had arrived on British shores, the commentary ran, 'what a roughhouse welcome he would have got'.

A generation later, the Obolensky legend was boosted to a fresh audience via the new little box in the corner of millions of living rooms. On the night of 15 November 1957, BBC1's *Sportsview* broadcast 'Hall of Fame', a 30-minute programme that profiled three all-time greats of sport: the boxers Joe Louis and Max Schmeling, and Prince Obolensky.

The much-loved commentator Raymond Glendenning spoke over newsreel footage of Alex's tries, describing the second as 'rugby's most sensational try of all time', while the narrator intoned: 'Though Imperial Russia is no more, nothing dims the memory of the Russian prince who scored the greatest try ever seen on a rugby field in England.'

Peter Cranmer, then 43 years old, spoke straight to the camera – straight-laced in jacket and tie, but smiling benevolently – as he recalled 'the England side played better that day than any team I've played with. We were all just that little bit keyed up.' And there was film of a contemporary Rosslyn Park match followed by the club's boozy annual dinner of the Obolensky Association, both of which survive to this day. Players toasted 'Obo' next to a framed photo of him on the clubhouse wall, with flagons of ale and choruses of the ribald rugby song 'If I Were the Marrying Kind'. 'This was the sort of rugby evening Obolensky lived for,' said the narrator.

As the years rolled by, the memories did not diminish – up to and including 2021, when the Rugby Football Union's film to celebrate its 150th anniversary on social media and during England's matches at Twickenham used Alex's second try to represent the inter-war years.

Each time England met New Zealand at Twickenham, newspapers and periodicals repolished the gem. The *Sunday Times* magazine in 1967 bracketed Alex with Lawrence of Arabia and the poet Rupert Brooke as 'the lost heroes'. Cranmer had not changed his tune, when he wrote for *Rugby World* in October 1972: 'During my time in international football, an England side never played better than in that game against New Zealand. It must have been full of drama for the spectators.'

In 1995, 86-year-old Bernard Gadney was interviewed by the *Evening Standard*. 'I can remember the match pretty well – being presented to the Prince of Wales under the main stand before we came out – and I can remember that try. I played only a small part in it but it really was a remarkable run by Obo. It was the first time we had beaten the New Zealanders and it was something special.

'I go back to [Alex's resting place in] the cemetery in Ipswich from time to time. It is what's in your heart that counts.'

And readers were inspired to get in touch with their personal memories. This letter from Peter Moore of Derbyshire to the editor of *The Times* in July 2014 is typical: 'Sir, I was at Twickenham on Jan 4, 1936, to see England beat the All Blacks 13–0 thanks to two electrifying tries by Obolensky, the second and best in front of the seats where I sat with my father. We were there because my school master, Bernard Gadney, was captain of England and I was captain of the school team.

'I remember vividly Obolensky's second try, so audacious was it. He had blond hair and he ran very upright with the ball clutched to his chest. He cut through the New Zealanders in a long slanting run, curving round to touch down. I will always regard it as the finest try ever scored at Twickenham.'

When England's best-loved modern rugby hero, Jonny Wilkinson, beat a particular scoring mark in 2008, a mere 72 years after the great match, Mark Reason chose a comparator he knew would reso-nate in the *Daily Telegraph*: 'Wilkinson did not become the world record points scorer by running in tries from 60 yards. You need to be called Prince Alexander Obolensky to do that sort of thing.'

CHAPTER 19

VIV'S VIDEO ANALYSIS

ON 21 JANUARY 1936, Captain Teddy Wakelam swapped rugby commentary duties for a stint at St James's Palace, and the proclamation of the accession of the Prince of Wales as King Edward VIII. Unusually, the monarch watched the ceremony from a nearby window, with Wallis Simpson at his side.

Three days before that, Alex had his next assignment with England, facing Wales in the International Championship, and there was an opponent lying in wait to whom the brilliant film of the new hero of Twickenham was not just a matter of entertainment. Vivian Jenkins used the newsreel footage to become a kind of pioneer of video analysis.

The Bridgend-born Jenkins had been Oxford University's full back from 1930 to 1932, and he played in Wales's December triumph over New Zealand, two weeks before Alex and England repeated the trick, and trumped it.

Bright and stocky and wavy-haired, Jenkins was playing in a Wales trial on the day of Alex's heroics, and he possessed the inquisitive trait of a man who would become a popular and voluble rugby correspondent of the *Sunday Times*. He regarded merely reading the reports of his fellow Dark Blue as inadequate preparation.

One afternoon at a news-flick cinema in the Strand in London, Jenkins, who was teaching classics and games at Dover College in Kent, paid a shilling for his entry and settled down to watch an hour-long reel of cartoons and news from 1 p.m. There were about three minutes allotted to the England–New Zealand match, and although Jenkins's eyes traced Alex's every move and shimmy, the action passed in a flash. The only way to see a replay was to view the entire programme again. And again. And again. Jenkins stayed in the cinema for four hours, sitting through 'all those damned Mickey Mouse cartoons', as he viewed the tries four times over – and even then he felt he would have liked to have seen them more.

For the second try, he instructed Alex, in an inner monologue: 'Just go straight for the corner flag – there is someone coming across. Oh, but you are cutting inside . . . and continuing to cut inside . . . and through the lot to the other corner!'

The International Championship was a simpler affair in those days – no trophy, no cash rewards, no building for the next World Cup. Nor was the scoring of tries a guarantee of selection. Oxford's Geoffrey Rees-Jones had nabbed two in Wales's 13–12 win over the All Blacks, but he was replaced in the Welsh team by a faster runner, B.E.W. 'Barney' McCall of the Army and Hampshire, to oppose Alex directly. There would be two famous Oxford full backs in the match, in Jenkins and England's Tuppy Owen-Smith, the pugnacious South African.

Meanwhile England were being acclaimed as the country's best team since the war, and Alex had a Saturday off, on the same day his brother Teddy made his debut for Rosslyn Park on the wing in a loss at London Scottish.

In the lead-up to the match between Wales and England at Swansea's St Helens ground, Alex's name was at the top of almost every news-paper piece, and his face appeared in most of the press photos. He was snapped with Bill Weston, Ray Longland and Bernard Gadney at Paddington Station, and pictured again, flanked by Owen-Smith and Ernie Nicholson, smiling on the steps of the hotel at the seaside resort of Porthcawl on the eve of the game. This picture, incidentally, gave rise to possibly the first use of what would become a popular monicker for Alex, as the *Star* – one of London's three main evening newspapers – gave it the headline: 'The "Flying Prince" Takes the Air.'

Kenneth McMillan's preview for the *Herald* was typical: 'Whatever combination the Welsh backs appear in, their one danger spot is

Obolensky, the Prince of Rugby fliers . . . Nor can they really take [Claude] Davey away from the centre to police Obolensky, without having things a bit more easy for Cranmer and Gerrard in the centre . . . The stage is ready, therefore, for the "match of the century".'

In the event, Davey did not make it, as he failed a morning fitness test on a pulled muscle. So Swansea's John Idwal Rees switched from the left wing to the centre, B.E.W. McCall of the Welch Regiment swapped from right wing to left, and Alex's Oxford teammate Geoffrey Rees-Jones came in on the right.

Wakelam took up his commentating position for the BBC on top of the cricket pavilion that was 'convenient and commodious, but a long way from the play'.[1] The weather was fair and the snow that had fallen in Swansea had been kept at bay by a thick covering of straw on the pitch.

A record crowd, estimated at 'nearly 60,000' in the *Morning Post* and 'at least 70,000' in the *Daily Sketch*, crowded the narrow entrances and eventually hemmed the pitch, with adults and schoolchildren standing or sitting cross-legged with their feet on the touchlines, singing lustily along to the Ystalyfera brass band. The *Sketch* reckoned another 10,000 were stuck outside. A spectator joked of Alex pre-match: 'You'll need somebody on a motorcycle to catch him.'

England's pack varied their formation, starting with 3-2-3, but also adopting a 3-4-1 and even a 3-3-2, while Wales started with 3-2-3 but converted to 3-4-1. At scrum half for Wales, Haydn Tanner was still at school, and in the 0–0 stalemate that unfolded, the Russian teenager in the visiting team barely had a run until the final quarter.

In the 66th minute, Alex made a clean break in his own half and was confronted by Viv Jenkins, working to the plan formulated during his four-hour cinema stint. He anticipated Alex would try the manoeuvre that had worked for his first try against New Zealand. When Alex attempted to veer into Jenkins, before swerving towards the corridor of space near the touchline, the Welshman with the letter A on his back crabbed carefully right to left, eyes trained on his prey. He lined Alex up as he reached halfway, tackled him hard around the midriff and bundled him into the pile of straw surrounding the pitch.

'When I finally got up,' Jenkins wrote later, 'there underneath me was little Cliff Jones, who had come across to cover as we had planned.' Alex picked straw out of his mouth and muttered: 'Good tackle, old chap.' A minute later, he had another go, cutting inside and striving to break tackles but succumbing to superior numbers.

Wales's two dangermen – Jones, the fly half, and centre Wilf Wooller – were similarly shackled by England's defenders, so the tall and elegant Wooller resorted to short, probing kicks, but Owen-Smith cleaned up everything, including a kick and chase by Wooller when the Welshman fumbled the ball and went head over heels as the England full back dived at his legs.

In other incidents, Alex made a switch of direction for a weaving wander from the right wing to evade two Welshmen and he proved his selflessness by passing to Hal Sever near the Wales 25-yard line. Sever punted a cross-kick infield towards his forwards, and it bounced near the posts, which had Wales scrambling frantically. In the third quarter, Alex hovered expectantly but first Peter Cranmer then Peter Candler kicked instead of passing. In defence, Alex made a notable tackle on his opposite number, McCall. The scoring blank persisted when Cranmer missed the target with a late drop at goal.

'I was sorry for Prince Obolensky,' wrote D.R. Gent for the *Sunday Times* on the first scoreless draw between England and Wales for 50 years. 'Very few chances came his way but he did most clearly show the tremendous Welsh crowd that he is a mighty dangerous three-quarter.' Gent blamed the 'extremely disappointing exhibition of football' on 'dull, scrappy scrummaging, with all the formations imaginable, and when one side did get the ball out it came so slowly it was a wonder Gadney or Tanner got it away at all.'

By the time Wakelam filed for the *Morning Post*, the forwards were definitively the villains of the piece. 'With two such brilliant back divisions behind them, it was quite reasonable to expect that they [the forwards] would get on with their necessary duties as quickly as legally possible, but instead they chose to indulge in an orgy of scrum slewing, clumsy mauling, and man-handling, and they seemed quite unwilling to allow the ball into the scrum at all.'

On the Tuesday after the match came the news the British public had dreaded. The death of King George V was announced by Buckingham Palace. He had passed away at Sandringham the night before, after a reign of almost 26 years, starting before the Great War. A million mourners would file past his coffin at Westminster Hall.

CHAPTER 20

JOINING THE *ISIS* AND IRISH UPSETS

KEITH BRIANT, THE editor of the *Isis* weekly newspaper, was no great enthusiast of games and pastimes, but his readership included many who were, and in the aftermath of the England v. All Blacks match, he appointed Alex as his new sports editor with a cultural remit.

'Following out our policy of making the *Isis* a completely representative paper,' Briant wrote, 'we are able to announce that we have secured the accession to the staff of Prince Obolensky. He will keep his eye on the sporting pages, cast a glance at the theatres, and give you the inside on "Twentieth Century Blues". Next week, exclusive to the *Isis*, we announce his impression of the England v. Ireland match.'

It made Alex a kind of work colleague to his pals Paddy Disney, George Galitzine and Franzi Hohenlohe, as they were all part of an *Isis* editorial staff as eclectic as Oxford in the mid-1930s was likely to get. There was Briant, the editor with his long walking stick, and George Joseph, a diminutive Scottish-born mature student who had been brought up in New Zealand and was a solicitor, barrister and boxing blue at both the University of New Zealand and Oxford. Now a Brasenose man, he had written four plays and could produce a completed article in the time it took others to think of a first sentence. Joseph penned film, play and book reviews for the *Isis*, which quipped that he 'looks his best behind half a pint'.

There were also K.M. Andrews (literary editor), W.A. Nield (assistant editor), Hon. Peter Wood (hunting notes) and Edith Shawcross, the film and theatre critic, tennis blue and 'expert on feminist opinions'. Hohenlohe had a column, 'Oxford Through the Keyhole', that Briant promised would be 'the death-bed of many a reputation'.

Briant had already reflected Alex's rugby feats by choosing him as the 'Isis Idol' in the edition of 21 January, for which Paddy Disney was the interviewer and writer who urged him to 'tell me your life story yet again!' – and so the tale of the escape to Riga and the voyage on the *Princess Margaret* were revealed to the Oxford student body in a piece that was warm and intimate and revealing.

> Those who look for signs of conceit in Alex will be staggered by his modesty and any press man will tell you how he hates publicity. As is natural in one who has had to struggle against misfortune and bear great burdens on very young shoulders, Alex has at times a dreamy air of reserve which is often misunderstood. But once show him you are a friend, and you will see his eyes twinkle and his face crease into that broad smile which his friends know so well.
>
> By his successes in serving England on the Rugger field, Alex has achieved a task much harder and much dearer to his heart – he has reflected honour on all his fellow-countrymen in exile in this country.
>
> At the same time he has already given us two brilliant tries and a superb tackle [against Cambridge] with which we can bore our grandchildren – and there are many more flashing tries and crashing tackles yet in store.

Alex was soon included in a collection of cigarette cards titled 'British Sporting Personalities', produced by W.D. & H.O. Wills, alongside fellow rugby stars Bernard Gadney, Wilson Shaw and Cliff Jones. Among the 48 names in the set, only the tennis player Fred Perry and the cricketer Wally Hammond are as well remembered as Alex today. Other domestic sporting heroes in 1936 included football's prolific goal-scorers Ted Drake and Dixie Dean, the champion golfer Henry 'King' Cotton and the record-breaking flat-racing jockey Gordon Richards. But Perry was arguably pre-eminent in this year, as he won his third successive Wimbledon men's singles title in July.

Alex was not, however, about to make a name as a sharpshooting journalist. He was more a hapless ingénu in the mould of William Boot from Evelyn Waugh's *Scoop*. In a misfiring start to life with the *Isis*, the apparently straightforward task of reporting the match between Ireland and England in Dublin on 8 February – straightforward because Alex played in the match – went awry because he was too whacked out by the trip.

In the lead-up, Alex had gone tryless for Oxford in a 20–3 loss at Richmond, when he was closely marked by Peter Cranmer, among others. In the evening, the England team to meet Ireland was announced with two changes, both in the pack: Harold Wheatley, a 23-year-old debutant, ousted Ernie Nicholson to join Longland and Kendrew in the front row, while John McDonald Hodgson, 26, would earn his third cap at flanker in place of Bill Weston. The changes were attributed by *The Times* to the 'general dismay and surprise [that] the scrummage was so ragged and ineffective at Swansea'.

The England team's ferry journey across the Irish Sea was choppy, and Alex and several colleagues suffered seasickness. Only Cranmer had come prepared. He had been very ill travelling to the corresponding fixture two years previously, and this time he requested a deck cabin from Sydney Coopper to mitigate the effects.

On the morning of the match at Lansdowne Road, the *Manchester Guardian* printed a solemn Bassano portrait of Alex and predicted an England victory unless Ireland were saved by 'rain and mud'. In fact, a strong east wing dried the pitch but, despite the fair conditions – visible in the surviving Pathé newsreel film, together with the black armbands worn by both teams to mark the passing of the king – the visiting backs never made it into full flow.

Gadney had an off afternoon, sending poor passes over Candler's head or behind the whole three-quarter line and along the ground towards Tuppy Owen-Smith. The centres Cranmer and Gerrard dropped pass after pass, and the Irish tacklers had a field day. One superb chance for Alex to score can be seen on the film as Candler breaks into the Ireland 25 during the first half. Alex, in his white number 11 jersey, is perfectly placed on the fly half's right shoulder, ready for an easy run-in if Candler had simply drawn his man and passed.

Instead, Alex was denied a sniff of decent possession until the last 20 minutes – and then he was beautifully tackled, four times, by his opposite number Vesey Boyle, as well as by the full back George Malcolmson, an RAF man who played for North of Ireland, and the scrum half George Morgan of Clontarf, a future Ireland captain and Lion. Twice Alex got away and twice Boyle kept up with him on the inside and timed his tackle perfectly.

In defence, Alex saved England from a kick-through by the centre Aidan Bailey, and England led when Hal Sever bundled through a forest of green jerseys, with the arguably illegal assistance of a couple of blocking forwards. Owen-Smith missed the easy conversion then Boyle scored a try with a dive just before the ball rolled into touch-in-goal, and Bailey grabbed a second, and Ireland won 6–3. It was done in spite of Seamus Deering, one of the best Irish forwards, being off the field for more than half the game with blood pouring from a cut over the eye and Morgan, the best Irish back, carrying an injured leg for the last half hour.

One report grumbled that 'the English backs played just about as badly as they had been expected to play before the New Zealand match', while the *Manchester Guardian* damned the Irish with faint praise: 'There must be some magic in the green shirts of Ireland's Rugby team. For years they have astonished friend and foe by playing far above their known club and trial form.'

Tatler supportively proclaimed Alex and Sever as 'the finds of the season' and blamed Alex's lack of opportunity partly on the referee allowing opposing three-quarters to stand yards offside. 'Speed as registered by stop-watches for sprinters . . . is by itself only a part of the three-quarter's pace,' the *Guardian* noted. 'Eric Liddell, Ian Smith and A. Obolensky could not run round the opposing wing three-quarter or full back by speed alone. Speed on the football field . . . depends so much on natural cunning, experience, determination, and the whole combination of almost unidentifiable qualities known as football sense so that the only reliable way of judging a player's speed is by results.'

It was a compliment to Alex to be bracketed with Liddell, the Olympic 400-metre champion of 1924 who was capped seven times by Scotland at rugby, and one of the central characters portrayed in the movie *Chariots of Fire*.

Even a master sprinter could be waylaid by dodgy transport, and Alex called in sick to the *Isis* after the voyage from Dublin, although the magazine hinted the heaving seas had not been the only liquid afflicting their new recruit: 'We regret that we are unable to print Obolensky's account of the Irish International. Alex arrived on Monday morning from Ireland, having fought the Irish on the field, kept them in order off it, travelled all night, and had 12 hours' sleep in four days – and that before the match. So the Editor and the Assistant Editor gently picked him up, carried him home and sang him to sleep, and do not propose to wake the weary hero in time to go to press.'

When Alex eventually turned in his report a week later, he wrote: 'A virtue of the *Isis* is that it is always right up to date, and as ill health incapacitated the writer from formulating any impressions on the England–Ireland international, it is with some hesitancy that I now write on a subject which is over a week old. No doubt those interested have long ago read the details of the match among other daily wails and depressions of our morning journals.

'Let me just add that the game was sadly reminiscent of this year's inter-Varsity match, when the better side failed to win and very nearly lost. Yet there are no excuses for the England XV except perhaps a rather unhappy trip across the Irish Channel. There is an old saying that if there is anything in a man the sea will bring it out. It certainly did with a large majority of the England team!

'Ireland well and truly deserved her victory. The men of Erin had two opportunities of scoring, and twice they scored. England had many more chances, especially in the first half, but only one was taken.'

Alex continued submitting sporting updates and lampooning his rugby pals in his 'Twentieth Century "Blues"' column, topped by a caricature drawn by Tom Webster of him in England kit, grinning and hair flying, chest puffed out and arms flamboyantly akimbo.

There was a tale about an enquiry Alex had taken from an American magazine: 'The questionnaire included: "Do you prefer to go out with a simply dressed woman or one whose attire draws general attention?" "Do you prefer phone calls or letters from girls?" "Would you hesitate to commit adultery if you knew the woman's husband?".'

Alex reported: 'These and many others will have to be answered (*chacun à son goût*, of course) by all members of the OURFC and the OU Lacrosse Club.'

Alex's efforts at light-hearted writing were at odds with the often world-weary tone of *Isis* editorials. One portentous polemic appeared in the edition of 5 February 1936, on the subject of the Olympic Games to be hosted by Germany in the summer. Entitled 'Soldiers and Sportsmen', it cited Dr Joseph Goebbels, the Reich's minister of propaganda:

'The Olympic Games, in the view of Dr Goebbels, are but a prelude to a more serious contest on the field of battle.

'The participation of Great Britain and of Oxford . . . cannot be otherwise construed than as an acquiescence by our representatives in the breaking of the Olympic Charter, and the perversion of Sport to political ends by Dr Goebbels and the Movement whose doctrines he spreads.

'It is no reply to say that refusal to participate is dragging politics into sport. We must lift Sport out of that mire into which Dr Goebbels would thrust it.'

CHAPTER 21

ONWARDS AND UPWARDS

MARCH 1936 WAS a red-letter month for Alex. He made his fourth successive appearance for England, against Scotland at Twickenham, and he received his certificate of 'naturalisation granted to a minor' from the Home Office, under the British Nationality and Status of Aliens Act 1914.

Alex pored over the detail in the document (which is kept now in the National Archives in Kew): 'He shall . . . be entitled to all political and other rights powers and privileges, and be subject to all obligations duties and liabilities, to which a natural-born British subject is entitled or subject, and have to all intents and purposes the status of a natural-born British subject.' It was dated 13 March, and signed by R.R. Scott, Under Secretary of State, and Alex's address was given as Brasenose College, Oxford.

The next day, Alex spoke the oath of allegiance to his adopted country before Frederick Vincent, Justice of the Peace for Oxford City: 'I, Alexander Obolensky, swear by Almighty God that I will be faithful and bear true allegiance to His Majesty, King Edward the Eighth, His Heirs and Successors, according to law. Sworn and subscribed this 14th day of March 1936.'

Two months after his glory match against New Zealand, Alex now possessed a *bona fide* qualification to play rugby for England, in the minds of those who regarded naturalisation as the key. And there was something more serious to it: the obligations mentioned in the citation included being called up to active service in the event of a war.

Alex's growing popularity was a double-edged sword, and in the six weeks between the Ireland and Scotland international games, he could not keep everybody happy. He played for Brasenose in the semi-final of the inter-college 'Cuppers' competition, scoring five tries against Jesus College, whose players must have been thrilled to be sharing the same pitch, rather than accept an invitation from Cliff Jones to join a team packed with internationals in a police charity match in Pontypridd.

Even more regretfully, Alex declined a first appearance for the Barbarians, the world-famous invitational club, in their Mobbs Memorial fixture against the East Midlands. The 'Baa-baas' announced Alex in the team 10 days ahead of the match, alongside seven fellow England players and Wilf Wooller of Wales, but Alex chose the Cuppers final instead. He scored a try, as Brasenose had come to expect, but they lost to the holders, University College.

Alex next enjoyed two matches for Oxford – a win over Harlequins, when he scored a try by making 'the best use of his speed to slip past two men', as the *Observer* reported – and a 16–6 loss to Gloucester at Kingsholm. For the latter, Alex captained the Dark Blues for the first time. He was also blistering on the athletics track, clocking 10.2 seconds in winning the 100 yards in Brasenose's inter-college semi-final against Oriel.

On 8 March, the England team that would meet Scotland on the 21st was named. There were no changes in the backs, despite a clamour for Bernard Gadney and Peter Candler to be replaced, but the forwards were given a big shake-up. Pop Dunkley moved up to the second row in place of Allen Clarke after playing well there for the Barbarians in the match missed by Alex. There was a new cap in Herbert Toft of Waterloo at hooker, and Joe Kendrew was dropped in favour of Northampton's John Dicks, who had been ever present in 1934 and 1935. Edward Hamilton-Hill and John Hodgson made way for the returning Weston and Reggie Bolton (the latter's first Test in three years), and Dunkley's vacancy was taken by Harlequins' Peter Brook.

Alex must have had a good idea his place was secure, as he had written to Irena as early as 12 January: 'I hinted (rather successfully

I think) to Lady Weigall, that you & mother should come & watch big brother Alex perform for England against Scotland on March 21st in London. She was v. enthusiastic. I wonder if anything will happen. I hope she offers to pay your fares over to London. The little holiday would do you both good.'

The trip Alex had planned for himself, to America with the Oxford team, was fated not to happen. Malcolm McGregor Cooper received a cablegram an hour before the departure of the main squad, telling the captain the trip had been cancelled because the hosts' treasurer had run off with £2000 worth of the funding. The money had been raised by Boris Karloff, the Hollywood horror movie actor who had played rugby at school, and squeezed donations out of pals including David Niven and Errol Flynn. An alternative offer to play in the east of the United States raised no enthusiasm, despite the offer of another fundraising drive by Karloff, who was in London, and Cooper told the players they would be going to Wales instead.

A photo from the England–Scotland match that survives in an Obolensky family album illustrates the hit-and-miss life of the inter-national wing. It shows Alex perfectly positioned to score a try that would have been his third in two Tests at Twickenham – if only his fly half Peter Candler had passed him the ball.

But Candler did not pass, just as he had not done in a similar position in Dublin. While England's 9–8 win regained the Calcutta Cup and left Scotland with the wooden spoon at the bottom of the International Championship, the *Manchester Guardian* reflected that 'Sever and Obolensky . . . [were] starved almost from start to finish by Cranmer and Gerrard, who would have been dropped from any school side for showing such stupid selfishness'.

On a March day warm enough to be 'borrowed from June', the Twickenham crowd was agog to see Alex return to the scene of his magnificent debut. The England scrum delivered quick ball but Gadney peppered the touchlines with kicks rather than launch his backs, which might explain the hesitancy of Cranmer and 'Gerry'

Gerrard. Alex twice made cross-field runs – one to pass to Hal Sever and the other to find touch near the left-hand corner, after he had run into a packed Scottish left wing, doubled back and skirted the oncoming forwards. *The Times* said Alex 'has been a wasted force ever since the match with the All Blacks', and he was marked relentlessly by Scotland's Ken Fyfe.

In the wake of what must have been a partial let-down, Alex finished this still astounding season freed by the cancellation of Oxford's American trip to play in the Middlesex Sevens for Rosslyn Park in late April, boosted by a notification of an exciting tour in the offing during his long summer 'vac'.

Meanwhile, at university, he had discovered an engaging hobby, a clue to which was visible in his next appearance in the cinema newsreels.

The annual ceremony of the 'Ivy Beer' was – and remains – a quaint little tradition, typical of Oxford. At lunchtime on Ascension Day [in 1936, this was 21 May] a tiny door between the Old Quad in Brasenose College and the next-door Lincoln College is flung open and members of Brasenose pour through, to be treated to free beer by their neighbours. The door is open for 10 minutes and it is the only time during the year it is unlocked. British Movietone's cameraman and several newspaper photographers were sent to film it, and of course they zeroed in on Alexander Sergeevich Obolensky.

In the film and photos, Alex radiated health and happiness in the May sunshine, while his friend George Galitzine smiled broadly in a fashionable polo neck sweater. A bespectacled bystander punched the air as Alex played for the cameras. The 'Oxford and England rugger star', as the commentary had it, guzzled the beer with a cigarette in his left hand, a pewter tankard in his right and 'a particular nose dipped into the sconce' (a sconce was a fine paid in ale).

Alex wore a shirt and tie and his customary Oxford rugby jumper, but his blazer was new, with bright gold buttons and, on the top pocket with a pen and handkerchief poking out of it, the crest of the Oxford University Air Squadron: the crown and wings of the Royal Air Force above the coat of arms of the university.

The squadron had been formed on 11 October 1925, the same month as one was established at Cambridge. It was a publicly funded flying club for undergraduates, aimed at recruiting peacetime officers for the Royal Air Force from the universities, and tapping into academic research to build better, safer aircraft.

In the mid-1920s there had been an order at Oxford against undergraduates flying, and Britain's Air Ministry trod carefully at first, rejecting the idea of a 'service' approach to squadrons based on Officer Training Corps, and instead offering courses during term, and attachments to RAF units during vacations. Nevertheless, flying was gradually seen as the perfect recreation for the vibrant young man – and still fairly novel and unusual, as manned flight had been around for just over 30 years.

Oxford's air squadron had a wing commander and a flight lieutenant posted to it, and the RAF provided good instructors and the finest trainer machines to fly. Conveniently for Alex, it was all for free – as an equivalent to the Royal Air Force Reserve, it included payment of the annual retaining fee of £25 – and he was one of around 25 members admitted each year.

Alex's first commanding officer in the OUAS was Wing Commander (later Air Chief Marshal Sir) Keith Park, a New Zealand soldier and Great War flying ace who had won the Military Cross, and was educated at the rugby-playing King's College, Auckland, and Otago Boys' High School. The chief instructor was none other than Cyril Lowe, who had also worked at the No. 2 Flying Training School based at RAF Digby.

Once a week, weather permitting, Alex and a handful of fellow undergrads were driven to an airfield, where rows of trainer planes sat on the grass while others buzzed in the sky. There was action and fun to be had here. Having grown up on grim tales of the Great War, the students immediately pondered the merits of this alternative to combat in the mud with the Army or on the water with the Navy.

They trained on the multi-seat biplanes – Hawker Harts, Hawker Hinds, Hawker Audaxes and Avro Tutors – that dominated the RAF up to the early 1930s, in an era of tight budgets and an assumption the country would not be fighting a war any time soon.[1]

Up close, some of the aircraft looked fragile. The Avro Tutor had a light framework of wood and steel covered with tightly stretched fabric held together by wire; the wings trembled in the breeze.[2] The Hawker Hart was more of a silver-winged monster, reeking of oil as it rumbled with the ticking-over of the engine. The Hind 'felt like a cross between a bulldozer and a bucking bronco'. The bright yellow Tutor was easy in the air but tricky on the ground, having no brakes or steering tail-wheel.

For a new recruit like Alex, there was flight familiarisation: a 30-minute trip in which the instructor explained the controls and basic manoeuvres, reminiscent of his elementary lessons in Trent College's Officer Training Corps. The OUAS also had summer camps at RAF Ford in Sussex, between Littlehampton and Bognor Regis, a couple of miles inland from the English Channel.

The instructor sat in the front and Alex in the back, communicating via the rubber Gosport speaking-tube, as the throttle was opened and the plane rattled its way across the grass and then into the air, rocking this way and that, as the ground fell away beneath them. There was no canopy, only a tiny windscreen in front of each cockpit. Alex poked his head over the side and a freezing blast of wind smacked him in the face. The instructor came on to talk about the stick, the rudder and the throttle and how the plane's nose should be positioned in relation to the horizon during turns, climbs and descents.

Alex soon knew he was going to enjoy this new and liberating view of the world. He signed off a letter to his sister Irena with an airy description: 'Must end now as have to fly among the clouds.'

Not all his pals were as keen. Franzi Hohenlohe paid for flying lessons but he gave up before getting his licence. George Galitzine, like his brother Nicholas, was colour blind, and he did not qualify for flying – instead he would become a major in the Welsh Guards. The third Galitzine brother, Emmanuel, was the flyer of the family: a Spitfire ace who set a record for the RAF's highest-altitude combat with the Luftwaffe.[3]

Alex had a sportsman's good balance and hand-eye coordination, peripheral vision and judgement of distance. He learnt to fly straight and level, to execute medium turns and climb, glide and stall, and take off into the wind and land. There were tight vertical turns with and without engine, and spinning, forced landings and low flying.[4] The key with the controls was to relax and move gently, coordinating his hands on the stick and throttle with his feet on the rudder. After 10 hours' dual training he was judged to possess the 'practical knack' to be allowed to fly solo.

The pattern for the first solo flight was to fly four sides of a square: take off into the wind, climb to 500 feet, turn left through 90 degrees while still climbing to 1,000 feet, then flatten out. Fly across the wind clear of the airfield boundary, turn 90 degrees downwind, fly past the take-off boundary, and turn across wind. At this point cut the throttle, trim the gliding speed to 65 mph, lose height to 500 feet and turn for the last gliding approach to land on the airfield. The skill was judging the cross-wind approach – counteracting the drift in a strong wind or keeping further away in still air. The famous RAF fighter pilot Ray 'Arty' Holmes wrote of this stage of development: 'I was a pilot! Or so I thought. Little did I know. Lord, how very little.'

CHAPTER 22

TANGOS AND TOMATO SAUCE

T HE SUN BEAT down on Tilbury Docks as the ship's horn blew a deafening blast and the engines rumbled into action. Irena Obolensky stood on the quayside, gazing up at the open deck, and waved frantically at her brother, who grinned and shouted, 'Cheerio!' and waggled a white handkerchief that he used to mop his brow, as it was a boiling June afternoon on the Thames estuary. Alex turned on his heel and with a cry of 'right, down to business' he headed for the bar in the smoke room.

Twenty-three rugby players were on board the *Andalucia Star*, a smart ocean liner of the Blue Star company who advertised voyages as 'luxurious comfort – no emigrants and second class – £101 for a 54-day cruise', departing for a 10-match trip to Argentina; in Buenos Aires, mainly, as only one game would take place outside the capital.

They were known as 'the British team', but they would eventually become formally designated as 'British & Irish Lions' by the directors of the professionalised organisation, who in 2017 gave each of the players a sequential number to include them in the 125-year history of the famous touring side. Alex's number is 296 and, in 2019, his niece Alexandra received a commemorative cap from the Lions board as a memento.

Douglas Prentice, the England selector who was the team's manager, knew what a rugby tour was all about, having captained the Lions to New Zealand and Australia in 1930. This 1936 team's playing kit was the same as it had been six years earlier, and would be seen again when Sammy Walker's counterparts went to South

Africa in 1938: smart blue jerseys with a badge of three lions rampant, stitched in gold.

Alex had his pristine British passport in hand, and foreign travel was a treat. The ship's captain hosted a farewell dinner the night before departure, which Irena attended. 'Don't fret, I've got the Oxford men to look after me,' Alex said, as he nodded to past and present blues John Brett, Paul Cooke, Peter Hordern, Denis Pratten and Robin Prescott. In the many photographs taken on the tour, which would last almost three months until the middle of September, Alex was rarely apart from Brett or Hordern. Alex's old pal and mentor Bernard Gadney was there, too, as the team captain.

These Lions were a quality selection, if only loosely representative of British and Irish rugby, with the non-English contingent comprising Wilson Shaw and Jock Waters of Scotland, and Vesey Boyle and Charles Beamish from Ireland. Only three men from this trip – Unwin, Boyle and Waters – would be in the Lions party two years later. There again, the Lions of 1930 and 1938 also lacked players who had business or other commitments. Ray Longland, Hal Sever and Peter Cranmer, to name just three, missed the 1938 trip. Such were the ways of amateur rugby.

Eleven of the squad of 23 were capped internationals, and five more – Cooke, Jim Unwin, George Hancock, Fred Huskisson and Prescott – were destined to achieve that status for England. None of the seven who remained uncapped – Harold 'Boy' Uren, John Moll, John A'Bear, Owen Chadwick, Peter Hobbs, Brett and Pratten – could be described as a makeweight. Brett was a captain of Oxford and Uren would play two non-cap matches against Scotland in 1946. Uren's father, also Harold, had been the first footballer to transfer directly from Liverpool to Everton.

Dr Hugh Llewellyn Glyn Hughes, the president of Blackheath FC, was the tour's honorary referee. There were no coaches or physiotherapists, and if any player was injured, he called on Hughes's medical training or the locals would help out. Tactics were looked after by Gadney and the 37-year-old Prentice, and the latter was also the tour banker, paying the bills and handing out expenses.

As the *Andalucia Star* built up speed and the white cliffs of Dover appeared on the starboard side, the purser intercepted Alex's pursuit of a drink: 'You might want to stay your hand, sir. Company of the Folies-Bergère coming aboard at Boulogne.' The players looked at each other and laughed. This was going to be a splendid trip!

The purser's information proved slightly inaccurate. It was a theatrical troupe from the Comédie-Française, not the scantily clad singers and dancers of the Folies-Bergère.

'It's the next best thing,' said Alex, and in a quiet moment he may have reflected how Tilbury had been one of his family's first sights of England all those years ago. But there would not be many quiet moments. The author received an account of another player on the trip who, in an interview decades later, said: 'We couldn't keep Obolensky out of the brothels.' There is no corroboration, unless perhaps a hidden meaning in the account Alex wrote for the *Isis*: 'The womanhood is a veritable bevy of beauty, and was responsible for the enthusiasm we displayed in learning the tango silently and passionately "*à l'Argentine*".' The opportunity to visit brothels was certainly there, as Argentina in 1936 was moving out of a long period of regulated prostitution into a moderately covert system under police control of rooms in nightclubs and hotels, rented out by the hour.[1]

During the 10-day voyage via Lisbon, Madeira and Tenerife, and across the Atlantic to São Paulo, Rio de Janeiro and finally Buenos Aires, the players made the most of a modest drinks tab in the smoke room. With its wood-panelled walls, leather armchairs and Doric pillars, it was like being at Vincent's in Oxford. A 'gala dinner' on 2 July comprised nine courses, from caviar to fruit salad via grilled salmon and roast turkey. The next day the ship's radio received news of Fred Perry's singles title win at Wimbledon, and the trip overall afforded a partial break from oppressive political developments. Germany had applied to re-enter the League of Nations, having stated in March: 'The restoration of her full territory to the German Reich has now been attained.' Despite this, suspicion of Hitler was growing, and by July it was clear the British cabinet was not united behind the prime minister's policy of appeasement. The players' cameras filled with black-and-white film clicked joyfully at the various ports of call, but the atmosphere in Tenerife was eerily quiet, amid rumours of a revolution in Spain.

'We'll train every day,' Prentice told the men, 'but early rising is not an essential.' Most mornings, the players took the ocean air in their multicoloured dressing gowns and bedroom slippers, then exercised in the limited space available: A'Bear, at a hefty 15 stone, made energetic stretches and runs on the boat deck. One of the many stories to live on from the tour is of Alex systematically kicking all their rugby balls into the ocean – the implication being he was uninterested in practice. The only photo of rugby on deck shows the players practising handling moves. Would they really have kicked all the balls away? A likelier scenario is of golf balls thwacked into the drink.

Alex had packed light, and where others wore club jerseys for training – Vesey Boyle, the quick-witted Dubliner, showed off his Leinster harp, and Brett donned his dark-blue Oxford jersey – he exercised in a white England match shirt, which he had either squirrelled away instead of returning it as he was supposed to, or had inherited from another source. The players joined in their fellow passengers' games of quoits and ping-pong and bridge, and for a fancy-dress party they larked around in make-up and monocles, bowler hats and women's frocks plucked from a box of props.

Tom Knowles, the fly half from Birkenhead Park, had toured with the 1930 Lions without playing a Test. Now his rival for a starting place was the excellent Shaw, who had played against Alex for Scotland and was on the way to 19 caps.

When the team reached Rio, they gaped at the beautiful harbour and the Sugar Loaf Mountain. 'An awe-inspiring precipice surmounted by a gigantic figure of Christ,' Brett jotted in the notes he kept for his college magazine at St Edmund Hall. There was a quick practice on a local ground, before the players headed into the city to sniff out the casinos, nightclubs and a German restaurant. 'Hitler salutes, chaps!' someone shouted as they walked in. The staff took it to mean drinks all round for the orchestra.

The ship next put in at Santos, 300 miles down the coast, where Alex donned his white swimming shorts with a high waist and black belt for a dip. Next stop was Montevideo in Uruguay, where a reporter from the English-language *Buenos Aires Herald* boarded and enthusiastically described 'the British Rugby touring team, the strongest ever to visit the River Plate . . . Their typically British healthy appearance testified to the excellent physical condition of every individual member of the team . . . among them the famous Russian Prince Obolensky.'

Brett, the reporter was told, had impressed passengers with his strength by tearing a telephone directory in half. Prentice said 'speed will be the team's chief characteristic', and they would be better than any club team and not far short of a top Test XV. He confided that cigarettes were not forbidden but smoked in moderation. Alex would not have stood for a full ban.

From departure on 20 June and with the first match set for 15 July, they reached Buenos Aires. 'An Army of Giants' was the newspaper headline, reporting: 'Few of the team do not top six feet.'

Alex would be beguiled by the place. 'It was dark when we set foot on Argentine soil,' he wrote later, 'but the following morning revealed the full beauty of Buenos Aires. The city derives much of its charm from its contrast of old and new. Modern skyscrapers clash with tumbledown buildings; mud tracks, cobbled streets and wide tarmac roads all afford means of circulation for primitive buses and modern American taxis; beautifully planned parks bristling with modern sculpture are within a stone's throw of desolate, untidy patches of land.'[2]

The players were given railway passes and honorary membership of athletic clubs, and every day brought a cocktail party or a dinner or dance. Unattached daughters and sisters of British expats delighted to greet the men from home. Uren met his future bride, an Anglo-Argentine named Dorothy Knight. The kilt-wearing members of the St Andrew's Society latched on to Shaw and Walker.

Alex revelled in the eminence of sport in Buenos Aires life, and in the city's sculptures depicting rulers and generals on the backs of horses often rearing in the air. 'It eternally glorifies physical strength whether in man or beast.'

On their only sustained venture outside the city, the players spent a week in parties of five or six on the *estancias* of British friends. Alex was in his element on horseback in a hat and jodhpurs as he and Brett and Hordern had a go at lassooing and playing polo, and gauchos initiated them in dipping and branding cattle, and shooting with revolvers. Another pursuit required mechanical help. 'Can there be anything more thrilling,' Brett wrote, 'than hunting ostrich in a Ford car travelling at almost 50 mph over the rough grass enclosures, with everyone shooting in all directions! You would not believe an ostrich could run so fast or was so hard to hit.'

Argentina was a world power in football and polo, but rugby was a less popular sport, based in well-to-do clubs around Buenos Aires and outposts such as Rosario, where the British team were scheduled to play their sixth match. Even so, the opposition was expected to be stronger than those faced by David McMyn's British team of 1927, who scored 295 points and conceded nine in winning nine matches out of nine.

In Britain, coverage of the tour was scarce. The cost of sending a reporter or transporting news film footage was prohibitive, and the Lions concept was in its infancy. *The Times* carried only a brief agency report of each match, but if they had gained access to the team's photos, the public could have seen players swimming or swinging polo sticks or shooting ostriches or posing in Madeira hats with glasses of beer.

The squad were guests of the River Plate Rugby Union, and based for training at the Belgrano Athletic Club. The majority of the matches were to be played at the Estadio Gimnasia y Esgrima (GEBA), which had smart new concrete grandstands.

Gadney as captain and scrum half was guaranteed to start every match, while the forwards Fred Huskisson and Bill Weston, and full back Harold Uren, would play nine times each, and Brett and Chadwick and Shaw eight.

Alex's contenders on the wing were Unwin, his Rosslyn Park club-mate, and Boyle, whom he had faced in Dublin in March. All three relished the firm and fast grounds. Unwin and Boyle played the first two matches, racking up five and four tries apiece in wins over a Combined Buenos Aires XV by 55–0 and a Combined Argentine XV, essentially Argentina A, 27–0. Shaw and Brett shared the goal-kicking, and John Tallent scored one try in the first match and three in the second.

Tallent was a stocky man with a dainty moustache, a triple blue at Cambridge with five England caps in the centres, who would eventually earn a military OBE and be one of the most enduring rugby administrators, earning a CBE for services to the game. Chadwick was another interesting character, on the way to graduating from Cambridge with firsts in history and theology while earning three blues, and eventually vice chancellor of the university.

Alex made his first appearance of the tour in the third fixture, and the press and a crowd of 3,000 hailed his 'brilliant debut' of two tries against the Olivos club on a Wednesday afternoon, including one to open the scoring in the 27–3 win. Unwin and Hancock scored twice each and 'Pop' Dunkley kicked three conversions. Dunkley and Bill Weston did the same back-row battering job they had done in England's win over the All Blacks six months earlier.

The locals knew Alex's name, and a cartoon of him in a Buenos Aires daily carried the caption: 'The prince, despite being only 20 years old, has established himself as one of the best rugby players in England. Due to his running speed, he has been nicknamed The Lightning Strike from Heaven!'

Alex went on to play the next four matches, including a try to set the British score going again when they beat another Combined Argentine XV, Argentina B, 28–0 the following Sunday, and Gadney scored three tries in the second half. John Moll and Jock Waters went off injured and neither played again on the tour. These blows and others – including, eventually, to Alex himself – scuppered the plan for Wednesday matches in the final fortnight.

The squad was hosted by Nevile Henderson, a Scot who was Britain's ambassador to Argentina. He believed that resistance to Nazism should have begun when Hitler promised 'guns instead of butter' in March 1935. Now Henderson believed that a militarily weaker Britain should appease the German leader. The following year, Henderson was posted as Britain's ambassador to Germany, and was a prominent government figure in Berlin through the Munich crisis to the outbreak of war.

Gadney's pastimes in Argentina included giving lectures on rugby. 'Play hard, tackle hard, play clean, back up and go all out every minute to win' was his theme one evening at the English Club on Calle de 25 Mayo, hosted by Oswald St John Gebbie, president of the River Plate Rugby Union. Alex watched in admiration and noticed how his friend rubbed his nose from time to time, as a nervous tic. Gadney never lost the shadow on his conscience from a tackle he had made on an opponent who was left paralysed with a broken neck.

Gadney talked about full-back play – 'Never sacrifice length for accuracy in your kicking' – and tackle technique. He did not mind putting the boot into a player lying on the ball. 'Don't infer that I'm advocating dirty play, but if a player has his hands lacerated by the boot of a forward he will learn to allow the ball to become free in future.' He advocated seven-a-side rugby to hone backing-up and quick judgement, and the scissors move of a player cutting against the grain to take a pass. 'Pay keen attention to our Mr Peter Hordern,' Gadney said. 'He's here, there and everywhere.'

Hordern, the 29-year-old Gloucester back-rower and the son of a captain in the Royal Indian Marines, was nicknamed 'Shrimp' and very much in the 1930s rugby mould of solid citizen and all-round sportsman. (His younger brother Michael was destined for a fine career as an actor.) Peter had four caps for England from 1931 and 1934, a blue at Oxford, and he had played for Blackheath and the Barbarians. He was also a competition sailor, and when his interpretation of yachting rules was questioned, he would say: 'I'm a rugby player and when I see an opening I have to go for it.'

Alex found Hordern unerringly entertaining, and heard tales of his role as a pilot officer in the Royal Air Force Reserve (Hordern went on to be a flight lieutenant, squadron leader and wing commander during and after the Second World War, winning the Air Force Cross in 1944.)[3]

Together the pair cooked up an infamous episode at one of the post-match dinners. Hordern accepted a wager from Alex to shampoo an Argentinean guest with tomato sauce. The guest needed a lot of talking round and several glasses of sherry before he saw the funny side.

The tour continued with a 62–0 win over the Pacific Railway Athletic Club, the highest score by a visiting team in Argentina at that time. Unwin scored five tries as a centre, while on the wings Alex managed two and Boyle none. Then the team travelled 190 miles north by rail to Rosario and won 41–0 at the Plaza Jewell, with two tries each for Alex and Unwin, and three for Hordern.

Back in Buenos Aires, Unión de Litoral were beaten 41–0, with Alex scoring twice, then the Old Georgian club by 55–6, with four tries to Alex and three to Boyle. This hoisted the British team's points scored to 295, with just nine conceded, neatly equalling after seven matches the totals managed by McMyn's 1927 team in nine. Rugby followers back home read in a Press Association 'Foreign Special': 'The game was outstanding for its keenness and cleanness.'

The Olympic Games in Berlin had opened a few days earlier, and on the day of the Old Georgians match, Jesse Owens collected his third gold medal, winning the 200 metres in a world-record time. There was a report in the Buenos Aires press. 'The secret of speed is the knack of always keeping the foot relaxed with the toes slightly spread,' Owens said, 'and then snapping hard with the calf muscles as soon as the foot touches the ground. Imagine you are running on a red-hot stove.'

Alex was feeling the strains in his own joints from the unyielding surfaces and five straight matches, twice a week. He was left out of the next two fixtures on successive Sundays: the 37–3 win over the Belgrano club, when the hosts scored the only try conceded on the tour, and the 23–0 defeat of Argentina in the quasi-Test match, when Boyle scored two tries, and Shaw scored one and dropped a goal. Chadwick kicked two conversions, and reports vary as to whether Unwin and Tallent had the other two British tries, or Tallent scored them both.

The international match in front of a record attendance of 15,000 at GEBA was scrappy, with an occasional punch thrown by the home players wearing the sky-blue-and-white-hoops of Argentina and captained by 'Jumbo' Francombe, alongside an Elliot, two Talbots, a Logan and a Cameron. Some of Hughes's refereeing decisions were booed and whistled by a raucous 'soccer element' in the crowd. Unwin left the field with injured ribs in the first half, after scoring his side's second try, and his place was filled by taking Hordern out of the pack.

Alex returned for the final game, a 44–0 win over a Combined Buenos Aires Suburban XV representing the CASI, Hindú and CUBA clubs. He scored a try to finish the tour with 12 in six matches, a ratio superior to Unwin's 14 tries in eight appearances (assuming Unwin did score in the 'Test').

This last match in Buenos Aires was watched by friends from the *estancias* who brought along two armadillos to be smuggled into a player's bedroom as a prank. On returning to his room, the player found the animals making a terrifying noise, and in a panic he grabbed their tortoise-like back legs, hoisted them into the bath and slammed the bathroom door. The poor man then retired to night-mares of being eaten alive, even though he was informed amid gales of laughter the next day that the armadillos, while possibly repulsive in appearance, were harmless and often kept as pets.

The tour was a clean sweep for the Lions, with 10 wins out of 10, and 399 points to 12 – in contrast to the Olympics, which ended on 16 August with Great Britain and its dominions having suffered, according to *The Times*, 'one bitter disappointment after another'.

There was a farewell dinner including cocktails at the City Hotel in Buenos Aires, and on 25 August, the squad boarded the *Avila Star*. So many friends came to wish them 'God-speed' that Alex joked: 'The smoke room might run dry before we've sailed!' The well-wishers were eventually persuaded down the gangplank, singing loudly, the *Avila Star* pushed away at midnight, and Alex listened as the voices faded from earshot. Even then Argentina seemed reluctant to let them go. A heavy fog 'did its utmost to hold us to her bosom', Alex wrote, and they had to anchor in the River Plate until dawn. Then a violent storm broke between Montevideo and Santos.

At Rio the players played an impromptu pick-up match with a Brazilian team on a pitch variously described as hard ground or a patch of concrete. The tourists scored 82 points and a lingering tale is that Alex ran in 17 tries. If he did, he chose not to mention it in his post-tour write-up for the *Isis*. Relatives of Unwin, who have spoken often of the trip, state that Jimmy was unsure if it was he who had scored 17 times or Alex – or maybe neither of them.

The old world had moved on in their absence and they found the island of Tenerife mobilised in anticipation of an attack by the Spanish government. At Lisbon an Argentine cruiser awaited South American subjects fleeing from Spain. Reaching Tilbury on 17 September, the team was welcomed by Sydney Coopper on behalf of the RFU. They were hailed in the press as 'bronzed athletes singing lusty choruses'.

As ever, the reporters were keen to hear from Alex. He restricted himself to speaking of firm grounds being conducive to his pace, and Argentinean players who might have done better if they had not got so excited in a scoring position. The ostriches and armadillos and tangos and tomato sauce were reserved for other accounts.

Alex wrote in the *Isis* of a day when Argentina might 'also become supreme in the Rugger world – and if they take advantage of the lessons we endeavoured to teach them, then the tour will have accomplished its purpose.' He had felt a 'spirit of progress' while he was there. To John Brett, the six weeks had seemed like six days, 'so overwhelming' was the hospitality.

Asked about the crowds' treatment of Hughes's refereeing, an unnamed forward said: 'They were better gentlemen than the spectators who go to Association football matches out there. On the soccer grounds they have to have wire netting all round the pitch.' Prentice said the abnormal number of injuries to the players was due to bad luck as much as hard grounds.

The ships that ferried the team back to Blighty met a grim fate. The *Avila Star* was torpedoed by a German submarine U201 on 5 July 1942, off the coast of Africa. The *Andalucia Star* was travelling from Buenos Aires to Liverpool when she was torpedoed by the German submarine U107 and sank, also off the coast of Africa, on 6 October 1942.

CHAPTER 23
TANIA AND TEDDY AND THEOLOGY

'SIT STILL, I want to see all that strapping!'

Tania Vorontsov-Dachkov is giggling at Alex's misfortune.

'Come on then, be quick!' he says as he leans forward in a beaten-up old armchair and waits for the click of the shutter on his girlfriend's camera.

Alex is wearing a crumpled jacket and a university rugby-club tie that is skew-whiff and knotted off-centre. A pair of bedroom slippers sits on the floor, one of them surplus to current requirements. He pulls up a baggy trouser leg to show a gauze bandage wound round his right ankle, down to the middle of the sole.

'Just one more,' says Tania, moving to make better use of the light from the window and capture Alex's toes protruding from the bandage. Outside in St Margaret's Road, cars and bicycles and pedestrians pass by. From here to the city centre it is a mile's jog or cycle ride south along Woodstock Road. Inside number 30 – a four-storey 19th-century building, Alex's digs for his third year at Oxford – the walls appear bare and a little grubby. There are no pictures or photos, and paint peels in the corners next to the skirting board. Two tassles hang from a curtain that can be unfurled to draw a veil over the door.

This softly intimate scene of an injured Alex appears among a collection of photos kept faithfully to this day in a beautiful country house in Shropshire. On a polished Georgian table in a tastefully decorated drawing room, there is one in a frame, recognisable from the set of portraits produced by Bassano in 1935, and it bears the handwritten inscription: 'All my love, Alex.'

Another photo shows Alex in timeless university garb, with a square mortar board cap on his head, a sleeveless gown draped over his tweed jacket and a white sweater bearing the initials OURFC. He is apparently mid-stroll on the street outside St Mary's Entry, with a couple of books and a sheaf of papers under his arm, and his right hand thrust casually in his pocket. The cap and gown were normally worn for graduations and examinations, but they were useful as props whenever a press photographer was in town.

This particular copy was unique. In the bottom right-hand corner, it bore a loving dedication, written in ink by Alexander Sergeevich Obolensky: 'If the walls on the left could speak, they would relate some very happy memoirs of Tania! Alex.'

To discover the picture in its modern resting place was immensely touching. The Shropshire house set in 20 acres belongs to John Richards, a retired former high sheriff of Cheshire who married Helena Hewlett-Johnson in 1968. Helena was the daughter of Tatiana Vorontsov-Dachkov and Gordon Hewlett-Johnson. And Richards and his family believe Tatiana, known as 'Tania' to all her friends and family, was the love of Alex Obolensky's life. None of the two families' descendants know precisely how long the affair lasted, but we know the end of it broke his heart, and hers.

'I think marriage was proposed; I think it was, yes,' John Richards told the author. 'What we do know for certain was that their bond was very strong. They were glamorous times and the players were on a world scene. They were quite a star couple at Oxford; they did make considerable waves together.'

To visit John and his daughter Camilla – Tania's granddaughter – was to probe into delicate family history. They did not want to detract from the great joy Tania found in the life she made with Hewlett-Johnson, whom she married in 1939. Tania was not sporty but she liked the company of sportsmen. Gordon had been at Wadham College, Oxford, and he won World and European Championship medals playing ice hockey for Great Britain in Davos, Switzerland, in 1935. The couple had three daughters: Monica, Helena and Jessica.

After Oxford, Tania spoke only rarely of her time with Alex. She died in 1985, at the age of 73, and many of her personal papers were destroyed soon afterwards.

'Whatever happened between Obolensky and Tania, they had a deep-seated relationship, and whatever happened as it was broken off was very painful to both of them,' says John Richards. 'She always had these photographs of him, but they were put away because she was married to Gordon and they had a very happy life.'

Alex and Tania probably began spending more time together in the latter part of 1936. Alex had returned from South America tanned and fit and full of stories. Tania, too, had travelled overseas that summer, to the United States with her mother and stepfather. Alex's pal Michael Berresford had summered (or wintered) in South America and, on the *Queen Mary* on his way home, he met his future fiancée, Mary Whistler.

On Alex's return, he and Paddy Disney moved into St Margaret's Road, where there was more flexibility for meeting the opposite sex than in the rooms at Brasenose with its rule against female compan-ions – although Alex had probably flouted that, to judge by his cheeky message on Tania's mortar-board photo.

The ankle injury that Tania was keen to memorialise was a sprain picked up while playing for Oxford against the Greyhounds at the end of October. It meant one missed match away to United Services – the *Sunday Times* described it as 'Hamlet without the Prince'. He travelled to Portsmouth anyway, to catch up with Jim Unwin, the United Services vice captain. Well-wishers crowded round them in the pavilion.

When Alex was not at Oxford, he was in London staying with his brother Teddy, who had left Trent College but not gone up to university, and was intending to go into business while playing for Rosslyn Park. Their parents and Irena had recently returned from

France after 11 years, and Lubov had joined the committee of a Russian Cabaret Ball at the Dorchester Hotel.

Alex probably looked to Tania for help in a new project, a 4,500-word essay he contributed to a book named *Be Still and Know: Oxford in Search of God*, edited by Keith Briant and George Joseph, and published by Michael Joseph in autumn 1936.

The book's title came from Psalm 46:10, which proclaimed the power and security of God, at a time of fear of another war. Briant had recently written a portentous editorial for the *Isis*, entitled 'Whither Oxford?': 'Far from bringing the world closer to the millennium, the progress of science and the unhampered growth of industrialism has only brought the peoples of the world to a state of barbarism and inter-racial hostility unparalleled in human history.'

Briant included Alex – now a 20-year-old who might in modern terminology be described as an 'influencer' – among the dozen students contributing to the book. It had a foreword by William Temple, the Archbishop of York.

Alex was keen to lend the perspective of an outsider, a refugee. Tania had an interest in religion and a sharp mind honed in the Sorbonne. Later in life she started writing a history of Russia. She and Alex saw how being forced to grow up outside the country of their birth made them different from previous generations.

In his essay, 'Through God – The Renaissance of Russia', Alex grappled with the provable truth that there was more than one religious model. 'Ardent Christians will argue that Christ is the only God,' he wrote. 'I do not believe this and in my opinion the Christian Church has much to learn from the spiritual and mystic side of other creeds. It is written, "Thou shalt have none other gods but me". This surely implies that there ARE other gods!'

Alex attempted to plot a rational, logical, not quite secular path. 'A regrettable fact of present-day Christianity is the antagonism between the different sects,' he wrote. 'Catholic shuns Protestant and the Baptist holds a contempt for the Greek Orthodox. This attitude should not exist.

'I have attended a church twice since I have been at Oxford but on both occasions I went of my own free will . . . I have friends from all different churches and sects and, to me, their difference in creed has no effect on my friendship. I do not mind whether my friend is a Christian or a Hindu . . . Having been born a Christian myself, I shall remain one – [because] one cannot go through the terrors of a revolution without feeling grateful for the existence of a benign Providence. What has been good enough for ten centuries of Obolenskys is still good enough for me.

'But my ancestors were not refugees, and some modifications in my religious views have been the result of circumstances which did not beset my forefathers . . . Faith is essentially a matter concerning each individual's heart of hearts.'

Alex reconciled the constitutional relationship with religion in his adopted country, where the newly crowned King George VI was supreme head of the Church of England, and the willingness of nation to wage war against nation.

In doing so, he declared – for the first time publicly, but not the last – his readiness to take up arms for Britain. 'We all detest the idea of war and yet when it comes, we willingly fight. I suppose that one's country provides one with an ideal so much greater than self. I know that if ever England has another war, I shall fight, not only because of my love of the country which has adopted me, but also in gratitude for all she has done for me.'

He concluded: 'Patriotism is emotional and, in times of war, often hysterical. Deism is the result of a spiritual urge. I believe that to worship God, one must serve Him, and the mode of service is the love of one's fellow men, irrespective of colour and creed.

'The battle cry of "we fight for God, King and Country" is an old one but I fail to see how any war can be a war for God. The Crusades were largely political, in spite of the religious causes attributed to them.

'So the Russian Church and its traditions still go on. What will happen to it eventually, we do not know. We can only put our faith in God and, through Him, in the renaissance of Russia. Some of my compatriots have unfortunately yielded to circumstances without a fight. Others have carried on the task of adapting themselves, believing that God helps those who help themselves. I am determined to be like the latter because, well, because – "Credo".'

A year or so later, amid the shattering pain of a break-up from Tania, Alex would miserably conclude God did not exist.

CHAPTER 24

LOVE AND LOSS

AS THE 1936–7 season kicked off, the press made a beeline for rugby's most obviously interesting interviewee. There being no such thing as an agent to act for him, Alex took a telephone call direct from the *Sunday Express* and he agreed to meet W.R.G. Smith, the sports editor, just before resuming his studies in Oxford's Michaelmas term.

Smith, a huge fan, found Alex in apparently reflective mood, mulling a desire to work hard to keep his place in the England team while stating he was hoping for honours the following June, in his studies of Philosophy, Politics and Economics, and contemplating his career beyond university. This was almost certainly a stylised view projected by Alex, who was always uncomfortable with journalists' questions.

'If I gain my degree next summer, I'll probably try for a post in some colonial service abroad,' Alex said. 'If I do that, it will be my last season in English rugger.'

Smith showed his surprise.

'What I mean is,' Alex said, 'I ought to be fit for at least five more years of first-class play, but if the offer of a good job comes my way, football will have to take a back seat.'

Smith asked Alex his height and weight. 'Six foot and about 12 stone 9 pounds,' was the reply. 'I'm going into intensive training when I get back to Oxford. Down to the ground at Iffley Road four or five times a week, not including the routine practice or club games. There's no special diet, because it is not necessary. But I'll be cutting down on the old ciggies and it'll be "early to bed" from now on.'

Smith was thoroughly charmed and, under an eye-catching head-line of 'Obolensky's Last Year of Football?', he wrote: 'One of the major excitements I hope to experience this winter is the spectacle of the most picturesque personality in Rugby football today – I refer to Prince Alexander Obolensky, England and Oxford wing three-quarter – tearing down the wing at Twickenham like an express train to score one of the particular brand of tries that have made his name a subject of discussion wherever the oval ball is handled . . .

'Obolensky brought glamour to last season's Rugby programme. He revived the glories of wing three-quarter play that had been dormant since the departure of I.S. [Ian] Smith and C.N. [Cyril] Lowe. He is as fine a specimen of sporting manhood as you could wish to see, and in the close season he seems to have filled out wonderfully across the shoulders. May he have a great season!'

The mention of an 'express train' soon gained a different conno-tation. Alex may have been training and playing hard, but he had not become a hermit, and one Tuesday in late October, he pulled off one of the tricks for which he was always remembered.

On this evening, at the United University Club near Trafalgar Square, Alex was enjoying the kind of easy soirée at which the lack of ready cash could be put to the back of his mind, although he was due back in Oxford for a lecture on the Wednesday and, even more pressingly, the Greyhounds' fixture – six weeks ahead of the big meeting with Cambridge – on the Thursday.

He had a plan, of sorts: one last drink, then hail a cab outside the Club House at 1 Suffolk Street, shoot down the Haymarket, along Pall Mall, all the way up Regent Street, across Oxford Circus to Portland Place and be into Marylebone Station in time for the last train. Give or take a little traffic, it would take, what, 10 minutes. Wouldn't it?

Thirty seconds before the train's advertised departure, Alex sprinted through the station entrance, alcohol and cigarettes on his breath, a wide grin on his face. The loud hiss of steam at the far end of the train quickened his pace. Waving a piece of paper that may or may not have been a ticket, Alex burst past the inspector hovering at the platform gate. An alert passenger held a door open as England's best-known rugby player ran alongside, made a final leap into the carriage and landed spread-eagled on the grubby floor while cheers rang round him. 'Made it!'

There was an ever-present urge in Alex to be brash and maybe a little silly. Charles 'Bloggers' Bloxham, his Oxford rugby contemporary, witnessed a similar escapade when the team was returning from a match in the west. The train made a 15-minute halt at Reading Station and the players stretched their legs. The whistle had blown and the locomotive was pulling away as Alex appeared at full pelt, dived through the window and was hauled in by his friends. 'A good chap,' was Bloxham's description, 70 years later. 'Those were the days!'

Kicking off his third season as a senior player more like a skyrocket than a locomotive, Alex scored seven tries in six matches up to and including the meeting of Oxford's first XV and the Greyhounds in which he left three defenders standing with a change of direction. He was a certainty to be selected for his second Varsity Match, which as usual would double as a trial for England. This season there was no incoming tour, just the customary sequence of International Championship matches, starting with Wales at Twickenham on 16 January 1937.

Alex began with two tries for Bob Oakes's International XV against Durham in Sunderland, to mark the county side's diamond jubilee, where he played in a high-quality backline including Tuppy Owen-Smith, Peter Cranmer, Vesey Boyle and Haydn Tanner. It was third time lucky as Alex had pulled out of Oakes's annual fixture twice before.

Returning to Old Deer Park, Alex put two tries past the Old Blues for Rosslyn Park, before starting the term at Oxford with a try for the Probables in a 29–10 win over the Possibles. The strength at Oxford's command was shown in the try-scorers: Disney, Errol Button, Charlie Grieve, Mervyn Hughes, Alex and John Brett. One of the Possibles' wings was Hugh 'Buzzer' Percy, on whose rugby prospects Alex was soon to have a significant influence.

A trip to Newport brought no try for Alex in an 8–5 win for Oxford, although he set up one for Button, and a supportive essay in the *Illustrated Sporting and Dramatic News* described how to make use of Alex's great speed. Alex next played for Oxford against Leicester at Iffley Road on 4 November and, within two minutes, he scored in the corner with 'three men hanging on to him', according to *The Times*.

The bad news out of this match was that Alex had torn a muscle in his thigh. He came off the field with a sharp pain, and soon the telltale sign of blood seeping from the injury was a contusion of dark purple across the back of his leg.

What had hitherto been a simple plan of a second Oxford blue and a fifth appearance for England was now flipped into a frantic race to get fit. Alex missed Oxford's trip to Richmond and matches at home to Blackheath and away to Harlequins, and the *Daily Mirror* reported: 'Obo's injury is giving Oxford the Blues.'

Meantime, in the family home of Hugh Percy, there was mounting excitement. Percy played as a stopgap right wing against Richmond and Blackheath, and when he turned out for Oxford A versus Edinburgh Academicals, a report by E.H.D. Sewell described him as 'a cleverer player than Obolensky', and almost as fast.

Micky Walford, the centre and defensive rock who was also a fine hockey player and cricketer, took against Percy but Alex championed the newcomer's cause. The tale handed down in the Percy family, and gratefully recorded in a scrapbook kept by Percy's mother Gertrude, is that Alex threatened to resign from the Oxford rugby club if 'Buzzer' was not picked for the team.[1]

Alex watched Oxford's matches while he waited for his leg to heal, and he told 'Mac' Cooper, the captain, that William Renwick on the left wing was too slow and Percy should be tried there against Major Stanley's XV. In Oxford's 12–9 win on 26 November, Percy marked Hal Sever and played well. Renwick, incidentally, eventually played twice for Scotland.

As Cooper announced each blue for the Varsity match in succession, and he sent cheery cards with a call to 'assist in Tab Slogging on Tuesday December 8th . . . I trust that this invitation will not interfere with your social arrangements', he clung to the hope of Alex being fit.

England's selectors were in attendance at Iffley Road on the last Saturday in November, for Alex's first match in almost four weeks. Gloucester were the opposition as Alex started on the right wing with Percy on the left and Renwick omitted.

On a nightmarish afternoon for Alex, his still troublesome thigh ruined his efforts to impress. Gloucester's forwards dominated and by the second half he was limping badly, with his chances of the Varsity Match obviously gone. Percy was one of three freshmen picked by Oxford for Twickenham, with Renwick instead of Alex on the right wing. Oxford lost 6–5, and Percy never had a sniff of a try – but he had at least made it onto the pitch and he referred to Alex respectfully as 'The Russian Prince' forever more.[2]

Alex attended the post-Varsity match party, understandably glum. Modern physiotherapy would have helped him recover more quickly, but in December 1936 he would be *hors de combat* for almost a month.

It was a grim time for Britain, too. Edward VIII abdicated on 11 December, after a tumultuous few weeks during which the public discovered more about Wallis Simpson.

'At long last I am able to say a few words of my own,' Edward said, in a speech from Windsor Castle broadcast live on radio. 'I want you to understand that in making up my mind I did not forget the country or the empire which, as Prince of Wales and lately as king, I have for twenty-five years tried to serve.

'But you must believe me when I tell you that I have found it impossible to carry the heavy burden of responsibility and to discharge my duties as king as I would wish to do without the help and support of the woman I love.'

He took the title of Duke of Windsor, and moved abroad.

CHAPTER 25

BACK IN THE ENGLAND SQUAD AND TIME WITH TANIA

TO PLAY RUGBY for England in the 1930s was not a career move with the potential to earn life-changing money; the prizes Alex was chasing were the pride of being picked for his country and the challenge of testing himself against the best players from other nations.

Missing the Varsity Match had been a big setback, and an Oxford tour to Ireland came and went without him before, on 19 December 1936, the teams for England's first trial were announced, with Sever and Unwin on the wings for the Probables, and Guest and Harry Faviell, a former Harlequin now at Redruth, for the Possibles.

Alex arranged to play for Dr Hughes's International XV at Blackheath on 26 December, but while his summer-tour pals Unwin, Moll, Tallent, Cooke, Chadwick, Hordern, A'Bear and Hobbs made it an enjoyable reunion, Alex watched it from the touchline, fit only to be a touch judge. 'I think I'll be ready in a few more days,' he told Dr Hughes, who fixed up a guest spot in the Blackheath Wednesday team at home to Kent Public Schools on the 30th, a normally very minor fixture which now attracted the attention of the media.

Just over a month since Alex had limped through the Gloucester match, he scored two tries and the *Daily Express* ran a stirring story of his 'brilliant runs', adding: 'He hesitated once or twice but finding his knee [sic] stood up to the strain in the heavy going, he went on to play at top speed.'

On such a day, direct quotes in post-match reports were rare, and sometimes pieced together from second-hand accounts. 'Everything went off splendidly,' Alex was reported as saying. 'There was no recurrence of the trouble. I am perfectly fit again.'

In theory, Alex was England's incumbent right wing from the previous March, but as with the first national trial at Workington, so the second one at Bristol went by without him. Still he kept at it, heartened by the England selectors continuing to declare an interest. He scored for Rosslyn Park in heavy conditions at Bedford on 2 January 1937 – the same day as the third and final trial at Twickenham – and, a week later, England arranged for him to be included in Leicester's team at Gloucester. 'If the clubs concerned do not object, it is hard to make out a case against RFU interference,' one reporter wrote.

The interference failed to do the trick. Alex did not play well and, when the England team was finalised the next day, Hal Sever and Harlequins' Arthur Butler were the wings, with Cranmer and Candler as the centres. There were six new caps as the selectors rubber-stamped the dropping of Gadney at scrum half in favour of Jimmy Giles. England's captain throughout the 1937 Championship would be Tuppy Owen-Smith.

Some of the newspapers ignored Alex's injury and observed merely he had been 'unable to satisfy the selectors he has regained his form of last season'. Others regretted his absence as England scraped a 4–3 win over Wales, with Sever's dropped goal outdoing a try by Wilf Wooller.

Alex put two tries past London Scottish in a new-look Oxford side at Iffley Road, and after another try against Edinburgh University, *The Times* reported: 'Prince Obolensky was easily the most dangerous attacking player in the game; whenever he received the ball a try seemed probable.' A fourth try in three matches for Oxford, against Bristol at Iffley Road, came on the day England edged a win in their second Championship match, 9–8 over Ireland at Twickenham.

Still the national selectors kept looking, and a full complement watched Alex play for Oxford against the Army at Aldershot three weeks before England's final Championship fixture in Scotland. In a strong wind and driving rain, Alex's defence stood out as he beat his old pal Jimmy Unwin to a try-saving grounding of the ball.

There was no media fanfare for the wider England squad in those days, only for the XV itself, but Alex's try on his debut for the Barbarians against the East Midlands at Northampton convinced the selectors to choose him as a reserve for the Scotland game, and he was one of 22 players who took part in a practice match before the trip north, with fellow wings Sever and the recalled Unwin. The week before Murrayfield, Alex scored for Leicester at home to London Welsh. Still the England selectors stuck with Sever and Unwin, and a 6–3 win in misty Edinburgh secured a Triple Crown and the Championship title. Owen-Smith was chaired from the field in his final international before retirement.

For Alex, it was a tale of so near and yet so far. Howard Marshall in the *Bystander* – a weekly magazine reviewing the arts, politics and sport – reported: 'An Obolensky in Sever's place by using his speed and swerve might well have scored two or three more tries.'

During his chat with W.R.G. Smith for the *Sunday Express*, Alex had spoken of 'two other main interests': flying and the theatre.

'I'm seeing all the plays that come to Oxford and reading the works of the chief authors,' Alex said. 'I plan to write some reviews for the *Isis* – you know, like a theatre critic – and I do like to hook up with the actors and actresses who play in Oxford to get the "atmosphere".'

There is no evidence of this coming to much, as neither his name nor his initials are attached to any theatre reviews in archived copies of the magazine, but he continued to indulge his other favourite activity with the Oxford University Air Squadron, headquartered at Shippon near Abingdon, about six miles from the city.

'My great ambition now is to gain my "wings",' Alex said, referring to becoming an operational pilot in the RAF, and Smith immediately formed the write-up in his mind: 'For a man who is just about the fastest runner with a Rugby ball the game has seen for many years, flying is a peculiarly fitting hobby.' The *Auckland Star* of 19 January 1937 also made the link, headlining a piece on Alex with 'wants to fly in the real sense', with a photo of him in a cockpit. The connection was equally obvious to *Tatler* when they took press pictures of Alex and his pals at Shippon in autumn 1936.

Back at Brasenose, there was pressure on Alex from Sonners and the dons to attend to his studies. No record survives of his third-year exam results, so we must guess they either went unsatisfactorily or perhaps he was excused from taking them on the basis that rugby had dominated his time at Oxford. Either way, Alex was enrolled for an extra, fourth year.

His injury-afflicted rugby season had a brief revival when he scored for Leicester at Bath at the end of March 1937, and again in the Tigers' final match at home to Blackheath three weeks later, to take his total of tries for the club to an impressive 11 in 13 appearances.

The newspapers reported Alex as lined up for R.F. Oakes's charity team in Harrogate and Hartlepool, for Rosslyn Park in the Middlesex Sevens, and for Wavell Wakefield's International XV, but none of these appearances transpired. Alex kept saying an optimistic 'yes', but he was stymied either by his lack of fitness or by needing to attend to his books. At this time, too, his friend Bernard Gadney decided to move to work at Malsis Hall Prep School in Yorkshire, and play for Bradford.

Progress was much more promising with Tania. In June 1937, Alex wrote to Irena, who had taken an office job with Norman Hartnell, fashion designer to the royals, in Mayfair: 'I am absolutely in heaven just now as Tania arrived back last Friday. I met her boat-train and we thought of going over to Hartnell's to take a drink off Norman and say "what-ho!" But it was rather an awkward time so finally decided to return straight to Oxford.'

Tania gained her degree that summer; the couple holidayed at a villa in the Cap d'Antibes and visited Cannes, and Alex went to the

Italian alps north of Milan. The heat of late August made him feel lazy, and he felt 'the mountain air will brace me up a bit'. They returned to London in the third week of September, via a break in Paris. In November 1937 Alex wrote to Irena: 'Hope you will be able to visit Oxford some time. If you come later in the term Tania will be here again, so we could have a small party together.'

The mythical figure of a young swashbuckler winning the hand of a fair lady has featured in epic tales from the *Odyssey* to *Star Wars*. To their friends and admirers, Alex and Tania fitted that bill. 'They were a celebrated couple, very much the toast of the town,' John Richards says now of his mother-in-law and her boyfriend. 'Tania was a big socialite, and in the dramatic society, and they were glamorous times.'

Alex's mother, Princess Lubov, had other ideas.

CHAPTER 26

DISASTER AT LEICESTER AND A PARTING OF THE WAYS

A LEX WINCED AS he climbed out of bed, racked with pain in his chest, sweat around his temples and neck. He shuffled to the wooden desk in the bedroom of his digs at the rear of a red-brick building on Iffley Road, lit a cigarette, located a piece of fresh blue writing paper in one of the drawers, and sat down to write.

Tears of fury pricked at his eyeballs and sarcasm dripped from his nib.

> Dear Papa & Mama
> You will be very pleased to hear that the Tania–Alex friend-ship has been broken by Mama's persistent & distasteful anti-Tania campaign. The poor girl couldn't help hearing about it. It may also interest you to know I am very unhappy. I gave you a very fair & clear warning against the anti-Tania campaign, so you must now face the consequences. During the past days I have been suffering great physical pain but it doesn't compare with the spiritual agony you have caused me.
> Alex

The physical pain was due to an alarming injury Alex had suffered the previous Saturday, 22 January 1938, making his 14th appearance for Leicester against Richmond at Welford Road. It had confined him to bed and ruined his hopes of winning back his place with England.

With his 22nd birthday imminent, Alex had never felt at a lower ebb.

*

Alex imbibing the 'Ivy Beer' with friend and fellow Brasenose undergraduate Prince George Galitzine at Lincoln College, Oxford, May 1936.

Alex the horseman, on the right, playing polo on the British & Irish Lions' tour of Argentina, summer 1936.

Alex in Argentina with Bernard Gadney, the captain of the Lions.

Alex posing in university garb in St Mary's Entry, outside Brasenose College.

The 1936 Lions squad. *Back*: Waters, Weston, Shaw, Cooke, Alex, Prescott, Moll, A'Bear, Hobbs, Unwin, Tallent, Uren, Pratten, Dr Hughes. *Front*: Beamish, Dunkley, Knowles, Gadney (captain), Prentice (manager), Hordern, Boyle. *On ground*: Hancock, Chadwick, Brett. *Not in photo*: Huskisson.

"MISS SKETCH'S" DIARY.

WEDNESDAY, JULY 13.

To the Dorchester for the POLO BALL in aid of the Chelsea Boys' Club. An excellent evening, for the dance had Lady Margaret Drummond-Hay as president and chairman, which meant that its success was a foregone conclusion. The Duchess of Hamilton's children are all energetic, talented and full of organising ability—moreover, they have hosts of devoted friends, so it's easy for them to get up anything, specially for a really good cause like the Chelsea Boys' Club, which is for the benefit of the boys of the "World's End" area of Chelsea—a poor and very crowded district.

Houp-là, "Motor-racing," and other games and side-shows provided alternative amusements to dancing—a modern fashion which everyone enjoys. Miss Diana Lloyd a very successful Houp-là thrower, as I saw she had captured at least one bottle of something through her display of skill.

Princess Natasha Bagration one of the decorative dancers. I liked her brocade dress, and noticed that she wore one of the heavy gold curb bracelets which have made such a come-back to favour this year. Mrs. Rhodes Moorhouse (the former Amalia Demetriadi) attractive in her high evening dress embroidered with silver.

MR. DENNIS BLACK, MISS DIANA DRURY and the COUNTESS OF WARWICK.

Alex on the town with girlfriends Nancy Harmood-Banner and Catherine Heywood, top left – as featured in '"Miss Sketch's" Diary' in July 1938.

Alex's beloved sister Irena, with her first husband, Edward Beddington-Behrens.

Alex, second from left, with rugby pals at a party given by MP and former England captain Wavell Wakefield (third from left), July 1939.

Alex, wearing his favoured white tie, with Tania Vorontsov-Dachkov at a post-match dinner.

Making a tackle for Rosslyn Park v Old Blues at Old Deer Park, October 1936.

The Rosslyn Park first XV, 1938–39. *Back*: H.A. Burlinson (hon sec), H.H. Cobb, J.V. Hartley, D.K. Huxley, W.C. Roff, W.M. Allen, J.R. Tyler, D.E. Martin, P.J. Halford, J.R. Patterson (referee), L.W.E. Hall (asst hon sec), J.E.S. Tyler (team sec). *Front*: P.F. Cooper, E.J. Unwin, K.H. Smith (captain), C.C. Hoyer Millar (life president), Alex, F.St.G. Unwin, F.G. Denman. *On ground*: R. Shepley, R.B. Comyn.

Dancing with Joan Wakefield at the Rosslyn Park Rugger Ball, Grosvenor House Hotel, February 1940.

Alex in his RAF uniform at Rosslyn Park's ground, Old Deer Park, 1939.

Catch him if you can: Oxford Greyhounds v Sussex County Rovers, at Lewes, March 1938.

Alex with fellow rugby international Trilby Freakes in the Oxford University Air Squadron in 1938.

Climbing into the cockpit of a trainer biplane.

'Prepared to fight for King and Country': Alex, sixth from the right in the middle row, and fellow members of the Oxford University Air Squadron in 1938.

Above: Alex's fatal accident card, in the files of the RAF Museum in north London.

Left: Harry Gray's statue of Alex, in Cromwell Square, Ipswich, unveiled in February 2009.

Leicester's Welford Road stadium was (and still is) one of the largest venues in club rugby union, but it had always been known for a lack of space between the touchlines of the pitch and the barriers in front of the spectators. Any player going hell for leather to finish a try or make a saving tackle ran the risk of colliding with the perimeter barricade.

The first 10 minutes of the Richmond match had gone well as Alex maintained his brilliant reputation as a prolific finisher with his 12th try for the Tigers.

In the second half, he was making a 'crashing run' on the attack when a Richmond tackler grabbed him and sent him flying into what looked like a pile of straw but was actually a thin covering to protect the grass from frost. Behind it was a concrete wall and Alex took the impact full in the chest. He stayed down for a minute, shocked and winded and maybe a little embarrassed. The club doctor came to examine him. He attempted to carry on playing for a few minutes, before being helped from the field. The newspapers were told he had damaged his ribs. Some reported that 'severe internal injuries had ended his sporting career'. Both Oxford and Leicester issued denials, describing those reports as 'far-fetched'.

Alex returned to his digs, where he was put to bed and told not to move for a few days. He had a haemorrhage on his left lung, and rib and knee injuries, and he was running a high temperature. Irena called to ask after him, and Alex let the landlady reply. In his subsequent letter he told his sister he was expecting to be strong enough for an X-ray the next day to 'see if any ribs are cracked and if everything is now in the right place'. He was 'a mass of bruises' but the fever was abating. He wrote to Eric Thorneloe, secretary of the Tigers, to say stoically he would be avoiding violent exercise for a few days but would resume training soon.

Alex's career was not over but the episode was serious at a time when England were one match into the International Championship, losing to Wales, and he fancied his chances of being picked to face Ireland and Scotland.

Alex had suffered injuries before, notably the torn thigh muscle in late 1936, but the greatest frustration now was down to the tremendous effort he had put into his rugby in the first half of the 1937–8 season. He scored two tries for the Probables in Oxford's final trial on 14 October, and racked up eight tries in 10 matches for the Dark Blues against Leicester, London Scottish, Newport, the Greyhounds, Richmond, Dublin University, Blackheath, Harlequins, Major Stanley's XV and Gloucester. Along the way, he made light of a minor back injury and a cold during a rainy spell.

Alex had moved from St Margaret's Road to share digs with Roger Kimpton and Desmond Magill at 290 Iffley Road. Magill had been to Eton and was a good cricketer who would tour Jamaica with a combined Oxford/Cambridge team in summer 1938 and play for the Army, while Kimpton was short and stocky with puckish features topped by a mop of curly hair. A sporting all-rounder, he took 160 off Gloucestershire in The Parks in his second first-class cricket match. He also won the Freshmen's lawn-tennis singles and gained a golf blue.

The three friends played bridge together in the evenings, and the *Isis* warned readers to give it 'careful thought' before wagering much money against them.

Alex's extra year at university had not been part of the original plan, but it delighted John Brett, captain of the rugby side, as Alex was an automatic choice for the Varsity Match on 7 December. A report of the match against Blackheath on their 75th anniversary stated: 'Obolensky, just as he seemed fated to be written off as a flash in the pan, has begun to score tries in the manner of 1936–7.'

For the big date with Cambridge at Twickenham, the wheels of royalty had turned and King George VI was the honoured guest. The players lined up to meet him on the pitch and he shook hands smartly with Alex. The king was a Cambridge man, so he was to endure a rough afternoon peering through thick fog to see Oxford win by a then record score and margin of 17–4. Amid thick fog, the Light Blues had plenty of possession but they squandered chance after chance with poor passing among the backs.

Alex wore a white number 2 in a curly font on his dark-blue

jersey (the system of numbering used to be varied, depending on what was agreed between the teams) and he had allowed his blond hair to grow; on the black-and-white newsreel film, it glimmered like a sheet of silver. He was also throwing in at the lineout, a task expected of a wing in the 1930s. The British Movietone footage shows him gently rocking the ball in his right hand like a butcher weighing a leg of lamb before he lifts it over his right shoulder and lobs it in the general direction of his forwards – who promptly have it nicked by their Cambridge counterparts. Ferocious defence and counter-attack were Oxford's lots, and scrum half Paul Cooke scored two tries, with another by Pat Mayhew after an adroit dribble on the left wing. Alex did not score but he was praised for his work as a decoy.

In the four-way tussle for England's two wing places in the 1938 International Championship, a three-part audition for Alex continued into the second and third national trials.

He was named in England's Possibles team to play at Ipswich Town FC's Portman Road ground on 18 December, when the Probables' wings were Jimmy Unwin and Johnny Macdonald from Cambridge University. A 10,000-strong crowd saw Alex strive furiously to make an impact. He and the slower but hard-working Macdonald mostly cancelled each other out, but Macdonald scored a try in the Probables' win by 23–11.

A minor injury kept Alex from playing for the Barbarians against Leicester on 28 December, and Macdonald replaced him and grabbed a try with a lively hand-off. Meanwhile the now 27-year-old Hal Sever, who had reversed a decision to retire from rugby, scored a beauty for Sale at Blackheath.

Alex's last bid to sway the selectors came on New Year's Day 1938, as he and Macdonald played for 'The Rest' opposite Unwin and Sever of 'England' at Twickenham. The Pathé newsreel teed it up: 'It must have given the selectors a few sleepless nights, before and after the event – but then it's always a gamble.'

As usual, Alex was picked out by the cameraman, pre-match. With his hands thrust in his shorts pockets for warmth, he was grinning but he looked focused and very fit. Whatever it was he said to the player in front of him in the team photo remains a mystery; indeed, there is no surviving audio of Alex speaking.

The Rest lost 13–11, with Unwin halting one run by Alex with a 'clothes-line' tackle round the neck that would have brought a penalty and possibly a yellow card today. Alex's skill in scooping up a loose pass and an awkwardly bouncing ball is seen in the newsreel, an instant before Sever comes in to block, about a yard from the pitchside camera.

The verdict in *The Times* was ominous: 'Sever's famous momentum promised more than Obolensky's famous speed. To be fair, Obolensky never had an entirely clear run away, but as he was being tried severely as a footballer and not as a track runner, the object lesson held good.' An accompanying photo showed Sever taking Alex down on the run, with a low, driving tackle beneath a fending arm.

Sure enough, Sever and Unwin were picked for England away to Wales at Cardiff Arms Park on 15 January. The Welsh won 14–8, although the teams scored two tries each, and there was a lovely try for Peter Cranmer made by Bill Weston and Unwin.

Back in Oxford, Alex was scheduled to captain the university in a BBC Radio 'Transatlantic Spelling Bee', facing members of Harvard University and Radcliffe College, from Massachusetts, representing the USA. Alex's teammates included Lord Oxford & Asquith, the grandson of a prime minister, and Miranda Tallents, daughter of the BBC's public relations officer. But the day beforehand, the shocking injury at Leicester intervened, and he was in no state to stand up, let alone spell 'pettifoggery' or even 'haemorrhage'.

Almost four weeks passed before he was able to have a run-out with Brasenose to test his recovery – a Cuppers semi-final lost to Christ Church in a snowstorm – but he missed Leicester's games with Newport and Swansea.

England's trip to Ireland was spectacular, and if Alex had played he might have been a beneficiary of the 36–14 win and seven English tries, including one for Unwin. Still, there was an outlandish reaction by the selectors as Cranmer was stripped of the captaincy in favour of the Waterloo front-rower Herbert Toft. With Unwin and Sever on the wings, England finished the Championship by losing 21–16 to Scotland, who claimed the Triple Crown and the title. It was the first rugby international match to be broadcast live on television, to a few thousand viewers around London. The winning try, scored by the Scotland captain Wilson Shaw in the corner, might have been prevented by Alex with his outstanding pace, but we will never know.

All the way through these rugby trials and tribulations, which were an extra burden on top of his studies and a lack of ready cash, Alex was increasingly upset by his mother's interference in his courtship of Tania. To Alex's extreme annoyance, Lubov Obolensky had taken against the pretty Russian on the arm of her eldest son.

A letter to Irena in early November 1937 demonstrated the hardening of Alex's attitude. 'Am dreadfully sorry I can't come to all the attractive parties you mention but have a tremendous amount of work to do,' he wrote. 'And contrary to the beliefs of most of the family I am quite a hard worker. I simply must get a good degree if my future is to be a success. Also am in very strict training now and so would not really enjoy parties. In any case my financial position is rather critical and can't afford travelling up to London.'

Alex wrote again a week later, to Irena's work address at Norman Hartnell's in Bruton Street, mentioning how Lubov had attempted to contact Tania's birth father, Alexander Vorontsov, through Countess Kleinmichel, a well-known member of Britain's White Russian community, having also chipped away at Alex's friend Paddy Disney, who had attained his second-class degree in PPE the previous summer. 'I am still v. much annoyed with Mama,' Alex wrote, 'as she persists in being unpleasant and making herself ridiculous. I hear she asked Kleinmichael to write to Alexander Vorentzoff and make inquiries re. Tania. Kleinmichael was furious as it is very awkward writing about these things, and besides everyone who was in Russia at the time knows it was a delicate and unfortunate affair. But although there was no marriage, everything was decently arranged and A. Vorentzoff sent money for Tania's upbringing etc. I cannot understand why Mama insists on washing the dirty linen publicly – especially as it only concerns her indirectly.'

Tania and Alex hosted Irena for Sunday lunch, the day after Alex had scored against Harlequins at Twickenham and then returned for a dinner party with a don.

Alex wrote to Irena: 'I was so happy to see you last week, especially as I feel that apart from you & Father, the family is rather anti-Alex. So glad to hear you still like Tania so much; am sure Papa would too if . . .' – he paused and crossed out the last word – 'when he meets her.'

Alex promised to send Irena tickets for the Varsity Match on 7 December while mentioning they were 'rather expensive' at 7/6 each. 'I am still on the rocks & can't see how I am going to pay my landlady for this term. Incidentally if I do send you tickets in the next day or two I think it would be best if you went with poor old Papa. After all Norman can afford to buy tickets of his own . . . Sorry I can't enclose 10/-. It makes me feel very miserable, but we are both in the same septic tank over this eternal cash question.

'Tania & I both send you our love. Also give my love to Papa. I think he is on my side because he is much more noble-minded than Mama & knows how I feel. Yr affectionate brother Alex.'

Alex put off the idea of meeting Irena after Oxford's next match at Blackheath in London, claiming he would miss it with a tutorial, a tea appointment, and a dance in the evening. And he added another reference to money. 'Perhaps it would be best if you got a lift here [to Oxford] with Norman . . . then he could stand us a dinner, as I myself am absolutely on the rocks & completely broke.'

In fact, Alex did play at Blackheath, running in two tries in a 21–19 win. Perhaps it was simpler to socialise rather than meet his 20-year-old sister. He threatened to go to Scotland after the Varsity Match and to spend Christmas with Tania and their friends instead of his family.

None of this was Irena's fault, and she was busy arranging to leave her routine job at Hartnell's, so the family trouble kept brewing. Alex began referring to Lubov as 'the Private Detective' and he warned his mother, through Irena, not to visit Oxford, citing her 'previous performance at Headington' and saying his uncle Vadim 'does not at all welcome her intention of coming up here. It is better she should make a laughing-stock of herself with a "starook" in Brighton than to be let loose here.'

It all led to the parting from Tania, and Alex's tempestuous letter. In response, his parents and Irena wired separately with greetings for his 22nd birthday, and he spent the day quietly, observing he felt 'definitely . . . much older and senile'.

Alex gave Irena an update in a second emotional letter. The siblings had seen each other a few days beforehand, when Irena brought flowers and fruit and cigarettes, but Alex had been too weak to venture out. In the meantime an X-ray showed his bones were intact and the haemorrhage had cleared.

'The only trouble is that the lung is still bruised on the outside,' Alex wrote, 'and in the photograph the whole of the left side of the chest is a darker colour than the right. However the doctor is most hopeful. He says the heart is in excellent condition & he expects to allow me to take exercise in the next day or two. At the moment am very busy with my work which lapsed rather badly while I was in bed. I simply couldn't do any reading with a temperature. The only exercise I have had so far has been a little flying (if that can be called exercise). The doctor allows me to fly providing I don't fly higher than 1,000 feet.'

Then he moved on, with evident fury, to address the news that Lubov had been prying for reassurance that the affair with Tania was over, and to remind Irena – as if she needed it – of his impecunious state.

> Please tell my dearly beloved parents not to pester and bombard Paddy with ludicrous correspondence. There is no need for them to prolong the hysteria – unless they think I am a liar.

It's rather getting on my nerves meeting people who produce ridiculous parental letters or stories. If they have failed so miserably to retain my affections, they might at least try to retain some of my respect; and also the respect of my friends.

You cannot imagine how sick I am of the whole business, and now that I have given way, they might at least be contented and calm. I sometimes think they take a devilish delight in making scandal and unhappiness. I am doing my best to forget a brief but happy interlude in my life, and they apparently wish to keep the memory alive now that the affair is dead. I often curse God for giving me such an incompetent, malicious, and misunderstanding mother. If God was here I should pull his beard very hard, but then I don't really believe in his existence.

By the way do you remember the little financial discussion we had? Is there any hope of your helping me out of the hole? Let me know soon because if you can't manage it, I shall have to resort to my own means. Let me know definitely, and don't make vague promises. I shall know, dear Irena, that you have tried and it is not your fault if you are unsuccessful. The whole point is that that [sic] something must be done quickly. I hope you are keeping well, and am looking forward to hearing from you. Must end now as have to write an essay for tomorrow morning.

Bless you always dear, Alex

CHAPTER 27

LUBOV'S OBJECTIONS AND OTHER FORCES OF NATURE

IT IS DIFFICULT to determine what lay behind Lubov's opposition to the relationship between Alex and Tania. The belief among Tania's descendants is that Lubov disapproved of Tania's illegitimacy, although Lubov was an illegitimate and adopted child herself. Perhaps she was just being practical. She believed in a matriarch's right to pick her children's partners, or at least influence their choices. Her solution to Alex's financial problems was that he should marry into money, and she may have thought it quite sensible and moral to point this out – and her daughter Irena would make just such a marriage, in 1944, with the partly Jewish-descended Edward Beddington-Behrens; they married in the Russian Church.

Irena possessed a serene beauty, inheriting the angular cheekbones of her father and a piercing stare from her mother. According to Felizitas Obolensky, her niece, she was 'sophisticated with a great importance placed on social life, though not too intelligent'.

Beddington-Behrens was one of the twin sons of Walter Behrens, President of the British Chamber of Commerce in Paris. Both brothers fought in the Great War – Walter died aged 20 at Ypres, while Edward received two medals for 'conspicuous gallantry and devotion to duty'. He mixed in the art world, and in the Second World War he would be a regimental officer participating in the British Army's retreat from Dunkirk.[1] Later he moved into politics and economics, working for the League of Nations and helping to found the European Movement, a service for which he was knighted in 1957, and he became an adviser to Harold Macmillan, a prime-minister-to-be.

Edward had been married before, to the daughter of a tailor, and he met Alex at a few London parties long before he bumped into Irena outside his expensive flat in Park Lane, and she quickly warmed to this cultured English gentleman with a pencil moustache and thinning dark hair.

In his autobiography, published in 1963, Edward Beddington-Behrens hailed his mother-in-law Lubov as the mainstay of the Obolenskys: a 'dark, active little woman whose old photographs showed her to have been very beautiful'. He recalled Serge Obolensky from the 1940s as 'small and shy with very charming manners', as Alex's father sat quietly doing crossword puzzles in a corner of 60 Muswell Hill Road, a rambling house that faced Highgate Woods, while Lubov busied herself finding lodgers for the empty rooms.

'It was difficult for me to get used to the haphazard *nitchevo* way of life in the Obolensky family,' Beddington-Behrens wrote. 'I remember admiring the garden of their house at Muswell Hill which, though neglected, was full of blossom in the early spring. "Oh, we never go into it any more," they explained. "The iron steps from the sitting room were broken a long time ago."'

Serge Beddington-Behrens, son of Edward and Irena, knew Lubov when he was a boy, in the 1950s. He recalled: 'I was very fond of my grandmother, who was a formidable matriarch doing her best to hold the family together. She had to do menial work while she was living in Paris in the 1930s, and did not complain. Later she had to have a leg amputated due to an embolism and she was incredibly brave about that too. She was a strong woman, although not too understanding about emotional issues. Grandfather [Serge] was a much more placid and accepting character; a quiet Russian you might have found in a Dostoyevsky novel.'

Geoffrey Archer, the boy who was at Twickenham to see Alex's great match in January 1936, had become a captain in the Army by the time he lodged with Serge and Lubov in Westminster Mansions, London SW1, in the early 1950s. They advertised for a paying guest and Archer, who had just returned from working in the oil industry in Australia and the Middle East, needed to find lodgings.

'The Obolenskys welcomed me as part of the family and I couldn't spend enough time with them,' Archer told the author. 'They were a charming couple and I gave them so much a week and they gave me breakfast. They both spoke very good English, although you could tell they were Russian. I felt inwardly sorry and concerned, because obviously they'd had this terrible change in their lives. They were elegant and intelligent and sophisticated, and suddenly to come down to this small flat in London, and with no transport, I don't know how they managed to adjust.'

Lubov was horrified when Alex's eldest sister, Maria, was lambasted in the tabloid *Sunday Pictorial* in November 1941 for breaking off an engagement to H.W. Norrington, a Canadian sapper. 'She belongs to those Russian titled folks who bolted when the Revolution came,' the paper wrote. Maria did not endear herself with the remark: 'I have broken it all off because there seems to be no chance of my fiancé getting a commission, and my family don't think we should marry until he has got one.' After Alex's brother Michael was divorced from his first wife, Anne Helbronner, in 1965, Lubov, then aged 75, reacted badly to his engagement to Felizitas Joerchel, begging him in a letter to break it off as 'she would never fit in our family, your set of friends and your firm'.

Felizitas recalled: 'I know many things about the Obolenskys' history, and for my mother-in-law [Lubov] to come down to the misery she had to live in, she became very difficult.' Michael stood his ground and, in her next letter, Lubov wrote: 'If this girl is nice, well brought up, well educated and of good background and suitable social standing, so all my blessings for your happiness.'

The day after Felizitas and Michael married, Lubov chided Felizitas's 'commoner' brother over giving his sister an innocuous instruction – something like 'Come over here a second.' Felizitas recalled: 'Lubov said: "No, you must say 'Dear Princess, may I ask you to do such and such." Even in straitened circumstances, Lubov insisted on protocol. She died two days later.

*

Two other forces of nature may have helped cleave Alex and Tania apart.

Alex's image in the press as a sporting titan had gradually been joined by a new portrayal as a party animal, and he had become a magnet for female attention. Tania might have felt jealous, and their differences in age and worldly wisdom meant the young countess with the sharp intellect might have grown tired of the boyish japes of his rugby set.

Alex had been elected to Vincent's in Oxford, and the papers reported him increasingly at society dances and rugby dinners. In the week of his non-selection to face Wales in January 1938, he was invited by Miss Catherine Heywood of the stately Caradoc Court in Ross-on-Wye to join 250 guests at the Monmouthshire Hunt Ball at the Rolls Hall in Monmouth. Alex wore his favourite white tie and, feeling comfortable among the horsey set – the Lysaghts and the Walwyns and the Twiston-Davieses – he danced Viennese waltzes with Catherine and with Nancy Harmood-Banner, the daughter of a Radnorshire baronet.

Catherine would marry, later that year, 'Johnny' Wakefield, a Gipsy Moth pilot and motor racing driver. And when Wakefield died on active service in the Second World War, she married Tony Gaze, an Australian flying ace and motor racing driver. As Katie Gaze, she was a vivacious and successful National Hunt racehorse trainer in the 1970s.

We know now that Alex was the kind of person others loved to tell stories about. Probably the most famous of these appears to have originated with Richard Almond, a forward in Oxford's Varsity Match team of 1937, and later a general practitioner in Henley-on-Thames, who described how Alex would 'consume a dozen oysters at the Sportsman's [sic] Club, St James's Square before every London fixture'.

In the 1930s, teams from Oxford or Cambridge visiting the capital to play a London side would often repair to an exclusive members' club for lunch, and return for dinner in the evening before a riotous train ride home. The Sports Club – its correct title – in St James's Square provided ultra-respectful service, and walls covered in fine art, its newspapers ironed flat and coins boiled clean. City workers popped in for a snifter or a game of bridge, while other members spent longer hours pondering the male-only tranquillity.

Almond's tale was quickly embellished by those who swore Alex quaffed champagne with his oysters. What could be grander or more amusing than the thought of England's most exotic sporting hero stuffing himself with fine food and wine as a pre-match loosener?

Whatever the truth of a complicated affair, we know how much Alex meant to Tania, as she held on to her photographs of him, with their tender written dedications, for the rest of her life. Her family say she spoke only rarely about those Oxford days with her flying prince. 'It was something that was mostly off the agenda, because it was painful,' as her son-in-law John Richards puts it.

We also know how much Tania meant to Alex because, after he joined the Royal Air Force, he gave them instructions that if he died on active service she was to be informed at the same time as his family.

On 28 January 1939, about a year after her split from Alex, Tania was married and the photo of her church wedding appeared as an inset in the *Bystander* of 8 February with the caption: 'Johnson–Vorontzoff-Dachkoff: Gordon Hewlett Johnson, of Canada and Earlscliffe, Bowdon, Cheshire, and Countess Tatiana Vorontzoff-Dachkoff were married at Altrincham, Cheshire.'

Alex's sister Irena cut the little photograph out and gave it a page of its own in the Obolensky family scrapbook.

In late 1937, Alex had been invited to contribute for a second time to a compendium of musings by Oxford graduates and undergraduates.

Would I Fight? was published by Blackwell in early 1938, as a follow-up to *Be Still and Know*, and it set out to examine the futility or otherwise of war and 'present the views of young men and young women on what they believe is worth killing and being killed for'. The editors were Keith Briant and Lyall Wilkes, a left wing future circuit judge and Labour MP.

The subtext was that Alex's generation would bear the brunt if another world disaster was to come and, if it did, it would almost certainly involve Germany, which had rearmed and strengthened economically out of the defeat of 1914-18.

The students suggested every conceivable antidote: religion, Fascism, socialism, Communism, pacifism, conscientious objection. Some of the language and mores are outdated now, but the book is a window onto a British society subjected to arguably the most extreme philosophical and political wrangling in its recent history. The 11 essays show the existential and emotional worries bearing down on these well-educated yet still youthful minds.

Alex was asked for an essay of 3,000 words and it would receive the strident title 'War is NOT Ignoble'. His main themes were the value of military might and a deep-seated disgust for the Soviet Union – his worldview was informed and dominated by a loathing of Communism and what Russia had become.

He began with a credible debunking of the infamous Oxford Union vote of February 1933, when the motion 'This House will under no circumstances fight for its King and country' was passed by 275 votes to 153. 'The whole of the Senior University was labelled with the White Feather, because some few curios had made the startling discovery that war was a bad thing . . . At least so it seemed to the outside world, but the three thousand undergraduates outside the Union received the great news with sardonic smiles and made no protest.'

In other areas, Alex was probably overreaching his wisdom, first-hand knowledge and years in an effort to appear wise and polemic. He praised the tools of modern warfare: 'There is something serenely majestic and noble about the sight of a battleship, a squadron of aeroplanes or a well-trained battalion on parade. All create an impression of might, efficiency and a kind of masculine beauty . . . I am not trying to propound that we should love war. I deny that it is ignoble.'

He mentioned his membership of the Oxford University Air Squadron and noted: 'Pilots take time to produce, and every pilot, we are told, is an asset to the country's safety.' He stated the defence of Britain's empire was 'the moral obligation of every Englishman' and, at the age of 21, going on 22, he attempted psychoanalysis: 'The Englishman is probably more emotional than the Latin or the Slav, though, of course, he will never admit it, nor ever relax his efforts to hide it . . . It is because of the Englishman's emotionalism that his patriotism is unequalled; his country means so much more than self that he will willingly die for it and consider his life well spent.'

This England of Alex's was mostly free from political extremes, yet in his short lifetime Communists had come to power in the Soviet Union, and Fascists had done the same in Germany and Italy. 'Frequently, I have been asked "What would you do if England declared war on Russia?" Not a hard question to answer, because there is no cause for which I would fight with greater enthusiasm than against Communism. The man who will restore monarchy to Russia will be greater than Napoleon, who restored it to France. Like most White Russians, I am a staunch Royalist.'

He warned Britain would be unable to withstand an 'entirely Red Europe', and while it was all very well to say every Russian refugee 'has the Bolshevist bee in his bonnet', it was Russians who had scoffed at the danger of Bolshevism 'and for that very reason they were its victims'. The League of Nations was faced with 'a super-human task' as quarrelling and dissent were endemic in the human condition. 'Democracy wants peace with liberty: it is more sober-minded and rather inert, possibly through lack of faith in the absolute genuineness of its doctrine.' This, he stated, was 'not so with Communism and Fascism. Both are mighty; both are open to criticism for fanaticism and the excesses of terrorism.'

Alex concluded his thesis with a promise of loyalty and a dollop of prescience: 'An old adage "Might is Right" still holds good. History shows that international treaties, agreements and guarantees are respected only as long as it is expedient to do so. Force is the agent which commands this respect . . . In the quest for peace England does not intend to impose her creed on others, as rival doctrines do.

To this peace, I attach security from absorption by aggressive rivals, and I am prepared to fight for King and Country.

'The era of peace and goodwill among all men is not yet at hand.'

By the time war broke out, less than two years later, Alex was a member of Britain's Royal Air Force, ready to fight against the Germans.

CHAPTER 28

QUESTIONS IN THE COMMONS AND OXFORD

THERE WERE WEIGHTY matters at hand in the House of Commons on the afternoon of Wednesday 22 June 1938. The green benches of the vaulted chamber were filled with MPs ready with questions for Neville Chamberlain, the prime minister, and Rab Butler, the government's regular spokesman on foreign affairs, on China and Japan and the Caliphate and Mexico and Italy and Palestine and the German citizens in the Sudetenland – to be followed by a debate on Alexander Sergeevich Obolensky.

Shortly before 3 p.m., talk turned to the young Russian and naturalised Briton who had recently been given a commission as an acting pilot officer in the Royal Air Force's Volunteer Reserve. The newspapers had reported it in May, and the issue in front of the holders of the highest offices in the land was whether Alex was barred from serving in the RAF by his father's Russian nationality.

Among the rows of men facing each other in suits and starched collars, opinions were divided broadly into support for Alex from the Conservative Party and sceptism opposite. Mr Robert Craigmyle Morrison, Labour and Co-operative MP for Tottenham North, and a parliamentary private secretary to James Ramsay MacDonald – the previous prime minister but one – rose to his feet to speak.

'Does the public announcement that Prince Alexander Obolensky has been granted a commission in the Royal Air Force Volunteer Reserve indicate that British-born subjects whose fathers are not British are no longer barred from entering the Royal Air Force as cadets?' Morrison asked.

Sir Kingsley Wood, the Secretary of State for Air in Chamberlain's national government, confirmed the rules were unchanged, but there were exceptions. 'There is no intention of modifying the present regulations under which the parents of candidates for commissions in the Royal Air Force, its reserves and auxiliaries must be British subjects,' Wood said.

'Under those regulations it is, however, open to the Secretary of State to authorise departure from this rule in suitable cases, and such authority was given in the case referred to.'

Lieutenant-Colonel Sir Albert Lambert-Ward, Conservative MP for Hull North-West, and a veteran of the Great War, chipped in with a point made more in spirit than in fact: 'Does not the fact that this gentleman has played rugby football for England indicate that he is tolerably well qualified to have a commission in the Royal Air Force?'

Mr Dai Rhys Grenfell, Labour MP for the Welsh constituency of Gower, asked: 'Can the Minister say how many Russians it is proposed to enrol in the Air Force?'

Then Morrison again: 'Will the right honourable gentleman see that equal consideration is given to other applicants who may not bear distinguished titles?'

Sir Kingsley slapped down these two barbs of sarcasm. 'I will give careful consideration to any case that comes before me. But I ought to say that, in this case, the individual referred to was already a member of an air squadron and his name was put forward by his commanding officer.'

Maybe it was no surprise Wood stood up for Alex. By the following year Wood was drastically ramping up the production of aircraft, and Britain needed pilots to go with them. By 1940, Wood was Chancellor of the Exchequer under Winston Churchill's wartime premiership.

The Auxiliary Air Force (AAF) and the Volunteer Reserve (VR) were the Royal Air Force's backup contingents. The Auxiliary was a constituted unit with a reputation as a social elite; the 601 of the AAF was known as the Millionaires' Squadron because you had to be wealthy to get in. The VR were part-timers and generally cadets or sergeants on entry, although a commission was open to those who proved their worth, or sometimes immediately.

The VR catered for bright sparks who had missed out on a posh education, but Alex's background of public school, rugby, Oxford and a noble heritage smacked of officer quality and he was commissioned from the off. The VR bore a strong resemblance to a flying club, much like the Oxford University air squadron. Pilots signed on for five years and began with a 10-week, 50-hour course of elementary theory and flying. Instruction was on weekday evenings at town centres and at weekends there was training or flying practice at an airfield, run by civilian organisations on contract to the Air Ministry. Of the first batch of 50 VR pilots certified in January 1937, 14 went on to be pilots in the Battle of Britain in 1940.

Alex was thrilled when a long buff envelope arrived, bearing the crest of Adastral House. The letter told him candidates for the Volunteer Reserve 'must have a high standard of fitness, British nationality, and give an undertaking never to go abroad without permission'. He was delighted to say 'yes' to all three, and was summoned to a local office for swearing-in.

There was an interview and a medical, and recruits endured six hours of jumping on and off chairs, balancing rods on rulers, handstands, headstands and press-ups, with a 60-minute break for lunch. In darkened rooms they manipulated switches to join pairs of lights, focus fuzzy beams and sort out jumbled figures and letters. Their hearing was tested by listening to watches, tuning forks and scrambled speech, separately and together. They held their breaths for 70 seconds and had their pulses read. They were told to say 'ahh' and cough, and open a thick dictionary as near to the middle as possible. Even as a regular smoker, Alex was physically super-fit, and he passed everything easily.

Choosing a uniform meant fishing around in cardboard boxes of RAF tunics, trousers, shirts, ties, sweaters, socks, underwear, boots and forage caps. If they fitted well, you were lucky. The recruits then added a gas mask and an identity disc on a piece of string.

Alex had learnt the layout of a biplane's cockpit in the OUAS, and how to get the machine into the air, control it, recover from a stall and practise 'circuits and bumps' (going up, going round and coming down). He would now add cross-country flying, navigation and landing at different airfields.

The ground syllabus comprised gunnery, bombing (the theory of making safe, fusing and dropping 20-pound bombs), engines, armaments, signals, Morse code by buzzer and by lamp, cyphers, theory of flight, aerodynamics, navigation, instruments and airmanship. He was shown how to fold an Irvin parachute, then made to pack his own and sign that it was his fault if it didn't open. And he saw the joke when he was promised a new parachute if the first one failed and he took it back.

There were inoculations and injections, and a wing squadron leader barked maxims: 'War is a very bloodthirsty business, and the sooner you realise it, the better.'

Through all this, the 50 hours' flying consisted of 25 dual and 25 solo.

In July 1938, Alex and 27 colleagues in the OUAS had gone for a fortnight's camp to RAF Ford. A group including Hubert 'Trilby' Freakes (the South African full back who would be capped by England), Hugh Disney (Paddy's brother) and a couple of rowing blues piloted Hawker Harts on solo cross-country flights as far as Yorkshire and North Devon, and there was fine weather until a 75 mph gale blew in and they had to line up a fleet of RAF lorries to protect the aircraft. They paid a fascinating visit to the aircraft carrier HMS *Courageous*.

Alex pasted photos into a scrapbook, with jaunty captions – 'Trilby gives a hand' and 'Brave man!' – alongside lovely prints of him in a cream-coloured flying suit with goggles, practising with his parachute and Sutton harness.

His commission meant he was saluted at camp, and expected to do certain ground duties such as inspecting the unfortunates 'on jankers' (punishment for a minor breach of discipline) in the guardroom, and overseeing the stores and the cleanliness of the kitchen.

The pilot officers and the flying officers (the next rank up) dealt with the dogsbody work and admin the commanding officers could not be bothered with. The compensation was piles of good plain food including jam butties and mugs of cocoa before bed.[1]

Membership of the VR was worth £25 a year, with travelling costs reimbursed too. By way of comparison, £25 could buy a good second-hand car at a time when Alex was on the lookout for hand-outs.

He wrote to Irena: 'If someone offered me £100 I could put an end to my deep depressions & general gloom.' His sister could not oblige, and Alex replied: 'Sorry to hear you couldn't manage to help me out of the septic tank of impecunity. Thanks all the same for trying. Am now faced with a major crisis so have to sink to writing begging letters. One of the people I thought of was Fr. Martindale but I don't know his address. Perhaps you could find this out for me. Not a word to the parents, of course.'

Martindale was a friend of Irena who was a renowned Jesuit author, scholar and Oxford philosopher. The son of an Indian civil servant, he had become a Catholic on leaving Harrow School, and he instructed converts to Catholicism or Catholics in danger of losing their faith. Serge and Lubov may have recoiled at Martindale's brand of converted Christianity.

Everyone in the Volunteer Reserve was aware their hobby put them in line for full-scale service, as they would be automatically mobilised by contract into the regular armed forces if war broke out. And Alex had enjoyed flying since he started in the two-seater biplanes of the OUAS in 1936, and his sister encouraged him. Even the very bleak Tania break-up letter concluded with a PS from Alex to Irena: 'The flying suit etc arrived safely. Thanks a lot.'

Other members of the family were less helpful. A condition of Alex's application was that his father should apply for British naturalisation, and Serge was dragging his feet. It meant taking an oath of allegiance and an implied betrayal of old Russia, and he had his Nansen passport if he wished to travel.

'Is anything being done about the family's naturalisation?' Alex wailed to Irena while she was visiting their parents in March. 'Mr Green has promised to stand the expense so I fail to see what is holding up the procedure. Try and brace up the old boy. After all he has nothing to do, so it shouldn't take him all these years to fill in a simple form. Really the inertia of the Obolensky family both amazes and depresses me.' It had the desired effect as Serge's application to the Home Secretary was made that month – two years after his son had been granted a British passport as a minor.

Serge also aggravated Alex by refusing to have his life insured by the trustees of the late Hardman Earle, to enable repayment of the Earles' loans to the Obolenskys in the event of Serge's death. 'It seems a somewhat unsound idea, but I can see no reason why Father should not comply,' Alex said. 'It will cost him nothing and place him under no obligations . . . I expect I shall have to go and pacify her [Mrs Earle] a little in the near future – in fact as soon as I can get away from Oxford – i.e. when I can pay my landlady!

'I seem to be sinking deeper and deeper into the mud of impecunity. It has taught me one very good lesson – that really one has only oneself to rely on, and I am doing this. You say I am impatient. "Active" would be a better word. It's no use sitting back and hoping that old God will do something. He never does.'

Alex was more kindly disposed to his 12-year-old brother Michael, as he posted 'Michenka' some stamps for his collection and autographs of rugby players, while apologising for not visiting him at school (St John's Preparatory in Windsor; Michael later attended Beaumont College in the town). Alex signed himself 'your loving brother', but they were never close, due in part to the 10 years between them, although Michael spoke later in life of a lasting adoration for his famous sibling.

There was a strange ambience to that summer of 1938, as Alex concluded his fourth year at Oxford, with an underlying mood of rising panic in Britain up to and including the pivotal month of September, when Prime Minister Neville Chamberlain made his fateful trips to Munich and peace was the headline, but war with Germany became all but inevitable.

Alex had been elected to Oxford's Phoenix Common Room, the university's oldest dining club, whose members wore a uniform of white waistcoat and tailcoats with facings of creamy silk. But he turned down Irena's invitations to parties in the Easter holidays. 'I'm going to disappear to some farmstead in Devon or Cornwall where I can lead a monastic existence with my books,' he told his sister, while enquiring after a 'Sylvia' whose surname he had forgotten.

In May, Alex popped into London to attend an exhibition staged by Franzi Hohenlohe at the Fine Art Society in New Bond Street. Hilariously, Franzi was selling what he admitted were works of modest talent – and his friends did not demur.

It kicked off with a luncheon in Bedford Square given by Lady Oxford, widow of Herbert Asquith, the former prime minister, and attended by 'all the better debs of the season', followed by the exhibition enhanced by a buffet and champagne.

One of Franzi's picture frames was made of ocelot skin cut from the collar of an old coat of his grandmother's. Another was wreathed in artificial flowers and a third had a white plaster thumb holding on to it. Chic private viewers, including a Lady Mount Temple dressed kaleidoscopically in 'gay blue glasses' with a green suit and red blouse, tottered in on the highest of heels. Franzi was described in the *Sketch* as 'verging lightly on surrealism'. He whispered in Alex's ear: 'The frames are worth 10 or 100 times more than their contents.'

Alex's second public examination for the final honour schools in Philosophy, Politics and Economics was set for 16 June and the oral examination – or the 'blooming viva', as he called it – for 25 July. No record of the exam questions survives, but the Oxford PPE equivalents from the year before, 1937, provide a guide: from 'If someone says that a thing is beautiful, is it possible to prove him wrong?' to 'How far was the growth of hostility between Great Britain and Germany the result of a conflict of economic interests?'

'Pray for me, you twerp, on Monday morning,' Alex wrote to Irena just before the viva, together with instructions to return a

latchkey he had absent-mindedly left in his dressing table at Muswell
Hill Road. He and his sister had been listening to records, until the
radiogram broke down.

When the exam results were eventually published, Alex attained
a fourth-class honours degree in PPE. His name was given in the
class lists as 'Obolensky Princeps Alexander e Coll. Aen. Nas.'; Aen
Nas being short for Aenei Nasi, the Latin name of Brasenose College.[2]

A fourth in 1938 was the lowest grade of pass, abandoned by
Oxford in the 1970s, but the word 'honours' indicated a notable
level of achievement and, in any case, obtaining a degree of any kind
from Oxford has never been easy. And Brasenose was fond of its
famous sporting son. A poem that was a paean to the joys of drinking
ale appeared in *The Brazen Nose* of June 1938: '[My deep love] doth
bid me come to share your lofty fame / who stand emblazoned high
in history./ What need to tell of Rugger? Our two wings [Alex and
Hugh Percy] / Are famed where'er the game a poet sings.'

CHAPTER 29

THE WORLD OF WORK AND 'PEACE IN OUR TIME'

A LEX'S FIRST STEPS out of full-time education included a break with friends in Cornwall. Then a pal at Rosslyn Park found him a post with an insurance firm in London, at a time when many an office in the West End was staffed entirely by 'honourables'.[1]

As an Oxford graduate, the 22-year-old Alex stepped in halfway up the working ladder, whereas many clerks started at 15. He would earn a weekly envelope and, as he noted in his essay in *Would I Fight?*: 'Most of us prefer being units in some business, service, or industry; monotonous though it may be, it means the comfort of a home and bread to eat.'

His socialising resumed at the Dorchester Hotel in July, with Lady Margaret Drummond-Hay's Polo Ball in aid of the Chelsea Boys' Club. Amid noisy games of houp-là and table motor racing, Alex ate dinner and chatted with Nancy Harmood-Banner and Catherine Heywood, both of whom wore summer gowns with plunging neck-lines.

Alex spotted a dark-haired woman with a prominent nose, wearing a brocade dress and a heavy gold curb bracelet that was an 'in' look. Princess Natalia Bagration, known as Natasha, was two years older than him, and as the daughter of Prince Constantine Alexandrovich Bagration of Mukhrani and Princess Tatiana Constantinovna of Russia, she was a descendant of two prominent royal dynasties: the Georgian Bagrationi dynasty and the Romanovs of Russia. She was also a cousin of the Duchess of Kent.

Natasha was tall and slender, with a wide smile of bright white teeth and 'legs like pillars of ivory and fine eyes set in a very level head'.[2] Alex frowned as guests giggled at her name, turning it into 'Buggeration'. He asked her to dance and they got talking. Her family had ruled Georgia until it was absorbed into Russia in the 18th century. Her father had been killed fighting on the Austrian front in 1915 and he was buried in Mtzkhet, ancient capital of Georgia.

For the young socialites, the weather and the social calendar were ever-present topics, but so too was the unrest around Europe. Yvonne Gaunt, the acquaintance of Alex's at Oxford whose boyfriend and future husband was in the university Air Squadron, observed later: 'Our generation were still free enough to enjoy life but we knew war was in the offing. I don't think it overshadowed everything – when you're young, you're young – but there was no getting away from it.'

When rugby resumed for the 1938–9 season, the *Evening Standard* bracketed Alex with Wilf Wooller of Cardiff and Wales at the 'top [of] all box-office attractions'. Alex was playing for Middlesex in the County Championship, and for Rosslyn Park. The club was celebrating its diamond-jubilee year, and it was a thriving hub of rugby, with 600 members and 11 teams fielded every Saturday.

In Alex's four years as a member of Rosslyn Park he had made seven appearances, scoring six tries. He missed the first match of this season when some fool misinterpreted a telephone message as being about his brother Teddy instead. But in the next two years, Alex would become a regular, and he reached a total of 21 tries in 25 appearances – a rate of around a try a match that was common to all the teams he regularly represented.

Paddy Disney was a teammate in the second match against Harlequins at Old Deer Park on 24 September. *The Times* reported that the bone-hard pitch threw up so much dust the spectators lost sight of some of the scrums. Alex was accompanied by three Royal Air Force men in Rosslyn Park's three-quarter line, but he was frustrated by a lack of service from his centres, P.J. Halford and S.G.

Walker, although they may have been playing bluff, with the Quins expecting the famous wing to see plenty of action.

A lady called Fay Cook was watching from the stands, her eyes fixed on a lean wolf in baggy clothing. Alex's hair was smoothed back, although a rakish quiff flopped on one side. His thick cotton jersey with the collar turned up hid a slim torso without a scrap of fat. Beneath his huge, billowy shorts, the quad muscles were prominently defined. Fay had met Alex in Cornwall and, as Paddy put it, had been 'duly dazzled'.

Post-match, as always, it was time for fun. Two friends of Alex and Paddy's named Moira and Wilfred were there, and afterwards the four of them and Fay had tea in the Old Deer Park pavilion.

Tea led to drinks and Paddy, whose girlfriend Marion Lake was away at her family home in Jamaica, drove Moira and Wilfred the short distance to Richmond railway station, and took Alex and Fay to a local restaurant called the Brasserie, which all agreed was chic and 'simpatico'.

It was pouring with rain and they chatted about events of the day, as any people in their mid-20s would. There were reports from the coasts of Sussex, Kent and Essex of human traffickers bringing desperate refugees from Germany and Austria across the Channel in small boats. 'Alien smuggling', the papers called it.

Paddy quickly twigged that Fay regarded him as a gooseberry, as Alex breezily kept including his pal in the conversation and made suggestions of another snifter. Paddy slid away, thinking to himself: 'I'll leave Alex to deal with the baby.'

Alex rented a flat for £2 a week at 13 Lancaster Mews, a pleasant, cobbled side street handily situated between Paddington Station and Kensington Gardens. His sister Irena, meanwhile, was staying with Franzi Hohenlohe at the magnificent Leopoldskron Castle near Salzburg. One day, Franzi heard Neville Chamberlain was on his way to see the Führer. 'If there is going to be a war, Alex would certainly have told me,' Irena said.

CHAPTER 30

UP IN COURT AND VYING FOR ENGLAND AGAIN

ALEX'S OFTEN WOUNDED tone in his family letters maybe proved the adage 'you always hurt the one you love', but in everyday life he maintained a front of indomitability. In November 1938 he was slapped with a speeding ticket and a £2 fine. Alex had been caught by a Sergeant Jones doing 38 miles per hour in a borrowed car down Fitzjohn Avenue in Hampstead, breaking the limit of 30 mph.

He wrote to the magistrates to graciously accept the immutable word of Sergeant Jones – and make a plea for public anonymity.

'I have driven for five years without a single accident or endorsement,' Alex wrote. 'If this is not an unconstitutional request, I ask that the Press be not informed of this shortcoming on my part, as it might cause me more pain than, in my humble opinion, fits the crime.'

Given that all these words made it into the next day's national newspapers, under the headline 'Obolensky fined for speeding', we can assume the magistrates were unmoved by the request.

Not that Alex was alone. Almost every day, the papers reported someone killed in a motoring accident, while on a single day that September, a radio star (Anona Winn), a well-known actor (Godfrey Tearle) and an England Test cricketer (Denis Compton) were summoned for speeding. Compton was fined £3 at the same Hampstead court as Alex. On the plus side, Alex's sporting life was going better than it had done for a long time and his name was bracketed with England in the press again.

The tries flowed with Rosslyn Park and Middlesex – he scored six in four County Championship matches against Eastern Counties, Surrey, Hampshire and Kent – and he played in International XVs against Bristol and Old Cranleighans. His England teammates for Middlesex included Peter Candler of Richmond, and Harlequins' Robin Prescott and Pop Dunkley.

Alex was watched by at least one England selector throughout a run of a county or club match every three or four days. A preview to Middlesex's 10–10 draw with Surrey on 2 November said: 'It is difficult to see how so dangerous a runner could ever be left out of an England side,' and 'in a possible British team, Obolensky would go straight into the right wing position.' (The 1938 British & Irish Lions had recently returned from South Africa with two losses and one win in the Tests.)

Cyril Lowe had stepped down from England's selection committee, which now comprised John Daniell, Bob Oakes, Harry Coverdale, Douglas Prentice, Eric Coley and Carston Catcheside. Two of them went to see Alex play for Major Stanley's XV against Oxford at Iffley Road, where he helped make two tries for Candler. Meanwhile Coverdale watched Alex and Tim Warr – another wing contender and a Middlesex teammate – when Richmond won the derby at Rosslyn Park.

Alex's tries for Middlesex, in particular, secured him a place in the senior 'England' team for the first national trial of the 1938–9 season against the Possibles in Manchester, with Cyril Holmes of the Manchester club on the other wing. The second and third trials were set for Bridgwater and Twickenham.

Holmes was picked on the basis of explosive pace. The 23-year-old from Bolton had won the 100 yards in the 1933 public schools' championship Alex had competed in, and went on to sprint for Great Britain in the 1936 Berlin Olympics, going out in the quarter-finals of the 100 metres in which Jesse Owens took the gold medal, and he won the double of 100 yards and 220 yards for England at the Empire Games in Sydney in February 1938.

Alex travelled in expectation of a reunion with Jack Harrison, his old pal from Trent, but Harrison withdrew with a pulled muscle, and the Coventry scrum half Jimmy Giles and Harlequins centre Basil Nicholson also dropped out, ruining a plan for Giles to partner fly half Harry Kenyon. Instead Paul Cooke was the scrum half, the fly half was G.F. Williams of Moseley, and Kenyon switched to the centres.

Newspaper previews explained of Alex that 'fortune swings once again in the right way for the Oxford blue of 1935–7' after the 'luck of injuries turned against him'. His opposite numbers for the Possibles were Dickie Guest, a pocket rocket who had recently scored six tries for Liverpool University versus Manchester University, and F.G. Edwards of Birkenhead Park.

And so on 3 December 1938, at the Kersal ground a couple of miles north of Manchester city centre, Alex pulled on the all-white kit of England for the first time since the win over Scotland in March 1936, albeit without the red rose that denoted an international fixture. He grinned for the team photo with Ray Longland, Herbert Toft and Cooke among an otherwise mostly new set of teammates. As usual, several contenders were engaged separately in the Varsity Match.

The rain and heavy going and sopping-wet ball restricted the plan for Alex and the new man Holmes to maximise their pace. Nevertheless, as *The Times* reported: 'Obolensky scored a try that probably only Obolensky could have scored. Kenyon, as he was tackled, got a long pass out to Obolensky, and the latter's speed carried him round what remained of the defence for a try wide out.'

A tremendous action photo of the try in the *Illustrated Sporting and Dramatic News* showed Alex with the ball gripped under his right arm, and his left arm splayed out for balance, as he surged out of the tackle of the Possibles' full back, Coventry's Harry Pateman. The spectators round the touchlines cheered a returning hero. But amid the muddled team selection, Guest prospered the most. The Possibles won 18–17, scoring four tries to two.

Alex continued to do all he could, scoring two tries for Rosslyn Park against United Services in Portsmouth the following weekend, when the *Telegraph* described him as 'the most famous player in this country'. He stayed in the top team for the second England trial in Somerset on 17 December.

Four players from the Varsity Match came into the Probables, including Trilby Freakes, the Oxford captain, while Jack Heaton of Waterloo and George Hancock of Birkenhead Park stepped up from the Possibles side at Kersal to be the new centres alongside a new fly half in Tommy Kemp, the rangy Oxford blue who had three caps. A pulled leg muscle for Harrison among the Possibles was sadly typical of his career. Alex's direct opponent was another flyer in Robert Carr of Old Cranleighans, and they fought a good duel, with Carr enjoying a key moment when he took a pass in full stride to sweep away for a try.

The team news for the third and final trial came through in the week before Christmas, and it was not good for Alex. He and Holmes were picked for 'The Rest', with Guest on the right wing in the 'England' team, and Carr on the left.

Alex prepared by laying a bogey with a try for the Barbarians in their annual fixture away to Leicester, with old rival Ken Fyfe as his fellow wing. Alex was a regular Barbarian by now, having twice played in the annual match with the East Midlands, and on the Easter tour to Wales eight months before this.

The wintry weather meant that at Welford Road, where Alex had such an unfortunate history, the touchlines were marked out in snow. 'All or not at all' was his only possible motto, and in the Baa-baas' 8–6 loss he collected a kick in his stride just short of the goal line to score in the second half, and missed another try by a tiny margin when he made a dive into the snow.

Alex next turned out for Rosslyn Park against Fettesian-Lorettonians on 2 January 1939, nabbing two tries, including one 60-yard sprint. A spectator named Ruth Walkden, a 19-year-old student at London University, was there with her parents. 'Every time the ball was passed to him, the spectators went mad,' Walkden later recalled.

The England team's final trial was at Twickenham on 7 January 1939, two weeks before the meeting with Wales. The papers reckoned it was 'tragic to waste the divine fire of Obolensky' and that he was 'playing better than ever before . . . the most dangerous scoring wing in the country'.

Alex's performance for 'The Rest' was spectacular; arguably the best of his rugby career. He scored two of his team's five tries as the supposed second string won by 17 points to three, and the second try in particular showcased his pace. *The Times* reported it was a Gus Walker dribble and breakaway that enabled Edwards to send Alex over for the first try, then a kick ahead followed up by Alex for his second.

Alex was entitled to a feeling of baffled frustration after the trials. The top team lost all three matches and used nine centres in the process. How could any wing give his best in these circumstances? The England selectors claimed, as they always did, that selection was not based solely on the trials and the Varsity Match. A critic might have replied: 'Just as well!'

Holmes had failed to prove he could grasp rugby's complexities, and now Alex and Dickie Guest were neck and neck. *The Times* speculated Alex might be asked to play on the left – an idea straight from the mouth of a selector, possibly over a post-match gin and tonic.

On the Monday, the England team to meet Wales was announced, with Guest and Carr as the wings among five new caps behind the scrum, with full back Freakes to win his second cap and the centre Jack Heaton, who had three caps from 1935, only marginally more experienced.

In a choice of conservatism over attacking threat, Alex's defence was still being cited as a risk. Alex reacted proudly and he inspired a remarkably florid report in *The Times* of his efforts for Rosslyn Park against London Scottish on 14 January, describing a moment of magical play by him, thrilling the crowd, as he caught the ball unmarked and 'was off diagonally across the ground and through the midfield press, apparently on its heels to a man – for all the world like a woodcock threading a birch plantation – then he straightened at the psychological instant when close to the corner flag to draw the last defence before passing to K.G. Evans, who appeared from nowhere as unexpectedly as a genie from a bottle.'

In the three years since his breakthrough for England, Alex had added game awareness to his sprinting ability. Injuries had interrupted at the most inopportune moments. Selection, he had learnt, was capricious and rarely easily understood. As it turned out, England beat Wales 3–0 at Twickenham with a try by the prop Derek Teden, another of the home team's eight debutants.

The England selectors kept fretting over their backline, with Ireland at Twickenham next. They reheated an idea from the previous season by asking Leicester to include Alex on the left wing against Richmond at the Athletic Ground on 28 January, two weeks before the Ireland match. It was Alex's only appearance for the Tigers in the 1938–9 season.

Roy Ullyett, the sports cartoonist in the *London Evening Star*, depicted a jaunty Alex with his blond hair flying, looking down on the shorter Warr of Richmond, with large eyeballs circling them to represent Daniell and Prentice in the stands. In another frame Ullyett had Alex saying 'an unexpected pleasure' as he plucked a slice of fruit from a plate proffered by a man in a flat cap: 'The only decent pass to reach "Obo" was when the lemons came round at half-time.' The elusive running of Warr, who was a schoolmaster at Mill Hill, allowed Ullyett a topical joke: 'R. Barr, the Leicester back, must sympathise with Mr Neville Chamberlain – he found that one Warr was heaps enough to stop.'

The Times clearly wanted Alex in the England team, saying he had done 'all that a man can do when the ball seldom comes his way'. The selectors delayed their picks until after the following weekend's fixtures, that included the semi-finals of the County Championship and the meeting of Rosslyn Park and London Welsh.

Alex hoped for a twist of fate to turn his way – a final nudge to persuade Daniell to give England a transfusion of the old Obolensky spirit.

CHAPTER 31

BITES AND BARBARIANS AND DELIGHT WITH THE DEBS

R UGBY FOLLOWERS WERE long accustomed to seeing Alex's name in banner headlines, but were not expecting the one they read in February 1939: 'Obolensky in Hospital, Bitten by Dog.'

The wacky episode that confirmed Alex would not be recalled to the England team was first hinted at in the papers on the morning of Rosslyn Park's match with London Welsh on 4 February. He was reported to be missing the game due to a cold, and therefore forfeiting the last chance to impress the selectors. Some versions later mentioned influenza, which was doing the rounds in Britain.

By the following Saturday evening, after Ireland had 'spread dismay and disruption' by beating England 5–0 at Twickenham, Alex had his left arm cradled in a black sling as he attended the post-match dinner at the Grosvenor House Hotel. He sat between a Miss Joan Mickie and a Mrs Hamilton Readman, and prised a cigarette from a case on the table. 'I was a passenger in a car in the country, and we ran over a dog,' he said. 'I was attempting to release the poor hound from under the wheels when it bit me. Beastly bad luck.'

The bite wound turned septic, and it must have been serious as Alex was admitted to the West London Hospital, in preference to the customary treatment of bed rest at home and sucking on a thermometer.

The injury and the dinner appeared in the diary of 'Miss Sketch', a columnist in the *Sketch*, who noted how her crinoline dress stayed unruffled because 'footballers know that a ballroom scrum isn't the same as a dance-floor crowd, and are gentler than some Lambeth Walkers I have met!'

Alex was ruled out of England's final Championship match, a 9–6 win over Scotland at Murrayfield featuring three penalty goals by Jack Heaton. The three-quarter line of Guest, Heaton, Hancock and Carr had been used for all three of England's games, while Freakes, Walker and Cooke at full back, fly half and scrum half respectively were replaced by Ernest 'Pip' Parsons, Kemp and Jack Ellis after the debacle with Ireland. The New Zealand-born Parsons was a 26-year-old RAF pilot who would earn a DFC before being killed in a Whitley bomber in August 1940.

The papers speculated that Alex's season might be over. In fact he reappeared for Rosslyn Park against Birkenhead Park in March after a gap of six weeks. As for the unpredictable International Championship, each of the home unions won the title at least once during the seasons of 1931 to 1939, but not one of them was able to retain it.

If picking a winning rugby team was a tricky business, judging the mood of the nation was tougher. Winston Churchill identified a 'wave of perverse optimism' as a cartoon in *Punch* magazine in March 1939 showed John Bull waking from a nightmare and the evils of the night flying out of a window. At the same time, there was a hugely worrying development as the Slovaks courted Hitler and declared independence from Czechoslovakia.

When Alex's sister Irena went skiing with Franzi Hohenlohe in the Austrian Alps over the New Year, the easy-going atmosphere had gone. They were told not to return to Leopoldskron because Nazi officials had confiscated the castle on orders from Berlin. From London, Stephanie Hohenlohe instructed Franzi to vamoose to the Continental Hotel in Munich. But Irena was travelling on her Nansen passport and forbidden to leave Ostmark, as the Nazis had branded Austria since the Anschluss of the previous year.

Irena hung on in Salzburg, looking after Franzi's dog, a Skye terrier named Katya, and waited for the necessary stamp. Franzi applied for a transit visa in the French Consulate in Munich, where he was trailed through the streets by a man from the Gestapo incongruously pushing a bicycle through heavy snow. After a nervous few days, Irena and Franzi departed for Paris and London.

In the middle of March, the Germans marched into Prague – the act supposedly prevented by the much-lauded Munich agreement. A shocked Neville Chamberlain made what Churchill perceived to be a despicable *volte-face* by saying the Czechoslovakian state as guaranteed by the British government no longer existed, due to the split by the Slovaks. Two days later, the prime minister shifted again, ranting at Hitler for reneging on his assurance that Germany had no further claim on Czech land beyond the original Sudeten carve-up. Chamberlain warned that Poland would be the next 'small state' on Hitler's list.

At Oxford University in April, the Union Society carried a motion in favour of conscription by 423 votes to 326. Churchill and students at Cambridge agreed, but Chamberlain did not, believing conscription would signal an acceptance of war as inevitable. Nevertheless, advertisements were widespread for the Royal Air Force and Royal Navy Volunteer Reserves, and the Territorial Army, while the Air Raid Warden Service had received 500,000 new volunteers since Munich.

The whims of the selectors and the bite of a dog had denied Alex the call from England he deserved. His reaction was to accelerate his socialising – influenced, perhaps, by the national mood and a realisation his flying might be leading to something vastly more serious. There was also his bachelor status and naturally outgoing attitude and lively libido.

Alex made a trip to Edinburgh to join four Scottish internationals in a Co-optimists team for a seven-a-side competition at Murrayfield on April Fool's Day in aid of the Royal Infirmary and Leith Hospital. The star-studded line-up were popular winners, beating Stewart's

College FP, Dunfermline, Watsonians and Edinburgh Police, with Alex scoring in both the semi-final and the 23–0 final win over the Police.

A slumbering train journey back to London was met by a message from the Barbarians confirming an invitation for their Easter tour to Wales the following weekend. These jaunts, based at the Esplanade Hotel in Penarth, ran from the Thursday afternoon to the following midweek, and attracted all the best players. Penarth RFC were almost always beaten by the 'Baa-baas', but Cardiff on the Saturday and then Swansea and Newport were trickier opponents.

'Players are asked to be in bed by 11 p.m. on the night prior to playing,' the itinerary said, 'and not to play more than nine holes of golf on the morning of a match.'[1] Well, the alickadoos could only ask. Peter Cranmer and Wilf Wooller had other ideas, and one night they shinned up a ladder to a window in the servants' quarters, seeking a red-headed maid. The ladder collapsed and the famous internationals crashed into cucumber frames below – but they were able to play at Cardiff the next day.

Setting off fireworks and riding a bicycle – both on the hotel's dance floor – was part of the fun, and Wilson Shaw, the Scot, merrily conducted the dance band despite being tone-deaf. 'It is quite amazing what beer can do,' Shaw said.[2] Wales's Claude Davey said: 'My career as a rugby player would not have been complete if I had not played for the Barbarians.'

Alex scored a try at Penarth on Good Friday and played again at Swansea on the Monday. It was possibly during this trip that he wowed the locals by roaring up to the Forest Arms hotel in Brechfa, Carmarthenshire, in a white Lanchester motor car – borrowed, presumably, as only the rich drove a vehicle whose marketing blurb was 'at 50mph, you can knit comfortably'.[3]

With rugby out of the way, Alex concentrated on the society 'season' and its 'carefully organised gaiety' revolving round the introduction of eligible young men to the 17- or 18-year-old debutantes who were being presented to the queen.

The first three courts in 1939 were held in the Throne Room of Buckingham Palace in March, in the presence of the reigning monarch, dukes and ambassadors. At the first of them, Queen Elizabeth, wife of George VI, dazzled in a dress of white satin, a gold lamé train and a diamond tiara.

Court ceremonies began at 8 p.m., and beforehand a fleet of Daimlers, Rolls-Royces and Bentleys swept down the Mall, carrying their precious cargo. Fashionable dresses with the bodice off the shoulder were bought directly from Harrods or Harvey Nichols, or from Mayfair dressmakers including Madame Claire, Paquin and Alex's acquaintance, Norman Hartnell. The debutantes wore head-dresses of ostrich feathers and hid their faces behind lace veils. A lady who wished to present a daughter or niece must herself have been presented before. The cost of more than £35 was 'not such a large amount,' a 1939 debutante told the *Evening Standard*, 'for the privilege of calling on the King and Queen.'

Once presented, the debutante embarked upon a long series of balls and dinner parties, where Alex fitted among a cohort of eligible males who had a title or a connection to an MP and had been to public school, which was taken as a guarantee of character and honour. Names were bandied about at tea parties in February, and the approved dancing partners and escorts were invited to the dances, to be crossed off only if they got married. Personality and disposition were assessed at gatherings that included the Royal Academy summer exhibition and the big events of the flat-racing calendar. The girls were more likely to have been home-schooled by a governess or attended boarding school, before the essential polishing at finishing school or in a spell spent abroad.

There were never quite enough men to go around, and a chap like Alex could scope a party out – quaffing the champagne and wolfing down the lobster, salmon and strawberries – before sloping off if the company was unengaging. Sometimes it was the worth the wait for scrambled eggs and bacon at 3 a.m. before making one's excuses.

In June or July, the dances moved out of hot drawing rooms into the gardens of town houses, and clouds of cigarette smoke accompanied the chatter and clinking of glasses as net curtains billowed at huge, open windows. The men were no longer expected to wear gloves, so there were sweaty hands on debs' bare backs as couples danced to 'The Lambeth Walk' and 'A Nightingale Sang in Berkeley Square' or romantic American tunes such as 'Night and Day' and 'Shine on Harvest Moon'.

Alex kicked off the season of 1939 at the grand reopening of the restaurant at the May Fair Hotel, one of London's dozens of swish venues. It was fine if you had the money for drinks and food and entertainment, but Alex tended to await the kindness of a free invitation.

At the May Fair, Alex met and dined again with Natasha Bagration, voluptuous in an electric-blue dress gathered at the waist and a multicoloured necklace of semi-precious stones.[4] Baron and Baroness von Bulow were at their table, and guests included Mark Tennyson, great-grandson of the poet, accompanying a debutante.

Alex laughed as he and Natasha danced, and a photo appeared in *Tatler* under the cheery headline 'On with the fun – and blow the axis!' – a reference to the alignment between Hitler's Germany and Mussolini's Italy soon to be formalised by the 'Pact of Steel'. Natasha would eventually marry Charles Hepburn Johnston, a British diplomat, in April 1945.

On 1 June, Alex attended a wedding at the Russian Church with a colourful crowd mustered from the tsarist exiles in London, as Prince Vsevolod, son of the late Prince John Constantinovitch of Russia and Princess Helene of Yugoslavia, married Lady Mary Lygon, third daughter of the late Earl and Countess Beauchamp.

With two or three balls being held in London every week, Alex went to one given for Doreen Davison by Lady St John of Bletso in Ennismore Gardens, near the Royal Albert Hall. Lady St John was the best-known of the less well off peeresses who made money presenting at court the children of the rampantly ambitious who lacked the requisite social qualifications or circle of friends. Almost a thousand people were invited, and more than a thousand turned up, on a rare fine night during an often chilly summer. One orchestra played waltzes, foxtrots and polkas in the drawing room and another played in a marquee in the garden. Fairy lights twinkled in bushes and a violinist moved among the beautifully dressed bright young things dancing on a smoothly manicured lawn. Steam and mouth-watering smells rose from piping hot sausages, next to a buffet of caviar sandwiches and champagne and a barrel of beer.

George Galitzine was at the party, risking dirtied knees as he gallantly crawled on the grass when his dance partner dropped her powder puff, while Alex peered admiringly at a stuffed 41-pound salmon caught by Lord St John. The *Mirror* reported Alex was 'as light on the floor as he is fierce on the Rugger field', and a photo showed him looking louche as he lounged on a deckchair next to a Miss Katherine Crofton, who was dressed in a billowy ball gown with a floral decoration. Alex had his hair slicked back, and a cigar-ette burned lazily between his thumb and index finger. There was a lascivious look in his hooded eyes as he gazed at his companion, who appeared faintly alarmed at the presence of the photographer.

In July, Alex joined rugby players and Members of Parliament at a dance for one of the debutantes of the year, at the home of William Wavell Wakefield and his wife Rowena in Avenue Road, close to the green expanse of Regent's Park. The deb was Joan Wakefield, the eldest of three sisters and a bright, vivacious 18-year-old with big bunches of blonde hair. She had been presented at court in March, having spent finishing time in Germany in 1938, studying the language.

Wavell Wakefield was one of the best-known rugby personalities of the preceding generation. He had 27 caps for England from 1920 to 1927; he had captained the side 13 times and was ever-present during the country's golden era of Grand Slams in 1921, 1923 and 1924. He pioneered a new theory of back-row play, interlinking the wing-forwards or flankers – of which he was one – through the lock at the base of the scrum. It spread the attack across the field and shaped the game we have today.

Wakefield had been a captain of Sedbergh School, the RAF,

Cambridge University, Harlequins, Leicester, Middlesex and the Barbarians. His book *Rugger*, published in 1927, was considered a classic. He was an accomplished cricketer, skier and 440-yard runner. In 1935, at the age of 37, he became Member of Parliament for Swindon (it does not take much guessing that he was a Conservative). He would be knighted in 1944, and become Baron Wakefield of Kendal in 1963, and serve as president of the Rugby Football Union, the Ski Club of Great Britain, the British Sub-Aqua Club and the British Water Ski Federation.

Nicknamed 'Wakers', this tall, upright man with thinning hair, a long, flat nose, arched eyebrows and wide smile can be seen as another surrogate father-figure in Alex's life. Wakefield had made money in radio diffusion and he spoke without the posh accent of a Harrovian or Etonian. He too was fond of white tie, which he had worn to the post-match dinner when Alex and England beat the All Blacks, and he had been the referee for that season's final trial in which Alex scored a hat-trick of tries.

Wakefield had also been in the Royal Naval Air Service in the Great War and he wore his uniform for his maiden speech as an MP. 'I had two fears,' he liked to tell his dinner guests. 'Either I might trip over my sword as I rose to speak, or I might sit down on the spike of my helmet when I had finished.'

In rugby matters, Wakefield was always on point. Fellow Harlequins related how he was kicked mercilessly while he was lying on the ball on his goal line at Bristol. 'I should have been penalised,' Wakefield said, 'and they didn't kick me hard enough.'

Alex had turned out for Wavell's invitational team in his final match of the 1938–9 season, and he possessed one notable trump card over this titanic figure of sporting and social life: Wakefield's England team had lost to the All Blacks at Twickenham in January 1925.

At this party for Joan Wakefield, feathers and finery decorated the ballroom. Katherine Crofton was there again, and Miss Annette Royds, daughter of Admiral Sir Percy Royds, came from a court at Buckingham Palace.

'Wakers' crackled with a relentless energy, and it radiated from Joan, too, in her opaque net dress spangled in sequins with elbow-length gloves. Alex, whose hair had never been slicker or shinier, adjusted the red rose in his buttonhole, and allowed Wakers to sling an affectionate arm round him for a photo that appeared in the *Sketch*. They smiled alongside fellow rugby players Jimmy Unwin, John Tallent and Robin Prescott – but it was the 'famous runner Obolensky' who was given the press's top billing among the 'well-knowns in the athletic world'.

Alex's social climbing reached its peak in that summer of 1939 when he joined a select group of eligible bachelors from the House of Commons and the worlds of sport and business attending a dinner party for 20 at the Wakefields' home.

The guests made their way to Regent's Park through a city on a war footing. Sandbags lined the doors of hotels and restaurants, barrage balloons floated above, and trenches had been dug in Kensington Gardens. In addition to the looming German threat, the Irish Republican Army (IRA) had been active in recent months, with 27 letter bombs in London in June, and explosions in Birmingham, Leicester, Lincoln and Manchester, in protest at British troops in Northern Ireland.

Conversation at the party began over aperitifs, and the guests might have tried out the new mnemonic for recognising air raid signals: 'Wavering sound: go to ground; steady blast: raiders passed; if rattles you hear, gas you must fear; but if handbells you hear, then all is clear.' Everyone had seen the government's 'Public Information Leaflet No. 1', describing precautions against fire and urging the population to carry identification labels 'made to last'.

The party then filed into the dining room, each man arm in arm with a lady on his left, to be seated, alternating between males and females, nine in a row on each side of a long mahogany table. The men were a clean-shaven bunch; beards at this time belonging to sailors, if at all. The table was laid with elegant candlesticks and flowers, a silver service of heavy cutlery, and plates of bone china ready for a meal of four courses: a dab of caviar or foie gras to start, a soup, then Norfolk duckling and Scottish salmon. The party drank wine of good quality from France, and it was the done thing to sip. There would be records put on later, maybe from a popular band leader.

At the head of the table, Wavell Wakefield in his husky voice spoke a few words about his roles on the Physical Training Council and in the House of Commons, where he had recently recommended the keeping of a stock of canned blood, and for all Britain's 42-million population to carry a note of their blood type, for use in a national emergency.

Facing 'Wakers', 20 feet away, was a 35-year-old with a slim face, thick, dark eyebrows and a confident smile. Gerald Palmer had been the Conservative MP for Winchester since the election in 1935 and, like Wakefield, he came from somewhere between old and new money, having inherited a huge estate from his father Eustace, who chaired the family business, Huntley & Palmer Biscuits in Reading.

Palmer had a fine rugby connection, as his grandfather Alfred was an uncle of the late Ronald Poulton-Palmer, the Oxford University centre and wing who scored a record five tries in the 1909 Varsity Match and went on to captain England, with eight tries in his 17 Tests up to 1914, before he died in the Great War.

The remarkable truth was that Alex, despite his émigré status, had something in common with almost all of his fellow diners. In his 20 years in his adopted country, he had adjusted and adapted and survived. And if by chance conversation did flag, he could rely on Mrs Rowena Wakefield, the redoubtable, kindly-faced woman sitting next to him.

Guests included Adrian Stoop, known as 'Bunny', the 20-year-old son of the England fly half of the same name who was an old friend of Wakefield's. Sheila, the Wakefields' 17-year-old middle daughter, sat one place away from the Honourable Anne Scott-Montagu, also 17, but already an experienced socialite as the eldest child of the widow of the second Lord Montagu of Beaulieu, who was now married to Edward Pleydell-Bouverie, Commander of His Majesty's Yacht *Victoria and Albert*. Charlotte de Rivoyre was the daughter of the naval attaché at the French Embassy who was busy coordinating Anglo-French naval plans. *Tatler* reported that Charlotte 'rides, swims and plays tennis with zest', and she was particularly striking with her hair worn 'up'. Alex might have sized her up as he popped an angel-on-horseback – bacon wrapped round an oyster – in his mouth.

Most interesting to the majority of the male dinner guests was a slim, pretty girl with dark curly hair and blue eyes. Miss Valerie Cole was living with her aunt – who had presented her at court on 16 March, the day after Hitler marched into Prague – and her uncle, of whom Valerie said: 'He has a reputation for being cold. He isn't cold at all. He is amusing and interesting and kind.'

Valerie was the daughter of the late Horace de Vere Cole, a Cambridge graduate and noted prankster who had died of a heart attack in 1936. Horace was the brother of Annie Vere Cole, who had married Neville Chamberlain in January 1911 – so Valerie's uncle and aunt were the prime minister and his wife, and her London home during her debutante season was 10 Downing Street. She lived on the second floor in servants' quarters recently converted by the Chamberlains into family apartments with bathrooms (as they have remained). The prime minister toiled on his speeches in his study, one floor below.

Valerie possessed an easy charm and Irish ancestry through her aunt, and if she fancied name-dropping she could start with the king and queen, with whom she had shared a dinner table at Downing Street earlier that year. Valerie was also a friend of Lord and Lady Astor among the 'Cliveden Set', the influential group that included the prime minister, the Lindberghs and Geoffrey Dawson, editor of *The Times*.

Amid the hum of conversation and clink of cutlery and glasses, Alex heard from Palmer how he had captained the cricket XI at Winchester School before attending New College, Oxford, and of his deep interest in the Greek Orthodox Church. While electioneering in villages around Hampshire in 1935, he gathered crowds after dark by pumping out gramophone music from a floodlit car. He had served as private secretary to Stanley Baldwin when he was prime minister.

Palmer's political views were typical of Conservatives of the day, and of White Russians such as Alex. While speaking up for boys' clubs in Portsmouth in June 1936, Palmer said Hitler and Mussolini had galvanised their countries' youth in a way Britain could not. Not that Palmer was suggesting Britain should go the same way, but he believed something similar could be done through the boys' clubs – using freedom not force.[5]

On 2 March, Palmer had attended an 'at home' at 10 Downing Street, and the day before that, Valerie Cole had accompanied Neville Chamberlain to the launch of the 'little season' – the parties, balls and dances before the season proper – in a grand reception at the Soviet Embassy when hopes were still high of an Anglo-French-Russian alliance.

Mingling and making friends with these people at Wakefield's party, on this evening of evenings, Alex must have felt closer than ever to acceptance into the British way of life and social hierarchy. His fellow guests may have listened to his views of the Communists in Russia, and nodded and agreed, even though they could never completely empathise. In late May, when Neville Chamberlain was still negotiating the defence pact, he had moaned of Stalin's government: 'I just wish I knew what sort of people we're dealing with.'

CHAPTER 32

ACTING PILOT OFFICER OBOLENSKY, READY AND WAITING

AMID THE 'GATHERING storm', as Churchill described it, Alex trained at RAF Ford in August 1939, enjoying himself in a place he knew from his Oxford Air Squadron days. He drank at the Southdean Hotel and Sports Club and he wrote to Paddy Disney to describe how a local reconnaissance had unearthed one or two new 'joints'.

The same month, Alex relinquished his commission in the Volunteer Reserve to become an Acting Pilot Officer on probation in the Auxiliary Air Force (AAF), and he joined the 615 Squadron based at RAF Kenley near the village of Whyteleafe in Surrey. The 615 had become a fighter squadron in November 1938 and received Gauntlets, which were replaced by Gloster Gladiators (the last of the biplanes) in May 1939.

The authorities may have decided it was not the done thing to have a prince in the Volunteer Reserve. Whatever the case, Alex had made a commitment to patriotic duty – remember his conclusion to the 'War is NOT Ignoble' essay: 'I am prepared to fight for King and Country' – although this is not the same as saying his innermost feelings were simple or straightforward.

The rhetoric of the time was not always of the banner-waving kind. Alex's favourite *Tatler* magazine carried an advertisement entitled 'This England' in January 1939, with a bucolic photo of a river babbling through wooded, rolling hills: 'Whether you love England as sweetheart or as wife . . . it is the earth itself and not the name that holds your heart. The Englishman is no aggressive patriot; some quiet corner of his land means more to him than flags.' The ad was placed by a brewer, with the pay-off line: 'Our Worthington . . . a marriage of English excellence with homely craft.'

A variation on the theme came from Peter Wood, the blond, bulbous-eyed Old Etonian whose father Viscount Halifax was now the foreign secretary. In Wood's piece in *Would I Fight?*, he dismissed pacifism in favour of patriotism, which he distinguished as being 'love of the country that is his by birth; pride in the country to which he belongs'. Wood would die aged 26 at El Alamein in Egypt in October 1942, having gained the rank of major in the Queen's Own Yorkshire Dragoons.

Alex articulated his sense of belonging in *Would I Fight?*, relating a story told to him by a fellow refugee in Paris who knew he was a naturalised Briton. The pair agreed 'Soviet Russia meant nothing to us except the grim and soulless destroyer of Tsarist Russia, our Russia'. Then Alex inquired why his compatriot did not adopt French nationality. 'You are lucky,' the man said. 'You have been adopted by a great country with a king. I prefer to remain without a country and hold on to my Nansen passport.'

Meanwhile in Alex's former homeland, Stalin was fatefully difficult to fathom. Through 1938, the Soviet Union had remained aligned with Western democracies. On 23 August 1939, influenced by developments in Czechoslovakia and Poland, Stalin shocked the world by signing a non-aggression pact with Nazi Germany.

Ray Holmes, the celebrated fighter pilot, wrote 50 years later: 'We did not really believe, in our hearts, that during that last week of August 1939, we were so near to war. All the threats, and promises, and prophecies . . . It still felt like bravado and shadow boxing. But suddenly we, on our Voluntary Reserve course, found ourselves flying four or five hours a day instead of two. Someone was pushing hard to get us as good as possible as soon as possible.'

The pledge from the generation of 1914 to 1918 that they had seen the war to end all wars was empty and useless.

Alex declared monarchy as 'dear to every Englishman, for it stands for something more than a mere figurehead of the State. It is something worth fighting for.'

The schoolboy of six years earlier who had carried bits of wood and nails and tyres to build a bonfire of Hitler was now a man ready to lay down his life for Britain.

Alex leaned towards a radio at RAF Kenley as the BBC announcer spoke: 'You will now hear a statement by the prime minister.' Then, after a pause, Chamberlain's weak and miserable voice spoke of dashed hopes and an uncertain future: 'This morning the British ambassador in Berlin handed the German Government a final note stating that, unless we heard from them by eleven o'clock that they were prepared at once to withdraw their troops from Poland, a state of war would exist between us.

'I have to tell you now that no such undertaking has been received, and that consequently this country is at war with Germany.'

It was the morning of Sunday 3 September, and the outcome feared for years had finally come about as a response to Germany's invasion of Poland at dawn on the 1st. All Britain's forces were mobilised on that day, and Chamberlain began to put a War Cabinet together. At 9.30 p.m. an ultimatum was sent to Hitler, to be followed by another at 9 a.m. on the Sunday. On the Saturday in between there was last-minute diplomacy and a debate in Parliament in which the mood was for war.

Chamberlain had scarcely finished his broadcast when the wail of an air raid warning sounded over London. Dozens of barrage balloons rose slowly above the rooftops. Residents hurried to nearby shelters where the mood was jocularity mixed with jarring uncertainty. The wail began again, and people looked at each other, unsure what to make of it, until a man on the street shouted: 'All clear!'

As the next few weeks unfolded, the impetus that yanked Britain into war disappeared almost in a flash. Poland was attacked from the east by the Russian Red Army, and the country was crushed. At Kenley, two concrete runways were being built to accommodate the new Spitfire fighters.[1]

Alex wrote to a friend (a relative of whom passed the author the correspondence on condition of anonymity) and the letter is a pointer to his flighty character, at 23 years of age, with national notoriety for his rugby and his socialising, and with active service looming – although, truly, to know Alex meant different things to different people. Edith Heap, a motor transport driver who met Alex at RAF Debden, later recalled: 'Amongst the pilots was the gorgeous Prince Obolensky, a rugger blue, but he wasn't interested in us, though always polite.' The pretty and well-connected Joan Wakefield had a plan to accompany Alex to a ball at the Grosvenor House Hotel just after the war began, and only cancelled it due to an air raid. Connections of university friends who attended the unveiling of a statue to Alex in Ipswich in 2009 cheerfully described him as 'all about the ladies' – which, it is fair to say, can mean anything from being jolly company at a party to a propensity for womanising.[2]

Alex wrote: 'I must say that I don't find life very amusing though it has its moments even in war time. So far I must confess I personally have found the whole business dull and boring beyond words but no doubt things will start humming all too soon.

'There's not much news to relate re my activities for fear of being court-martialled or divulging official secrets. In fact, this very nearly happened to me in the "Embassy" a few days ago when I was shooting a colossal line and was looking with an alcoholic gape at my watch and remarking "tut tut! It's 3 a.m. and I must be off now to drop some more pamphlets". All this while surrounded by a bevy of admiring beauty with eyes popping out like organ stops. Also within earshot of a Squadron Leader who didn't think it was at all funny.

'Do drop me a line – let me know how life's treating you, what you're doing, your mother's maiden name and the number of your dog licence etc. Don't tell me you've got a cushy job poring over a map of Europe moving little flags about it, generally winning the war.'

The same friend who received this letter would later be working at an airbase, and in a letter to his own wife he mentioned a female colleague who was a former prostitute and had been working in an administrative capacity under his command. He thought her 'a very remarkable woman who had gone astray through being badly brought up', and had a 'highly emotional make-up to control and showed signs of letting it run away'. She had a 'rascalish veneer', 'sex appeal' and 'charm', and other words he used to describe her were 'wayward', 'unstable', 'intelligent', 'fundamentally sound', 'courageous', 'very capable'. Encouraging her was like helping a 'lame dog over a stile' and 'she may go straight and she may not'.

Towards the end of the passage, he summarised her succinctly: 'She is a female Alex Obolensky.'

Meanwhile, Alex's friendship with Paddy Disney began to drift, understandably in the circumstances, and it was a surprise when Alex heard his pal had been married to Marion Lake earlier in 1939.

Alex nevertheless wrote to Paddy, wishing 'heartiest congrats and good luck to you with your "lottery ticket", though that is perhaps an unkind synonym for the "dead-cert" Marion. Bless you both my children, and all the happiness in the world.' And he ended affectionately: 'Nightie-night you newly-weds, and stick together through thick and thin.'

The 1939–40 rugby season kicked off as normal, although it was later reshaped by scratched fixtures and matches staged to raise funds for wartime charities, and Alex turned out for Rosslyn Park against Harlequins on Saturday 30 September. The local *Richmond & Twickenham Times* wrote: 'It is pleasing to find one club well known to Richmond spectators has literally started the ball rolling.'

Ivor Lambe, a diarist for the *Daily Mirror*, picked up on Alex's new role, writing: 'We certainly are adaptable, judging by the way people are doing their bit. Prince Alexander Obolensky, fair-haired naturalised Britisher [and] the fastest Rugger three-quarter I have ever seen, is now in the RAF, where he has a commission. His running speed won't be much use to him here, but he will be an asset to any mess for he is a cheerful likeable fellow.' This ran next to an advertisement for Izal Germicide, a disinfectant recommended to readers in their air raid precautions.

Being called up was worth £12 a fortnight in pay, and Alex was now running a small car, with petrol at seven pence a gallon. He had been voted as vice captain of Rosslyn Park's first team, and while he quickly dismissed paying 17 shillings for a club scarf, his earnings stretched to five shillings for a Rosslyn Park tobacco pouch.

A press photographer snapped Alex arriving at Old Deer Park in his blue-grey RAF uniform. The skew-whiff tie of old was gone and everything just so: four bright silver buttons down the middle of the single-breasted jacket, and one on each breast pocket, with a belt above the waist between the third and fourth buttons. Trousers with as sharp a crease as he could manage – he had never been crash-hot with an iron – and black shoes shining; neatly knotted tie and leather gloves present and correct. And the badge on his officer's cap – the crown, eagle and laurel wreath in gilt metal, with maroon in the void of the crown – fixed to a mohair strap above the chinstrap.

If Alex ran his thumb across the bird on the badge, facing to its left, he may have reflected it was reminiscent of Russia's double-headed eagle, and touched a connection deep within him to his father: uniformed, militaristic, ready to serve. Maybe there were memories of the sailor suit Alex wore as a toddler; of the blazer and cricket whites at Ashe, the rugby kit and OTC uniform at Trent, the gown and mortar board at Oxford, the flying suit of the OUAS. Pride in orthodoxy; confirmation through conformity. When he won his wings, he knew, they would be woven in gold wire on the breast-pocket badge.

On this bright autumn day, several of the players changed from service uniforms into rugby kit while the tea room buzzed with a fair-sized crowd, around a sixth of them women. The match kicked off late, but nobody minded as there was plenty of time before the blackout. In the near distance another few hundred spectators cheered the famous golfer Henry Cotton from green to green in a competition on the Mid-Surrey course.

The pitch was hard, and the pace fast and haphazard, amid familiar shouts from the spectators to the Rosslyn Park centres to 'give Obolensky the ball!' Harlequins had a try just before half-time, but

Alex got one back in the second half and Park won 11–5. He would not play again until the Major Stanley's match with Oxford University in mid-November.

At Kenley there was a visit from the Honorary Air Commodore of 615 Squadron, appointed earlier that year – none other than Winston Churchill, now First Lord of the Admiralty in addition to his seat in the War Cabinet. Maybe he favoured Alex with a variation on the memorable remark he later made to the actor David Niven, who served in the Army: 'Young man, it was a most magnificent effort, to give up a most promising career, to fight for your king and country . . . Mark you, if you had not have done so, it would have been despicable.'

Britain's air strength grew rapidly during 1939. Germany had previously leapt ahead in producing Messerschmitt 109s, but by July 1939, Britain had improved from five squadrons remounted on the recently introduced Hawker Hurricanes 10 months previously to 26 squadrons of eight-gun fighters. By July 1940, Britain would have 47 squadrons of modern fighters.

The planes needed pilots, for whom normal service training took almost a year, full-time, before they qualified. By late 1939, all courses were shortened.

Bombing raids began against German shipping targets on 4 September, and October saw the first German aircraft brought down on British shores. The Auxiliary Air Force squadrons were receiving fighter planes: Hawker Hurricanes went to 501, 504, 601 and 605, and Gloster Gladiators, Bristol Blenheims and Supermarine Spitfires went elsewhere.

The Auxiliary was bolstered by pilots from the Volunteer Reserve in considerable numbers, but only a few were sufficiently trained for immediate squadron service, so it was likely to be early or mid-1940 before they could make their presence felt. And there wasn't the number or size of Auxiliary squadrons to cope – they would have needed 50 or more aircraft, but instead they normally had 12, which equated to about 18 pilots.

If Alex had been in the Auxiliary in peacetime, he would have trained for an evening a week at his local town centre and on weekends at an airbase. Now the Auxiliary and the Volunteer Reserve were mobilised, and those who had yet to complete their training were sent to Service Flying Training Schools (FTS) before returning to their units. Alex was selected for fighter training; others were chosen for bombers. On 7 October 1939, he was dispatched to No. 7 FTS at Westwood, two miles north-west of Peterborough, on a bleak sweep of (then) Northamptonshire plain, dotted with hangars.

The school had been formed with 17 Hawker Harts in December 1935, joined the following February by Avro Tutors, Furies and Audaxes – the biplanes with which he was already familiar. Alex's transfer offset some possible criticism over his lack of training – the subject of the debate about him in the House of Commons – but he had to make up the shortfall now.

Alex was name-checked by D.B. Wyndham Lewis among the images of the day in the *Bystander* in October's 'fifth week of the Great Hitlerian War'. They included 'rugged Chelsea pensioners, none too decoratively posed by the camera-boys, scrutinising maps of Europe or jovially trying on steel helmets; British soldiers arm-in-arm with poilus and French tars arm-in-arm with British tars; Boy Scouts humping sacks of waste-paper; ATS girls stumping stolidly down Lambeth Walk – a rather half-hearted effort at whimsy, we thought; the Houses of Parliament by moonlight; Miss Hersey Baird, driver to Gen. Sir Walter Kirke (almost daily); Prince Obolensky, RAF, lacing up his Rugby boots; a Peeress or two sewing for the Red Cross; evacuated schoolboys picking fruit for farmers, and other matter of the type one may dismiss as mental gripe-water, like the stuff with which they soothe infants suffering from colic. And who is to blame The Ministry of Information to a large extent, still . . .'

In November, Alex wrote to Irena, who was staying in Manoir du Kerdouz, in Ambon in Brittany.

> No news here as we just work and fly seven days a week. I
> managed to wangle a little leave last weekend to play rugger in

Oxford and had a real blitzkrieg of a party in London that evening. The following day I spent with the family and then returned to exile. Have heard from Teddy several times & he seems to be enjoying life. Ditto Donda.

Looks as if I shall be here for at least another six weeks from now, though I take my intermediate exams on the 28th [November].

Am sorry this is such a dull letter, but as I said before there is no news of any interest in Peterboro.

Much love, Alex.

Donda was the family nickname for Alex's youngest sister, Lubov, the fifth of the six Obolensky siblings, born in London in February 1921, five years after Alex. She would become a nurse in Kenya in the war, and meet and marry Clive Wilfrid Salter, a divorced barrister from Scarborough.

The flying training school was populated by tough but good-hearted sergeants who were representatives of every class and calling – farmers, bank clerks, estate agents – and instructors who were firm but fair.[3] Some were nostalgic for Great War dogfights: the Red Baron and all that.

With Germany producing 800 trained pilots a month, compared with 200 a month in the RAF, training had been cut to as little as six months, or 150 flying hours, from an average 18 months to two years or 200–320 flying hours in peacetime.[4]

Days were long and Alex slept in a straw bed. Up in the air, instructors had ruses to throw you off guard with shouts down the Gosport speaking-tube just as a manoeuvre was imminent.[5] 'See that bloody great pub by the crossroads? They keep a wonderful bitter there – you ought to try it one night.' A stall, however, was no laughing matter. If the nose of the plane was too high and the airspeed fell dangerously low, it became sluggish and the whistle of wind through the struts died away. The instructor would watch for the student to make the necessary recovery, maybe with a comment: 'Things seem to be getting a bit quiet, Obo?' Alex was taught it was an error you made at your peril. Both pilots and instructors died.

On 11 November there was the armistice commemoration, and Yvonne Gaunt went to the war memorial in the Broad in Oxford. 'I looked around and thought "How many are going to survive?"' she later recalled.

Alex had leave for Christmas 1939 and he celebrated with rugby pals old and new by playing for a combined England-Wales team against Scotland-Ireland in a Services International match for the Lord Mayor's Fund for the Red Cross, at the Richmond Athletic Ground on 16 December.

Twenty-eight of the 30 players had been capped by their countries, and the band and pipers of the Irish Guards played for a crowd of 4,000. Squadron Leader George Augustus 'Gus' Walker (later an Air Chief Marshal and president of the Rugby Football Union) captained England-Wales, and Army captain Mike Sayers, with 10 caps for Ireland, led the opposition. Viv Jenkins played at full back, and Alex was joined in a starry three-quarter line by Jim Unwin, Peter Cranmer and Claude Davey.

Alex had a try from a cross-kick by Cranmer, England-Wales won by 17–3, and afterwards the teams repaired to a favourite haunt, the May Fair Hotel. As the main course of steak-and-kidney pudding was brought in, someone shouted 'Orderly Officer!' and forfeited half his helping.

In the Pathé film of the match, we see Alex jiggling his legs in a bitterly cold wind, and in another sequence his great pace is clear as he chases a ball. No opponent could outrun him on the ground. He was not yet a master of the air.

CHAPTER 33

INTRODUCTION TO A HURRICANE AND ENGLAND AT LAST

WHEN VIVIAN JENKINS became a writer for the *News of the World* and later a columnist on rugby union for the *Sunday Times*, he often told a story from the pre-war period, which was that his friend Prince Alexander Obolensky had said: 'My flying training is going well, but I still haven't got the hang of landing.'

In fact, it was a line Jenkins received second-hand from Arthur Rees, the Wales flanker who was training for the Royal Air Force at the same time as Alex, and became a fighter pilot and wing commander. It was never clear when Alex had said it, and whether he was being flippant or factual, or a little of both.

If Alex did find difficulty in landing, as 1939 turned into 1940, he at least had the honesty to admit it. If he had been incompetent at flying, per se, he would have been taken off it altogether. As an acting pilot officer – the lowest rank, below pilot officer and then flying officer – he was considered by the RAF to be a competent pilot in the making.

The acceleration Alex needed in his training stalled in the first weeks of the new year, when Britain suffered its coldest winter for 45 years and the RAF was grounded. Alex was laid up with flu and laryngitis as Winston Churchill broadcast his latest update as First Lord of the Admiralty on 20 January, amid tense debate about whether to fight the Germans in Norway and the Russians in Finland: 'Many illusions about Soviet Russia have been dispelled in these few fierce weeks of fighting in the Arctic Circle. Everyone can see how Communism rots the soul of a nation; how it makes it abject and hungry in peace, and proves it base and abominable in war.'

Principally, though, Churchill spoke confidently about how Britain and France were coping with the seaborne exchanges that had dominated the first five months of the conflict.

Alex was perked up by a week's sick leave in the country but a return to the No. 7 flying school restored him to the drab surroundings near Peterborough, made worse by being completely snowbound. Boots froze to the floor in the huts, and the trainee pilots dressed to go to bed, pulling coats on top of the blankets.[1] Everyone was 'binding' – the flyers' slang for whining about conditions – and maybe comprehending Churchill's aphorism that war alternates between acute discomfort and long, deathly boredom.

By early February, Alex was feeling jealous of his younger brother Teddy, now 20 and serving in the Royal Fusiliers, and writing with sketchy details of forays in front of the Maginot Line – the concrete fortifications constructed by France on their side of the borders with Switzerland, Germany and Luxembourg.

Alex heard rumours of his own next move, but he couldn't be sure which were duff or true. He might become a liaison officer to the French Air Force, or return to 615 squadron and get to fly sorties across the English Channel. There had been talk of night-flight training in Scotland but that was off.

All he knew for certain, he wrote to Irena, who was still in Brittany, was he would be in Peterborough until 19 February at least. 'I don't expect I shall be in France for some time yet. As soon as I do, I will get in touch and we can fix a rendezvous in Paris.' And he joshed with his sister, who had a new beau. 'Can't wait to meet your fiasco. Incidentally . . . what nationality is he? I'll help you both in any way I can, but I ought to have a little data to work on to enable me to form opinions before I come out.'

The war and the weather had stopped rugby fixtures for seven weeks. Rosslyn Park's matches with Metropolitan Police and Wasps either side of New Year's Eve were scratched due to frozen pitches, and the subsequent games in January and February were cancelled.

When the snows cleared, Alex was picked for a team titled the 'Empire' to meet the Army at Richmond on Saturday 10 February. The man whose selection for England had once been viciously opposed in some quarters would now pull on a white jersey in the name of King George VI's entire domain.

The Army side had a wonderful backline of familiar faces including Peter Cranmer, Jim Unwin, Viv Jenkins, Wilf Wooller and Dickie Guest. In the changing rooms at the Athletic Ground, amid the lacing of boots and the pungent muscle embrocation that stung the nostrils, it was not quite like old times. Light-hearted grumbles about exams or getting a girl had given way to news from the front. The Empire were well beaten, 27–9, but Alex's wriggling run set up a try cheered by a crowd packing the touchlines.

A fortnight later, he played for Rosslyn Park for the first time in five months, in a home win over Harlequins. A reporter wrote of the 'pleasing informality' of Old Deer Park. There was the formality, too, of Alex running in the winning try in the last minute, followed by that reliable standby of socialising, the rugby club dinner-dance, as everyone toddled off to the Grosvenor House Hotel in London for Rosslyn Park's 'Rugger Ball'.

Alex now eschewed his faithful white tie in favour of his RAF uniform as he gazed round the ballroom. He may have thought back to the festivities on the night after his great match against the All Blacks. Was it really four years ago? What a happy twerp he had been, expecting or at least hoping life would be all about rugby and girls and some kind of service to his adopted country.

Alex waltzed and polka'd and caught up with Joan Wakefield, who was 19 now, and a photo of them appeared in the *Daily Express* next to an article marking the start of British Summer Time: 'Sixty minutes of extra daylight and blow the black-out until 7 p.m.! The family torch – that's half a crown Hitler owes us – had an hour off . . . Arriving home at 6.50 p.m., I found the man next door in his garden . . . he cracked his new summer-time joke: "Now I can *see my way* to having the garden ready for planting."'

This spirit of forced cheerfulness was common among those who were old enough to remember the Great War and believed the worst was yet to come. In the evenings the street lights were dimmed or extinguished, and doors and windows covered by heavy curtains, cardboard or dark paint. Britain hunkered down with its gallows humour and did its best to say 'boo sucks' to Hitler.

In the last week of February 1940, which was a leap year, Alex received two pieces of wonderful, life-affirming news.

On the 28th, he heard of his long-awaited recall to the England team, to meet Wales in Cardiff on Saturday 9 March. The match was not regarded as an official Test, as some of the best players were busy in the services, yet the line-ups would have been worthy of full-cap status if the game had taken place in peacetime. The majority of the participants had won caps before the conflict.

The next day – leap day – Alex was formally awarded his wings, signifying the completion of his initial RAF training. He would be upgraded from 'acting' to 'confirmed' pilot officer and entitled to the coveted breast-pocket badge. Other than that, there was little fuss. A telegram read: 'Post 91075 P/O A.Obolensky to 504 (F) Squadron, Debden.' Alex had a brief period of leave during which he visited his parents in London, though his mother wasn't well. He showed his logbook to his father and received a quiet nod of approval.

Making the move he had been waiting for, the step up to operational training, Alex left the Peterborough flying school and joined 504 Squadron based at RAF Debden near Saffron Walden in Essex. The 504 was equipped with Hawker Hurricane fighters – between 15 and 20 at any one time.

Debden was a sector station where the majority of the personnel were based and the main servicing on the Hurricanes carried out. The 504 was alternating with another squadron, No. 17, to keep both accustomed to operating in different locations and dispersing aircraft.

The officers' mess at Debden was quiet and cool, and a row of smart cars stood outside. A mess servant took Alex's luggage and showed him to an airy room with a washbasin and two beds covered in crisp white sheets. 'Tea will be served in the anteroom at four o'clock,' said the batman.

The 504 was formed as a Special Reserve Squadron in 1928, and went over to the Auxiliary Air Force eight years later. In 1938 it was incorporated into the RAF's Fighter Command – the companion to Bomber Command and Coastal Command.

The squadron leader was Rupert Hartley Watson, a fresh-faced 28-year-old of fine English stock: alumnus of Sherborne School in Dorset, and son of a lieutenant colonel in the 3rd Dragoon Guards and a rector's daughter from Devon.

Hartley Watson had been in the RAF's Special Reserve, and when war broke out he gave up a career managing a textile-dyeing factory in Manchester. He was looking forward to marrying his sweetheart Prunella, an ATS girl in London and daughter of a DSO; their engagement was announced in *Tatler*. But the wedding would never happen. In April 1940 Watson died when he crashed his Hurricane serial number L1947 as he returned to Martlesham Heath from a night interception patrol.[2]

The 504 had its forward base at Martlesham Heath, 50 miles from Debden near the Suffolk coast, on the doorstep of mainland Europe. Once a week the pilots, aircraft and first-line crew moved between bases. Alex packed an overnight bag slung into an aircraft or a vehicle in a convoy, and had a bunk at Martlesham or stayed in a pub.

In the evenings the pilots of the 504 drank beer at the Black Tiles or Red Lion and chatted about restaurants and cocktail bars in London, second-hand cars and the merits of BBC comedy programmes. They met women who ranged from childish 'popsies' to those who moved alluringly in tight dresses at dances upstairs in the King's Arms at North Walsham. A chap might get 'waterlogged' and start singing bawdy songs to which he'd forget the words. After a few rounds the pilots fell to talking shop about the Hawker Hurricane, which at this time was receiving more publicity than its cousin the Spitfire.

The Hurricane was a shining example of British design and engineering, put into production by the Hawker Aircraft Company in 1934 and entering service three years later. Sydney Camm, the chief designer, had trekked continually from Hawker's offices in Kingston-upon-Thames to the Air Ministry in Holborn, with his ideas for Britain's first monoplane fighter at the time during 1933 when Hitler was rearming in Germany. The Supermarine company was thinking on similar lines with its Spitfire. The backing for these ventures was private as the RAF was undergoing cuts and still wedded to the biplane.

The Hurricane was the first fighter capable of a level speed in excess of 300 mph – 100 mph faster than the aircraft then in service – and it had an increased firepower. A centre section of round metal tubes created a strong, stable yet manoeuvrable platform for its eight Browning machine guns.

The Merlin engine made by Rolls-Royce in Derby, Crewe and Glasgow was of great quality, considering people were still ploughing with horses in the 1930s. If the Spitfire was the greyhound of the skies, the Hurricane was a bull terrier. There were 497 of them in service by the outbreak of the war and eventually 14,533 were built.[3] The Hurricanes and their pilots would destroy more enemy aircraft during the Battle of Britain in the summer of 1940 than all the other air and ground defences combined.

However, there was a damaging opinion about that it took an 'ace' to fly a Hurricane, which may have begun as a joke but was taken seriously by the public and the press.

Early in 1939 the pilots of 111 Squadron – the unit initially equipped with the Hurricane – had been bragging about the skill and guts required to handle it, saying it had to be 'tamed and constantly watched' and it was 'a killer-plane that only the dashing, devil-may-care elite were permitted to fly'. There was a story of an armourer in 73 squadron who let off two guns in a stationary

Hurricane and shot a corporal across the airfield. The man had been standing in line to receive his pay and the other 20 in the queue skedaddled. Many newly trained pilots held the 'Hurri' in almost superstitious dread, and trainees in Fighter Command were known to crash it through a lack of confidence or sheer nervousness.

The pilots did have confidence in the Hurricane's Hawker lineage and it was said you couldn't break one, unlike a Spitfire. The Hurricane's box-girder construction meant a shell or bullet might pass clean through the fabric fuselage, whereas they would have demolished the Spitfire's monocoque fuselage. Even when one 'Hurri' returned from a flight without a rudder (the vertical flap on the tailplane), with half an elevator (the horizontal flap on the tailplane) and with a 'great big hole in the wing a bloke could fall through', the pilot was unaware of the extent of the damage until he was back on the ground.

By coincidence, it had been Alex's old acquaintance King Edward VIII who gave an informal christening to the Hawker Hurricane on a visit to Martlesham Heath in July 1936. Now it was time for Alex to meet this fearsome machine, with the expectation of going to war in it, he was what aviation experts call a 'sprog pilot' in the 'type'.

The Hurricane was a single-seater, so the first time a pilot flew one was the first time he had been up in one. Up to the point of gaining his wings, Alex had accumulated flying time of 211 hours, made up of 142 'solo' and 79 'dual' with an instructor. Almost all of this was in biplane trainers: the Avro Tutors, Hawker Harts and Hawker Audaxes. These two-winged craft with fixed undercarriages were 'rheumatic old geese' compared to the Hurricane.

Since gaining his wings, Alex had spent another six hours flying solo in Harts and Audaxes, just over an hour in the Miles Master, a two-seated trainer, and gained his first experience of monoplanes with two hours 15 minutes in Hurricanes.

It was a hell of a difference to be confronted with a single-winged machine with a retractable undercarriage, closed cockpit, eight machine guns, flaps, and an engine twice as powerful as the trainer and capable of nearly twice the speed.[4] There again, many a flight commander believed flying required flexibility more than experience, and reasoned that young minds such as Alex's could absorb new ideas and techniques.

Climbing into the cockpit as the plane stood on trestles in a hangar, Alex saw the Hawker family likeness between the Hurricane and the Hart. The cockpit in both had the pilot sitting in space and lots of darkness below and behind him. But the Hurricane had many more instruments – there appeared to be at least three times as many – and the constant-speed Rotol propeller with wooden blades was different.

He was talked through the controls by a flying officer standing on the wing. Alex passed his fingers over the dials and switches and levers and handles – fuel selector, hydraulic pump, seat adjust, canopy jettison – and attempted to memorise the location and feel of each one. Almost nothing was labelled.

The central control stick between his knees had a circular hoop like the handle of a spade, and it pivoted forwards and backwards at the floor, but was also hinged laterally at knee height. He ran through the drills of take-off and landing, and the hydraulics squealed as he lifted and lowered the wheels and the flaps that were operated by compressed air. 'Now do it with your eyes closed,' the test pilot said.

Ray Holmes, who flew Hurricanes with 504 Squadron from 1940, had a motto: 'Trust in God, and live one day at a time . . .'[5]

Just under four years after Alex had won his fourth cap for England, he resumed his international rugby career. The Red Cross match with Wales at Cardiff Arms Park featured a batch of servicemen who believed they might be sent to war at any minute, to play before 40,000 spectators relishing the renewal of Anglo-Welsh rivalry and the first wartime 'Test' in Britain since the Boer War of 1899-1902.

Dickie Guest was passed over by England in favour of Alex, who was selected on the left wing with Jimmy Unwin on the right, and at fly half Tommy Kemp ousted Jeff Reynolds. The team included five of the seven Englishmen who had recently helped the British Army to a 36–3 win over the French Army in Paris, and there were four uncapped players in Gloucester centre Francis Edwards and three forwards: Clarence 'Gillie' Gilthorpe of Wasps and Coventry, Bedford's Rex Willsher, and Christopher Newton-Thompson, the South African captain of Cambridge University. Kemp and Jack Ellis were the half-backs who had steered England to victory over Scotland the previous year. Peter Cranmer was the full back.

Alex was wearing the treasured white jersey with the red rose on his chest as he clip-clopped across the wooden duckboards between the changing room and the pitch. There was a rousing clamour of shouts and applause from the Cardiff crowd whose hats and topcoats were interspersed with service uniforms, while schoolboys sat cross-legged round the touchlines. The familiar clipped voice of 'Teddy' Wakelam was on the radio commentary of the second half relayed from 4.15 p.m. by the BBC's Home Service. This was big-time rugby, again.

The crowd all had a fine view as Alex made a cross-field run, reminiscent of his greatest day in 1936, to help set up a try for the excellent Kemp, who went over on the short side of a five-yard scrum. At half-time, with the scoreline at 3–3, the newsreel cameraman moved in for a close-up of Alex mingling among the England players sucking restorative juice from their pieces of orange.

In the second half, there was a lovely move from a scrum and a lovely moment as Unwin scored. Kemp passed out of a tackle to free his centres Heaton and Edwards, both of whose pace might have suited Alex in earlier England teams, and Edwards handed on for Unwin to race clear behind the posts and find his old pal Alex clapping his hands in celebration. Edwards scored another try and England won 18–9.

The following Saturday, 16 March 1940, there was another charity match at Richmond, in which Alex played for Oxford University Past & Present against their Cambridge counterparts for the Army

Recreational Equipment Fund. The customary Oxbridge strength was shown in the presence of 10 internationals. Alex's full back, Viv Jenkins, played a blinder, Ken Fyfe was on the wing for Cambridge, and old friends in Micky Walford and Robin Prescott were at centre and prop for Oxford. Alex and his fellow wing Gerry Hollis were 'always a menace to the Cambridge defence'. Hollis scored twice and Oxford won 13–11.

The return international between England and Wales was set for Saturday 13 April, and Alex was picked to play for England again. The venue would be the Kingsholm ground in Gloucester where he had announced his talent to the audience beyond school and university as a freshman playing for Oxford's Greyhounds in the autumn of 1934. 'The star performer,' as the *News Chronicle* had reported of the then 18-year-old flying down the right wing.

Back at Debden, Alex was rising early for a 12- or 14-hour day, including the odd stint on the parade ground and entertaining visiting VIPs. The 504 were escorting convoys up and down England's east coast. The Germans were not yet bombing on land but they were attacking ships and convoys, and minelaying off the coast.

On Easter Saturday, 23 March, Alex found some table space in the mess and settled down to write a letter to Irena, who was now in Paris, staying at the Hotel Pierre 1er. He smoothed out a sheet of RAF headed paper, with its famous motto stamped in black: 'Per Ardua Ad Astra' ('Through struggle to the stars').

He began with a cheery greeting to his sister. 'My dear Irena,' then, in larger letters, '*Christos Voskriese!*'

The Paschal Greeting, also known as the Easter Acclamation, was an Easter custom among Eastern Orthodox Christians. Instead of 'hello' or its equivalent, a person would greet a friend or family member with 'Christ is Risen!', and the response was 'Truly, He is Risen' or 'He is Risen Indeed'. Had the Obolenskys been together, they might have exchanged a triple kiss of peace on alternating cheeks.

Sorry not to have written sooner but have been pretty rushed during the past few weeks. Managed to get some leave before being sent to this station and managed to see the family in London. Madrinka, as you probably know, has been ill, but has rallied round pretty well.

Am enjoying this place a lot. The flying is much more interesting and the surroundings infinitely preferable to Peterboro'. Have not had time yet to look up any of my friends who live in the district but hope to manage this anon. Trouble is we are pretty hard worked on the whole with pretty long hours.

Hope you're still enjoying life. Duty calls – so must rush off.

Bless you – Love Alex.

On Easter Monday, Alex drove the 40 miles to Bedford to play in a 'star-studded' London XV against East Midlands at Goldington Road, in aid of the Army Recreational and Comforts Fund. The *Bedfordshire Times and Independent* described it as 'help combined with entertainment, a most acceptable arrangement . . . excellent football in excellent conditions and it made those present realise more than ever what the war has robbed us of this season.' The band of the Bedfordshire and Hertfordshire Regiment's Infantry Training Centre added to the 'holiday gaiety'. The ATS passed round a bucket, collecting £10 and a few shillings.

Colonel Jack Hartley, one of the England selectors, was in the large crowd. Alex's new England teammates Kemp, Derek Teden, Fred Huskisson and Robin Prescott were in the London team, who won 13–6, and there was good old rubicund Ray Longland in the East Midlands pack.

Alex had no way of knowing this would be his final match of rugby.

CHAPTER 34

TRAGEDY AT MARTLESHAM

T HE SLENDER WOMAN in a knee-length dress takes the small, buff-coloured envelope she has been handed at the front door and walks into the kitchen to sit at a wooden table. Her jaws clench and her slim fingers shake as she holds the envelope and reads the words printed in black letters on the front: 'Post Office Telegram – No Charge for Delivery.' It is addressed, in handwritten blue ink, to 'Mrs Hewell Johnson, Mayfair Mansions, Fielden Park'. The misspelling of her married name passes her by in the tension of the moment.

She reaches for a letter opener and, turning the envelope over, slides the blade under the flap that had been stuck down a few hours earlier. The paper splits apart and she removes the envelope's dreaded gift: a piece of white paper, folded in two. She unfolds it and reads the message conveyed in clinical capital letters on tiny strips of paper pasted onto the note.

29/3/40 =

IMMEDIATE MRS HEWELL JOHNSON MAYFAIR MANSIONS
FIELDEN PARK WEST DIDSBURY MANCHESTER =

DEEPLY REGRET TO INFORM YOU THAT PILOT OFFICER
ALEXANDER OBOLENSKY IS REPORTED AS HAVING LOST
HIS LIFE AS THE RESULT OF AN AIRCRAFT ACCIDENT ON
29/3/40 FULLSTOP HIS FATHER IS BEING NOTIFIED =

UNDER SECRETARY OF STATE AIR MINISTRY LONDON

She rereads the message, and rereads it again: 'deeply regret . . . Alexander Obolensky . . . lost his life . . . aircraft accident . . . his father is being notified . . .'

She is aware of the instructions left by Alex, that in the event of his death while flying with the Royal Air Force, two people are to be informed before anyone else. One is Serge Alexandrovich Obolensky, and she is the other.

The RAF has observed the wishes of their young flyer, and now the telegram is in the hands of Mrs Gordon Hewlett-Johnson, née Countess Tatiana Vorontsov-Dachkov – or, in other words and at another time, Alex's 'dear Tania'.

She lays the telegram on the table in front of her, and weeps.

The night before the flight that ended his life, Alex sipped a cup of tea in the officers' mess of 504 Squadron, Fighter Command, at the Royal Air Force satellite base of Martlesham Heath.

Strolling towards him was Flight Lieutenant George Greaves, a disciplinarian who later trained pilots at British Flying Training Schools in Florida, where he was described as 'possessing a face contorted with fury as he gave cadets a dressing down, sprays of spittle from his mouth spattering their uniforms'. According to a cadet there, he was 'the sort of Englishman who makes the rest of the world loathe all Englishmen'.[1] He was short with thick, dark eyebrows and a broad nose; a scratch golfer, magnificent tennis player, and he could do the 100-yard dash in close to 10 seconds.

Greaves was also known universally as a superb pilot who at the age of 33 had survived two of what his fellow flyers might call 'spawny', or lucky, episodes.

In April 1936, Greaves was an observer pilot in a Westland Wallace biplane on a flight from Hucknall, when Pilot Officer Reginald Malcolm Broadhead, off course and looking to land, saw electricity cables ahead of him and put the nose down too steeply. Having careered across 30 or 40 yards of field, the plane turned a complete somersault and landed on its back.[2] The two men escaped with cuts and bruises.

And everyone in 504 squadron knew of Greaves's brilliant forced landing of a Westland Wallace in a snowstorm, on playing fields in Yorkshire one evening in November 1937. The aircraft had been flying to a bombing range on the coast when it had engine problems. Greaves circled the town before bringing the plane down in a field that was so small, there was no room to take off again. The plane was dismantled by RAF mechanics and taken back to Hucknall on a lorry.

As a fighter squadron, the 504 had a dozen pilots separated into two flights, 'A' & 'B', each led by a flight lieutenant and consisting of two sections of three: Red and Yellow sections in 'A' Flight, Blue and Green in 'B'.

Greaves now called together his Yellow section of 'A' flight: Pilot Officer Samuel Anthony Compton Sibley and Acting Pilot Officer Alexander Sergeevich Obolensky. 'Formation flying tomorrow morning, 10 a.m. sharp,' Greaves said.

Sibley, London-born and living in Sussex, had celebrated his 20th birthday the day before. He was a former cadet at RAF College Cranwell and had been granted a permanent commission as a pilot officer on probation the previous December. He was destined not to see the summer. Sibley died on 14 May 1940, shot down by flak as he piloted Hurricane L1941 near Brussels.

Flying in formation had been central to a military pilot's advanced training since the Great War. It offered a concentration of firepower in attack, and cover and backup in defence. For budding airmen such as Sibley and Alex, it was exciting and demanding. At 3,000 feet, the three pilots would see how close they could get their planes to each other, edging in until the wingtips overlapped, then holding position as if they were shadows of the leader's machine while they performed steep turns and dives and complicated battle moves. They might move line-astern and be positioned so the second and third were slightly higher than – and just to the right of – the one in front, while out of the slipstream. You had to be watchful for the leader trying a trick of slowing in a climbing turn that would put you at risk of stalling.

Greaves told them they would take three Hurricanes up, with Alex in serial number L1946. He hadn't been on the squadron long enough to have his own aircraft. Each plane had one fitter and one rigger looking after it on a day-to-day basis, checking it before it went out and when it came back.

Outside, near a hangar in the twilight, Corporal George Heard was the fitter in charge of the L1946. At 7 p.m. he inspected the engine and found everything correct. Thomas Henry Burton, a metal rigger in the ground crew at Martlesham, was alongside Heard for the daily inspection, and he found everything correct, too.

The day had been squally with snowstorms. That night before bed, Alex laid out his kit: the Sidcot flying suit with a fur collar and lining, a helmet with earphones, fur-lined flying boots and leather gauntlet gloves with silk inners.

They were the trappings of a participant in war. Yet Alex had never felt the 'zonk!' of a bullet through the fuselage. Someone once observed: 'Given a choice, the cool, steady types plumped for bombers. The "let's have a party" types chose fighters.' Alex wanted to be one of them. He wanted to improve. Everyone sensed the serious fighting with the Germans was weeks, maybe days, around the corner. As he drifted off to sleep in his iron cot he must have been looking forward to the challenge of putting on a good show for the experienced taskmaster Greaves. If there was a scintilla of doubt in his mind about his skill in handling a Hurricane, it was understandable. Alex's experience in one of the world's most famous fighter planes was less than a handful of practice flights for a total of 135 minutes.

The morning of Friday 29 March was cool and overcast at Martlesham Heath. The cloud cover was at 3,000 feet and complete – or 10/10ths as the RAF jargon had it. A wind from the south-west was breezy, but not troublingly strong, at 20 to 25 miles per hour. Visibility was the lowest it had been all week, but officially good, at two to five miles.

Dawn in early spring in this part of Suffolk could deliver a thick mist that would clear once the sun had come up. On this day the remnants of an overnight frost lent a pale, glistening tinge to the grass of the runways. It was cold on the ground, but you had to fly to 2,000 feet to encounter freezing conditions.

Greaves met Sibley and Alex at the dispersal. The planes were placed randomly on the tarmac, not lined up in nice neat lines as they would be after the war. 'We'll take off individually and land individually,' Greaves said. Heard, the fitter, ran the engine of Alex's Hurricane at 08.50 and satisfied himself everything was in order. Burton, the rigger, ran his eye over the plane 10 minutes later and gave the same verdict.

Alex walked over to the Hurricane. The trailing edge of the wing met him between waist and chest height. The wings of this Mark I version spanned 40 feet, almost nine feet more than the plane's length. Its maximum height with one blade of the Rotol wooden propeller vertical was 12 feet 11½ inches.[3] Rob Erdos, a Canadian pilot who flew Hurricanes decades later, described the wings as 'seemingly fat, as if it [the plane] had just eaten something'.

Alex fastened his parachute, fishing for the loop between his knees and bringing the two side straps round and through it to be clicked in. He pulled the stirrup-shaped step from the lower fuselage of the plane to pop the hand-hold open, the fitter gave him a leg up, and he began the climb to the 'pulpit', aka the 'office'. He placed his left foot on the port wing and made one step along so his right foot found the step that was set into the fuselage. Climbing over the canopy sill into the cockpit, he slid into a cramped space, the only padding on the seat being the parachute under his backside. Woe betide you if you dropped a pen or a checklist, as it would rattle out of reach amid the control cables, pipes and wires below. There was a little rear-view mirror on top of the cockpit, and the hood above the head could be slid open.

Heard started the engine at approximately 09.50. Burton helped strap Alex into his Sutton harness, locking the four straps together over his chest with the split pin. It was a quick-release safety belt; a separate item, shaped like a letter H as it passed over the top of the parachute harness, with a lap clip into which each strap was clipped. If you were taxiing the plane you would probably keep it loose, to have the seat at the highest level to help with visibility. When you flew and fought you lowered your seat and tightened the harness. Having the seat down helped put the legs up and enable the pilot to cope with some of the G-force in manoeuvres.

Alex hooked his booted feet into the rudder pedals and checked the panel of instruments. If his brow was furrowed with concentration or nerves, it was hidden beneath his face mask. He performed the final checks for take-off, going over the priming and starting procedures. Burton wished him well in a Nottinghamshire accent Alex would have found familiar from his schooldays at Trent College.

His head was above the side edges of the cockpit. The bigger the man, the more clearance you had. But you still couldn't see over the nose, to the front, in this standing position. And the sightlines from the Hurricane's cockpit were still unfamiliar.

Unlike the biplane trainers, there was no comforting bulk of an upper wing over his head, or latticework of struts and wires on either side, but there were similarities. Any kind of flying required the pilot to be aware of the different speeds, temperatures, pressures, revolutions per minute and other instrument readings necessary for take-off, climbing, straight and level flight, normal cruise, fast cruise, various rates of turn, approach to the airfield and landing. There were codes of letters to help remember the sequences of brakes, trim, flaps, contacts, petrol, undercarriage and radiator, and for climbing, descending and landing.

Greaves taxied his Hurricane out and took off, followed by Sibley. Then it was Alex's turn. He primed the engine, presetting the levers and knobs. Magnetos on, press the booster coil and starter buttons, and set the big propeller slowly turning. A puff of exhaust smoke coloured the same pale blue as Alex's eyes as the dragon awoke with a 'vroom' and a bang: the thousand horsepower of the 1,640 lb (744 kg) Rolls-Royce Merlin engine in front of him. Here was the rush of adrenaline Alex knew from the rugby field as the engine, indecisive at first, rumbled and gave a deep, crackling roar before it settled into a smooth, elemental rhythm.

Alex gave the mechanics a thumbs-up. They bent and pulled the heavy wooden chocks from under the wheels. On the cockpit dashboard the white needles of a dozen dials wiggled. Alex eased the throttle forward, opened the radiator wide to prevent overheating, eased off the brakes and taxied carefully to the side of the field, being careful with the brakes to avoid standing the aircraft on its nose. There was longer grass here, before the mowed smoothness of the runway, and it was blown and flattened in the Hurricane's slipstream.

As with all the single-seat fighters, it was necessary to zigzag while taxiing, so the pilot could see what was ahead by looking out of the cockpit at a narrow angle. The plane felt tight and bouncy, like a new car. There was a feeling of solidity, the wings especially being much thicker than he was used to, and the wheels widely spaced so that it sat on the ground firmly.

As he opened the throttle slowly, he used the rudder pedals to counter the veering caused by the slipstream from the propeller. He turned into the wind, stopped and began his cockpit check, a mental and physical task that helped take the mind off any collywobbles in the gut. One Spitfire pilot called this 'a stomach-clenching moment of black apprehension', in charge of 'a restless, trembling stallion at the end of a none-too-certain rein'. It was necessary to remember on take-off not to get the nose too far forward, as there was a matter of inches between the propeller tips and the ground. Tracking the centre of the runway would have been easy if you could see it. Instead you used peripheral vision to judge your position.

With his oxygen on and flowing, Alex had the hood open and secured for the sobering reason that if he flipped the plane over, there was no way of sliding the canopy back to make an escape. The problem was that even a six-inch gap in the open hood created a whirling eddy of turbulence in the cockpit from the slipstream of the propeller. It could snatch a map from your hand or slash the loose ends of the parachute straps against your face. Opening the canopy was 'a choice between being swirled or poached', because with the engine oil and coolant radiators mounted beneath the fuselage, and all the hot fluid lines running down both sides of the cockpit interior, with no ventilation it could be like sitting on a barbecue. The Hurricane was notorious for its cockpit fires.

At 10.05, Alex took off.

He climbed steeply, gaining height at more than 2,000 feet per minute. As a comparative beginner there was no way he could hold the plane steady, but he accepted the pitch and drift, kept his eyes on the airspeed indicator and the horizon, positioned the nose in the correct climbing attitude and reached for the lever of the under-carriage, pumping it steadily until he felt the clump under his feet as the wheels folded into their housings. Many a pilot forgot to do this and would reach the economical cruising speed with a wallow of sloppy controls and the threat of a stall before he snatched at the lever and jerked it into the 'up' position, making the plane instantly buoyant and manageable.

With the throttle opened again, the Hurricane moved at 180 mph in the climb. Feeling for the hood catch behind his head, Alex pulled the Perspex bubble forward on its rails and locked it shut with a little thud. It cut out much of the noise and all of the gale.

He turned his head cautiously to look around. At 1,400 feet, the airfield was below and behind him. He lifted the nose to continue to climb. This was where you could revel in the Hurricane's power and speed, flying at about 230 mph. He had not flown a Spitfire, but the field of vision was better in a Hurricane because its nose sloped downwards more steeply from the cockpit to the propeller. He could use the horizon – the pilot's friend – to tilt and rotate and level in the rightful place. The famous Hurricane pilot Stanford Tuck wrote of knowing 'he could make this plane almost a part of him, like an extension of his own body, brain and nervous system'.

The armour plate behind Alex's seat was a flat sheet of metal curved to fit the shape of the canopy.

The trio of pilots reached 3,000 feet above the Suffolk countryside and coastline, and Greaves called Alex and Samuel Sibley to join him in a 'V' formation and follow him in turns and dives, maintaining a close and consistent distance. They went through the motions of firing, then broke off either port or starboard, dropping away sharply. It made Alex's head thump against the Hurricane's Perspex hood, and his engine briefly ejected blotches of dark smoke.

Stories circulated years later that Alex had been doing 'loop-the-loops' but these were probably exaggerations extrapolated from the fact of formation practice.

After 30 minutes of physical effort and intense concentration, Greaves called the practice to a conclusion and instructed Sibley and Alex to 'break up and land individually'.[4] He turned hard and set a course for a return to the airfield. Sibley and Alex knew they had to follow suit.

Greaves landed and taxied round. Sibley came in after Greaves and he was taxiing as Alex, the third of the three, banked his Hurricane and fixed his sights on the grass runway. It ran from a point where a supermarket stands today to just short of the Foxhall Road, near a bomb dump. The runway had a drop at the end of it. Some have called it a ravine; others more accurately referred to it as a dip.

Alex needed to make a combat-style overhead break: a tight, 180-degree, continuous decelerating turn over the middle of the airfield. This had to be curved or you couldn't see where you were going.[5] The landing needed to begin downwind of the runway, abeam of its threshold, and things would happen fast from there. A heavy right foot on the rudder was required on a full-throttle climb and an even heavier left one on a quick descent.

With speed dropping below 180 mph, it was time to lower the undercarriage wheels, with an accompanying green light on the dashboard. Open the hood, feel that buffeting slipstream again and identify the Aldis green light winking the all-clear on the airfield. Extend the flaps down, as the speed lowers through 140 mph – not above, or they would not come out properly and might be damaged.

The airfield was marked by natural boundaries of ditches and hedges, and Alex looked out for the guide of Sibley landing before him. Speed down to about 100 mph on the final approach, and slowing. Now the drill was to keep easing the 'spade' grip back, holding the nose up, floating in, until the port or starboard wheel or both struck the ground with a bounce. It would be a rumble and a jig, keep her straight, slow to walking pace and . . . stop.

Alex was coming in too quickly. He was overshooting, too close to the end of the runway. Every pilot in aviation history would be familiar with the sensation. And every pilot would be aware of the two alternatives: pull up and go round again, or take a risk and attempt a fast landing.

What flashed across Alex's mind in these critical moments? Did he make a misjudgement through unfamiliarity with the controls, unused as he was to the weight and the power of the aircraft? Did he doubt himself, or did he decide to test himself? Was he rash or brash or simply hopelessly wrong?

He continued with the attempt to land.

The Hurricane had its tail up, and in the instant its wheels touched the ground and continued into the dip at the end of the runway, gravity and the weight distribution of the aircraft took over. The machine with its heavy engine housed near the front, behind the propeller, flipped violently through 180 degrees over its nose.

Inside the cockpit, Alex's head was whipped hard against the circular glass reflector sight in front of him, and in the next moment he was upside down with his canopy smashed into the ground under the two-ton weight of the plane. He was killed instantly. The machine skidded across the grass, upside down and backwards, roaring and flailing until the propeller jammed and stalled the engine. Sibley sprinted over, and the airfield's crash crew rushed out, with an ambulance and a fire engine. A Verey pistol cartridge was fired, shooting a flashing red light into the sky, to warn others not to land.

CHAPTER 35

AFTERMATH: THE REACTION, THE INQUIRY AND THE FUNERAL

A LEX WAS THE first international rugby union player to
die in the services in the Second World War, and it was a huge
news story around the Saturday morning breakfast tables of Britain,
reported and received with a mixture of shock and regret and grief.
The Times described him as 'killed instantly . . . while landing his
machine at an East Anglian aerodrome yesterday', and agency-written
copy appeared in dozens of local and regional newspapers. The
Birmingham Gazette combined reportage, irony and the standard
staccato phrasing with '"Flying Prince" killed in RAF 'Drome crash'.

A photograph circulated by a wire agency showed Alex in his
flying suit and cap, with goggles perched above the forehead and
the Sutton-harness strap hanging down. He cuts a serious figure,
with his head dipped forward slightly, a half-smile of pride on his
lips, and a logbook under his left arm. The *Daily Express* found the
words written by Alex for *Be Still and Know* in 1936: 'If ever England
has another war, I shall fight, not only because of my love of the
country which has adopted me, but also in gratitude for all she has
done for me.'

The Saturday papers also noted Alex had been due to play for
Rosslyn Park that day, against Aldershot Command at Aldershot. 'If
I can borrow a plane,' he was quoted as having replied. The *Star*
said his 'sense of humour [was] typically English' and a Sunderland
paper mentioned 'years of rugby lay ahead – What a Tragedy!' Most

poignantly, in terms of rugby, the *Irish Times* noted that Sydney Coopper of the RFU had written to Alex with the invitation to play for England in the forthcoming re-match with Wales, and added: 'The reply may be in the post now.'

Instead, before the Rosslyn Park match at Aldershot, the teams lined up in the centre of the field to join the spectators in a minute's silence in Alex's memory. It must have been particularly hard on those who knew Alex well – Jimmy Unwin, D.K. Huxley and Derek Teden were in the Park team who lost 22–8.

The *Observer*, two days after the accident, wrote of 'Rugby's Great Loss' and quoted Tommy Kemp, the England captain and fly half alongside Alex in Cardiff just three weeks previously: 'The rugby world has lost an athlete, a friend, and a splendid sportsman by the sudden and tragic death of Prince Alexander Obolensky. A fine sprinter is rarely a good footballer, but "Obo" combined these two qualities so well that he soon became the most popular player in the game today.'

The *Evening Post* in New Zealand wrote on 1 April: 'His death takes another of the picturesque figures from the Rugby field', while in a *Daily Telegraph* obituary he was 'a romantic figure capable of doing almost incredible things'. The *Sporting & Dramatic News* said: '[Obolensky was] simple in bearing, unaffected in outlook with a happy delight in the good moments in life . . . There was universal grief at the news of his passing, for he had become something of an institution in the country . . . His name was immediately a familiar one.'

The following Saturday, when Rosslyn Park played the RAF, D.R. Gent wrote: 'The death of Prince A. Obolensky . . . hung over this otherwise very cheery afternoon's sport at Richmond. So long has he been an outstanding figure, and so recently was he playing on this very ground, that we could hardly believe that we should see no more this fine, upstanding, spectacular and most attractive player providing us with the thrills he has been giving us for so many years. We all mourn his loss very deeply.'

By then it was known Alex had been killed by a dislocation to the cervical vertebrae in his neck and a fracture of the base of the skull.

*

The RAF's Court of Inquiry into the crash was ordered by the officer commanding No. 12 Group, and convened at Martlesham Heath at 10 a.m. the following day, Saturday 30 March 1940. It was held in private, as was normal for a fatal accident. Alex's mother was in attendance. Her emotions at the thought of her son's ghastly injuries and his body being eased from the wreckage and taken to the airfield's mortuary can only be guessed at.

The court comprised Wing Commander Leon Martin, Acting Flight Lieutenant Sydney Howarth Bazley and Warrant Officer Harold Lee, and they called five witnesses: George Greaves, Sam Sibley, George Heard and Tom Burton from 504 Squadron, and Flying Officer R.A.K. Hopkins.

Burton, the rigger on Alex's plane, was interviewed for radio in 1988, and recalled he was 'shaking like a leaf, with all these bigwigs there'.

Burton said: 'Prince Obolensky, hell of a nice bloke, what happened to him, he landed and overshot, and he was so big, over six feet and a rugby player, he hit a ditch or a dip or a rabbit hole or warren at the bottom of the runway, went straight over and broke his neck. You can see what happened, the aircraft just tipped over and he was big, he couldn't get down far enough and the armour plate at the back of his head wouldn't hold him.

'They asked me what I'd done to the aircraft, was it all right previously. The usual pilot had flown that aircraft earlier in the morning and it was perfect, nothing wrong with it at all.'

The court's minutes and witness statements and other relevant notes are held in an Air Ministry file in the National Archives. Sections of the statements and conclusions have been redacted, and the author made Freedom of Information requests to enable some of these to be lifted, but other redactions were maintained under a rule of data protection that says 100 years must pass before the release of information judged likely to cause harm or distress to any reader.

A three-line section of the file begins with the printed words 'the cause of accident was in our opinion . . .' and Wing Commander Martin continues in blue ink: '. . . having regard to Para 9 above and the weather conditions which gave the maximum alighting area, due to an error of judgement on the part of the pilot.'

A typed note summarises the salient points. 'Pilot's flying history – wings February 1940, total hours 221 [and] 30 minutes (Hurricane 2 hours 15 minutes). Inspection and maintenance in order. Brief statement of finding of court – in the opinion of the court, the cause of the accident was due to an error of judgement on the part of the pilot. Remarks by Station Commander – Agrees. Remarks by Air Officer Commanding – Concurs.'

There was no evidence of failure of the engine or the airframe, and Alex had not attempted to use his parachute. The Hurricane's weight distribution was a principal factor.

The court's report was sent to No. 12 Group and forwarded on 23 April 1940 to the Under-Secretary of State at the Air Ministry in London. Once it had been filed, several matters were brought up for debate or clarification. No. 12 Group asked RAF Debden whether Alex was properly strapped in, and were his straps tight or loose. They also wanted to know whether the windscreen and/or hood over the cockpit collapsed during the crash. The replies, if any were made, are not recorded.

There are, however, notes written into the file showing a discussion continuing into 1941 about the metal plate behind the pilot's head in the Hurricane cockpit. The officer commanding 504 Squadron stated that 'a strong piece of "U" metal behind the pilot's head might save lives in future accidents of this kind'. Air Vice-Marshal Wilfred McClaughry, the Air Ministry's Director of Training, wrote on 17 May 1940: 'I consider that some sort of structure around the fuselage, and above the pilot's head, might easily prevent death or injury in cases such as this. Will DD/RDT [Deputy Director of Research and Development, Technical] please remark on this aspect of the accident.'[1]

A reply in August describes the existing plate and states: 'It is doubtful whether it can be expected to stand up to such severe conditions as in this case but action has been taken to consider modification to the Hurricane and revision to the requirements to withstand the loads due to skidding backwards on its back.' In

January 1941 there is a reference to a 'modification 210' to the Mk I and II Hurricanes, but it is clear it will not be put into production.

There was speculation in later years that Alex had been thrown out of the cockpit. This would have been more plausible if he had been taxiing when he tipped over. A story handed down to Tania Hewlett-Johnson's descendants was that he finished in a tree and broke his neck when there was an error cutting him down. This may have been an attempt to take away attention from a fatal error.

The official report noted Alex's lack of flying time on the Hawker Hurricane but made no comment on it – at least, nothing that appears in the unredacted sections.

There is, however, a comment in the accident record card, which is marked 'FATAL' and can be seen at the RAF Museum in Hendon, north London. In a box titled 'Nature of Accident', there are notes in two sets of handwriting: 'Lack of judgement and inexperience on type. Overshot, turned over lndg: covered 2/3 of drome before getting down on which: ran tail up; over boundary and t.o.' The words 'overshot' and 'ran tail up' were underlined for emphasis.

Years later, Laurence Thorogood, a pilot and squadron leader, bemoaned in a documentary how he fought in a Hurricane in 1940 with just 20 hours' experience, and that a friend twice attacked German planes with his gun set on 'safe' and wondered why the weapon was so silent.

For an expert view on the extent to which Alex may have been hampered by a lack of experience, the author spoke to Mark 'Disco' Discombe, the squadron leader of the Royal Air Force's Battle of Britain Memorial Flight, who is an experienced pilot of reconditioned Hurricanes.

'Hurricanes are relatively straightforward when you look at the technical aspect of them,' 'Disco' said. 'But this was his first operational type, and both in performance and the technology it would have been a step up. The Hurricane is quite heavy to control. In pitch she is dynamically unstable, she is slow in roll but quite responsive. All aircraft have their own vices, and they were still in the early days of designing these things out.

'If you think about borrowing somebody's car, and you change gears, your hand doesn't fall where it would in your car – we call it muscle memory. You have to pause and think about it for a while – he probably would have been still thinking: "Where do I put the gear down, where is this or that button?" With sub-three hours under his belt, he would still have been thinking about what he had to do, using his conscious thought.

'For a pilot, that is one of the trickiest things. In training, a lot of your capacity is used up just trying to find the instruments and controls, and as you get better your eyes fall to where they need to fall, as do your hands and the grip between your knees. The more natural it is, the more time and effort you have to look out of the window, to either fly the aircraft accurately or, more importantly, fight the enemy.

'The accident – because he is new to the aircraft, he has come in too fast and likely too high. Too fast wouldn't surprise me as this is one of the first times he has been in a high-performance monoplane. An old-fashioned biplane had a lot of drag through the wind. You bring the power back and it will slow down a lot quicker. With a Hurricane, if he has got a bit high and he's coming in a bit steeper, you'll be bringing the power back but the speed won't be coming off because she's more slippery, more aerodynamic.

'As you go through your career, most pilots would look back on a landing and say "should have overshot on that, really". A lot of that is personal pressure and pride. You have just done formation with your mates, you are on final gear down, ready to land, and you're the one who goes round and they say: "What are you doing?" You want to get down with the boys, go to the debrief – it's professional pride and "all I am doing is landing".

'He has obviously come in fast, he's decided to force her down. She's not slowing down, she doesn't really want to land. The main wheels have touched but in a much more level attitude with the tail upright. How would he flip it over the top? One, is she is in such a nose-down attitude that the propeller struck the ground and that would cartwheel you over? I think that is unlikely. In a Hurricane you have to get the nose a long way down for the tips to strike. A Spitfire in France two or three years back did that on take-off.

'The other possibility is he's watched a lot of this ground going past, the start of the runway has gone past, he still isn't down, still isn't down, he's thinking: "Where's that hedge at the far end?" He's forced it down eventually, feels the wheels touching, he thinks: "Great, I'll brake." Well, if you haven't got the tail down, and you haven't pinned the tail down with the elevator, if you brake, that will mean you will roll forward and over the top.'

There was no post-mortem. Alex's death certificate submitted by Bernard Pretty, the Suffolk southern district coroner, recorded a verdict of 'misadventure'. It read: 'No. 108, Deben district in East Suffolk, Woodbridge sub-district. When and where died: Twenty-ninth March 1940 at the Royal Air Force station Martlesham. Occupation: 60 Muswell Hill Road, London N10, a prince of the Russian Czarist regime, and a pilot officer in the Royal Air Force. Cause of death: Fracture of the base of the skull and dislocation of the cervical vertebrae consequent on the accidental overturning of the single seater aircraft of which he was pilot in the course of landing. Misadventure. No P.M.

'Certificate received from Bernard Pretty Coroner for Suffolk (Southern District). Inquest held Thirtieth March 1940.'

The funeral with full military honours was held in Ipswich on Tuesday 2 April. The town had never seen the like of the cortège that wound the five miles from Martlesham Heath to his resting place in the New Cemetery.

The service in the crematorium church was conducted jointly by Archimandrite Nicholas of the Russian Orthodox Church, and the Reverend F.E. Doughty, an RAF chaplain, with an aircraftman at the organ. Alex's coffin was draped in a Union flag and carried by six RAF pilots. Serge and Lubov looked gaunt as they led the procession, heads bowed, accompanied by their 13-year-old son Michael, walking stiffly in suit and tie. Teddy was away with the Royal Fusiliers.

Lubov's half-brother Vadim Narishkin wore his Army sergeant's uniform with a black armband, alongside commanding officers from air stations to which Alex had been attached. Paddy Disney was there, together with D.K. Huxley, the captain of Rosslyn Park. The New Zealand Rugby Union and the All Blacks team of 1935–6 sent a wreath. A firing party shot a volley of tribute above the grave.

A memorial service followed at 11 a.m. on 11 April at the Russian Church of St Philip in Buckingham Palace Road, with a full Russian Mass conducted by Father Vladimir Theokritoff, and Serge, Lubov and Michael present again. The rugby fraternity came out in force: Sydney Coopper and the president of the RFU, and representatives of Rosslyn Park, Oxford University, Kent, Middlesex, Guy's Hospital, Old Merchant Taylors, United Services and Metropolitan Police. Eugene Sablin represented Russians in London, and the secretary of Old Tridents was there for Trent College, which had been dealt a double blow – Peter Blix, the 'sensitive, scholarly and lankily athletic' Norwegian in Alex's unbeaten team of 1932–3, had died the previous month, drowned when his ship was torpedoed on its way from Bergen to the USA. The crew made it to lifeboats and were picked up by the *Albert L. Ellsworth* before that too was torpedoed by a German U-boat. In attempting to reach a life raft, Blix was overcome by the freezing waters.

On 5 April 1940, Alex's name appeared in a list of 26 men 'Killed on Active Service' in an Air Ministry communiqué of 85 casualties. Such litanies became sadly commonplace in the five years that followed.

The next day, Ivor Brown, who had attended Balliol College, Oxford, around 1910, and would become editor of the *Observer* in 1942, contributed a paean of 1,500 words to the *Manchester Guardian*. It embraced a wide-ranging contemplation of sport's place in Britain, and the beauty and redolence makes it worth seeking out in its entirety. On Alex specifically, these excerpts summarise Brown's admiration:

> What the death of Prince Obolensky has taken from his relatives and his friends of Oxford and the RAF, the outsider cannot assess. From the experience of those who like watching

games something unique has vanished, a flash of beauty, an excitement of the senses.

Russians are expected to be temperamental and the great Obo could have his days off, when he seemed detached and nonchalant as though this running and kicking were inconsiderable matters for the piece of work that is man.

Then, on other days, he would so glory in the game, so outrace all opposition, so bewilderingly appear on the unexpected side of the field to make an uncovenanted rescue or an incredible score, that he swerved right away from and above even the highest class of the speedy and side-stepping players.

If you had any mind for these things he was, on his great days, unforgettable.

His use of speed could make the heart jump suddenly, start a shiver of ecstasy, and set the senses a-tingle. He and his fellows, whatever the turf, of Twickenham or Wimbledon, Lord's or Hoylake, put a glory into things. Are games so small, so trivial? Clumsy and coarse they may be: the method is all; but when the masters play our life is decorated and enlarged.

Ivor Brown also penned a moving poem, preserved in the World Rugby Museum at Twickenham, in which he raised a comparison of death in wartime by mentioning Ronnie Poulton-Palmer from a previous generation, and concluded with the verse:

> His play, his work, his death were on the wing,
> To the green English field, from Russia come,
> Now England's cap with deer's-foot grace he'll bring
> To that last field of bright Elysium.

The Times of 13 April previewed England's match with Wales at Gloucester: 'England's one change was brought about by the lamentable death of Prince A. Obolensky in a landing crash . . . Obolensky's popularity was not due merely to his success as a wing three-quarter of exceptional speed. There was something eminently likeable about him on and off the field, and his memory will not be confined to the books of records. Today's match will lack something pleasant because of his absence and the tragic cause of it.'

Guest took Alex's place in a 17–3 win for England, preceded by two minutes' silence among the 20,000-strong crowd. England had a dropped goal by Prescott and a try by Heden converted by Heaton for a 9–3 lead at half-time. Heaton and Unwin scored further tries in the second half. *The Times* later noted that Alex had also missed a chance to be among 30 of the best players in England, Scotland, Ireland and Wales, in a match played between the Army and Great Britain the following week.

The crashed Hurricane L1946 was restored to service almost immediately, despite the plane and its engine being described as damaged 'seriously', on the official sliding scale between 'totally' and 'slightly'.[2] It was eventually lost in a crash in October 1940 against a background of escalated aerial warfare.[3]

At Oxford University, there were loose ends. Brasenose College's bursar wrote to Serge at the start of April 1941, seeking £21 and two shillings 'in settlement of the late Prince Obolensky's batels [food and accommodation expenses]. I have not heard further from you since 18th May 1940, when you said you would be writing in due course.' Serge had replied that he would take out letters of administration as Alex had left no will, and he was also 'ascertaining what, if any, Estate was left by him'.

In a handwritten letter of 12 April 1941, Serge came clean:

> I regret to tell you that my son Alexander died in debts without leaving any money whatsoever. My financial circumstances actually do not allow me to meet this liability of my late son, which I sincerely regret.
>
> Yours faithfully, Serge Obolensky.

CHAPTER 36

THE LEGACY,
THE LEGEND

ALEXANDER OBOLENSKY'S DEATH at the age of
24 invites a romantic vision of him as a James Dean figure,
taken before his time, forever preserved as young and beautiful in
our consciousness, never to grow old or to be wearied or condemned
by his years.

To fully consider Alex's legacy, which as we have seen endured
powerfully down the decades, we can look first at his place in the
pantheon of rugby, and give his career an informed reappraisal. Many
a commentator has taken his total of four Test matches and two tries
as evidence he was not remarkably talented, or was merely a flash
in the pan, or just lucky. Some have almost turned his tumultuous
debut at the age of 19 against him, because his subsequent seasons
were not as fruitful.

First, it is important to compare the number of caps Alex was
able to accumulate with those available now. As a fixture in the
England team in 1936, he played in all four internationals that year,
against New Zealand, Wales, Ireland and Scotland. Of the other
countries that are England's annual opponents these days, France
had been expelled from the International Championship in 1931,
and although the decision was reversed in March 1939, the war
delayed France's rejoining, while Italy was yet to become the force
that saw it added to the Five Nations to make it Six in 2000.

Overall, England's Test fixtures have multiplied four or five times
in the rush for revenue that included rugby union abandoning its
amateur code to go 'open' in 1995. In the 1930s, the England team

played no internationals at home in the autumn and made no overseas tours in the summer. The fixtures with emerging nations such as Argentina, Canada, Fiji, Georgia, Japan, Romania, Samoa, Tonga, Uruguay and the United States began in the 1970s or later, and the Rugby World Cup was not inaugurated until 1987. That competition alone can earn a modern player half a dozen caps in the space of six weeks.

In the 1930s, Bernard Gadney and Peter Cranmer were picked for England year in, year out – and they mustered 14 and 16 caps respectively. The only time either man met opposition other than Ireland, Scotland and Wales was when they faced New Zealand in 1936. By 2020, England had three men in Gadney's position of scrum half – Ben Youngs, Danny Care and Matt Dawson – who had more than 75 caps each.

Under modern conditions, Alex might have toured two or three times with the British & Irish Lions, who on their 2017 trip to New Zealand took two specialist wings and five other players capable of playing in the position, and played three Tests. On the one Lions tour Alex took part in, to Argentina, he missed selection for the solitary international match.

Another factor was the Second World War interrupting organised sport. Alex was recalled to the England team in early 1940, but the players were not given full-cap status. Today, caps are awarded for markedly more dubious friendly internationals with mixed selections. And furthermore, of course, Alex died at the age of 24, or otherwise he might have played on when international rugby resumed in 1947.

A fourth element is the role of replacements. There were no substitutes in international rugby from 1871 until the regulations were amended in 1968. If a player was injured, he played on – and the spirit was to do so if possible – or his side made do with 14 men or fewer. By the 2010s, an international team was allowed eight replacements on the bench, all of whom could be used. The England hooker Luke Cowan-Dickie gained 25 Test caps as a substitute between 2015 and 2021. In Alex's era, that number would have been zero.

All these aspects of Alex's impact in rugby have been, at best, underrated. He was either injured or within a selector's pick of further caps for three seasons from 1937 to 1939. It is fair to speculate that, had he been around today, a career of 50 caps – sufficient for an England player to lead the team out at Twickenham as a special celebration – might have been within his grasp.

Thankfully, a sportsperson's legacy is never measured by numbers alone.

On the famous tries scored by Alex against New Zealand, the author sought the opinion of Rory Underwood, the great Leicester wing of the 1980s and 1990s who holds England's record of 49 international tries in 85 Tests, and coincidentally served as a pilot in the RAF for 18 years, flying Tornados, Canberras, Hawks and Domines.[1]

Underwood kindly watched film of the famous tries and was surprised to learn Alex's age when he scored them. 'You're joking, he was 19?' Underwood said. 'It's something that resonates with me. He was mentioned to us through the Air Force, him and Douglas Bader. He is somebody I have always known of and recognised that he was a pilot and also an England international and played for Leicester Tigers and was on the wing. Obviously the one thing that's missing is I wasn't a prince!

'The combination of it being a debut, against the New Zealanders, who had never lost any match in England, the final score was 13–0, to shut them out was one hell of a result. And talking about rugby – this is two tries that have come about from running out of your own half. The style England were playing was 15-man rugby. They are great tries; typical wingers' tries.

'The first try is a classical outside swerve. He takes the ball, it's popped off from the number 13, and you can see there isn't a gap there. He's got another 20, 25 yards to go. Obolensky is coming on a short line, straight at the full back, and that is what makes the try for me. If he'd gone on the outside in the first instance he'd have beaten his man easily, but he'd have been on the five-yard line. The fact he took the inside arc and straight away the outside arc, the full back was stuffed. You can see he doesn't think about it, he is straight into it. That would happen naturally and it's brilliant; you can tell he's playing with confidence, not frightened or anything.

'The second one is cutting back and just pure pace. There is no swerve, no sidestep – once he has changed direction, and gone on the inside, that was head down and go for the corner. When he got the ball he stopped because the guy was covering across. So he stopped, looked up and thought: "Well, the space is there, I'm going to run there." That is what you see him do. He thinks: "I'll cut inside." He sees the two other defenders, gets his feet right, then he just sets off and goes: "I'm going to beat them for pace." What's interesting as a right winger, he is holding the ball in his right hand when he is on for being tackled from the right-hand side. I would have put it in my left hand and used my right hand to make sure you couldn't get anywhere near me.

'Pace is something you can't train; you have either got it or you haven't. And if you have got pure pace, it doesn't half make a difference.'

The premature end to a colourful life spanning three of the great cataclysms in history – the Great War, the Russian Revolution and the Second World War – meant Alex did not see the blazing, screaming summer of 1940. He was one of three Russians believed to have served in the RAF during the war; the others were Emanuel Galitzine and Alexander Molchanoff-Sacha, aka Richard Marner.[2] Had he lived, he might have been fully trained to fly Hurricanes and Spitfires in the Battle of Britain, and known sorties and direct hits and collisions and fires and dunkings in the sea and bailouts over land.

After the war, who knows? Perhaps Alex would have found a rich duchess to marry and developed into an international playboy, spinning the roulette wheel in Monaco or bantering with Jack Kennedy on Cape Cod. He may have made his peace with the press and become a sports pundit, or reverted to insurance, or become a dutiful officer in 'some colonial service', or the civil service, as he had once imagined.

Instead, we are left with a variety of memorials. At Trent College, the Second World War stone plaque in the chapel carries the names of four members of the unbeaten rugby team of 1932–3: Alex Obolensky, John Harrison, Clive Carver and Peter Blix. A few steps away along a neat path, bright-eyed students meet to eat lunch and discuss the possibilities ahead of them in the Prince Obolensky Building, a dining and conference facility of airy modern design with panoramic views over the playing fields. It cost £4 million to build and was opened by Alex's niece, Princess Alexandra, in February 2008.

Alex is commemorated in an eponymous association and trophy at Rosslyn Park, and at Twickenham Stadium, where his name is engraved in the 'Walk of Legends', among 60 rugby greats from Wavell Wakefield and Dickie Jeeps to Jason Leonard and Martin Johnson. There was also for many years an Obolensky banqueting suite at Twickenham, and an Obolensky lecture series staged by the *Sunday Times*, while Oxford University Rugby Club toured Russia in September 2010 to mark the 70th anniversary of Alex's death.

Most striking of all is a statue 15 feet in height, erected in Ipswich in 2009, with British and Russian television news crews attending the unveiling. Crafted by Harry Gray, it was funded by Ipswich Borough Council and a variety of donors, including the Chelsea FC owner Roman Abramovich and many members of the rugby-loving public. It depicts Alex, still the only Russian-born person to have played sport for England, bare-chested, holding the ball behind him, leaning forward in a spirit of speed and a will to win, atop a shaft of Portland limestone inspired by the structure of a Hurricane plane. Grooves in the shaft represent the aircraft's sliding hood and the angular forms refer to the shapes of 1930s Art Deco.

*

Alex's passing left behind five siblings whose grief and love lingered, and to whom anxiety and upset were often companions, among an extended family scattered across four continents as a consequence of their parents' original exile.

Princess Alexandra, the daughter of Alex's youngest brother, Michael, by his first marriage to the Belgian-born Anne Helbronner, was the first Obolensky the author met. Had it not been for the surname and the family nose, Alexandra was every inch the charming, well-educated English lady. She was married to Stuart Hulse, a public relations expert and former Dulwich School boy with an appreciation of rugby and journalism. Together they were running a boutique, Obolenskys, in Odiham in Hampshire, and they were generous and excellent company. After leaving the Army, Michael, who was 10 years younger than Alex and had only vaguely proud memories of his brother, became an accountant for the World Bank, Coca-Cola and other companies, based variously in Toronto and several cities in South America. Family letters show how Michael had peered through the delivery-room door in a Toronto hospital in 1953 and been delighted to see that 'Alexandra has the nose of an Obolensky!' She was followed two years later by a baby boy, Nicholas, known as Nick, but Michael and Anne split up, and Anne took the children to London, where Alex's mother Lubov kept a grandmotherly eye on them.

Alexandra introduced the author to her cousin, Serge Beddington-Behrens, the son of Alex's sister Irena by her first marriage, and a psychotherapist and author who lives in Mallorca. A warm man who prefers a hug where a handshake might do, Serge loaned the author the batch of letters written by Alex to Irena between 1935 and 1940 – the last of them written and posted on 23 March 1940, six days before his death.

Serge Beddington-Behrens's family photos show Irena healthy and happy in the Swiss Alps in the 1950s, but she and Edward would divorce, and in 1958 Irena married a Scot, George Morton, with whom she had two more children, Anna and Geordie. Morton had a fantastic collection of art; in their Gstaad home they had a

Modigliani painting on the wall and a Henry Moore statue on the table. They also had a villa in Vienna and a place in Venice. In common with her brother Michael, Irena smoked, and she died of cancer in Lausanne, Switzerland, in 1996.

The third Obolensky brother Teddy, who played rugby in his youth, eventually got into the movie business. He made a film in 1956, *The Legend of the Good Beasts* starring Peter Ustinov, whose mother had worked for the Imperial Mariinsky Ballet and Opera House in St Petersburg. It was a Russian ugly duckling tale, featuring characters modelled by Fabergé. Teddy was also an uncredited film editor on six other movies, including *The African Queen*.[3]

Michael met his second wife, Felizitas Joerchel, in the 1960s while she was working for the World Health Organisation in Venezuela. Born in Silesia in 1939, Felizitas and her younger sister were split temporarily from their mother when they were young, fleeing to Bavaria to escape the Russian advance. Their father would die in a Russian prisoner-of-war camp. Yet Felitizas married a Russian, and she came to know several members of the Obolensky family well. Graciously hosting the author in her tastefully decorated apartment in Madrid, she shared her recollections amid books on Russian history and photos of Obolenskys past and present.

Felizitas had no real idea why she became Michael's second wife; she had considered him to be just a good friend, with a shared interest in books and music. But 'Misha' was at an airport to meet her flight one day in 1967, and insisted they be married. It had to take place in London, too, he said, because his mother Lubov was ill and frail. The engaged couple came to London with Michael wearing an old suit but with money in his pocket to buy a new one.

A few nights before the register office wedding he lost his cash, playing cards, so the new suit was never bought. The reception – thankfully, there was a wedding cake – took place amid the grim surroundings of Lubov's flat in Iverna Court, west London. Lubov had suffered an embolism the year before and had had a leg amputated. She was dreadfully sick, and the flat was 'terribly dirty'. Felizitas recalled Lubov possessing a deep, booming voice with a Russian accent, even though the lady was almost 80 and she had lived in England and France most of her adult life.

Michael's wedding night was an excuse for him to get drunk with Felizitas's brother and a big wheel from the Shell oil company. Between the four of them they scraped together enough money to settle the restaurant bill, and caught a cab back into London, where more drinking ensued, including the ritual chucking of glasses into a fireplace. Michael was eventually poured into the marital bed, to catch some sleep before the next day's honeymoon flight to Gstaad and a room lent to them in Irena's house.

Michael carried two business cards: 'Prince Michael' when he wanted a table at the Ritz, and 'Michael Obolensky' for business life. He was later taken on as a Russian adviser by the newspaper publisher Robert Maxwell. On a trip by executive jet to Moscow, the man at passport control stood to attention and said: 'Welcome, my prince.' After Michael was also feted at a party, he and Maxwell quickly parted.

Felizitas inherited a collection of around 300 letters sent between Michael and his parents from the 1940s to the 1960s. The author went through them one long night in a Madrid hotel. Serge's letters to his son, written in French, were concise and unfussy, in black ink and a tiny font. The letters written in English by Lubov read like a runaway train: a battering-ram in blue biro, scrawled over page after page of strident opinion and instruction. Here was a matriarch gripping tenaciously on to her social retinue and dispensing family advice even as her health was failing her.

Maria, the eldest of Alex's siblings, known as 'Masha', was separated from her husband Sydney Ranicar by now. She appeared to Felizitas to be 'small and bird-like and very shy', and kept in Lubov's kitchen like an unpaid servant.

Alex's father Serge had died seven years before this, in December 1960 in a London hospital, nine months after having a fall. Serge was described by Michael as a wonderful person, a saint; quiet, cultured and warm-hearted. He could not help one contradictory opinion: as a White Russian émigré, he desperately wanted the

Germans to win the Second World War, as it would mean a defeat of the Soviets, even though his sons Alex and Teddy had joined the British RAF and Army respectively.

Felizitas met Alex's youngest sister, Lubov, in Mallorca in 1972: 'A lovely person, one of the brightest of the bunch, but a sad alcoholic. She went through the Mau-Mau period in Kenya.' A letter among Michael's correspondence described how Lubov and her English barrister husband Clive Salter had split up.

Felizitas bore two sons to Michael, and she is fiercely proud of Sergei and Andrey, describing them as rare Obolensky men who turned out well. She spoke with the author about the concept of the Russian soul, a subject also close to the heart of Serge Beddington-Behrens, and much debated throughout history. Felizitas's son Sergei takes a particular view that if there is a Russian soul it must be 'something to do with irresponsibility'.

Michael died in 1995 from lung cancer, overweight and having smoked three packets of cigarettes a day. There is a picture of him on the wall of the Rosslyn Park rugby clubhouse looking grey and flabby but happy, with his son Nick at his side, taken when they were guests of the Prince Obolensky Association in 1994.

Nick recalls how the Obolensky family retained an entitlement to estates of land in Russia, the largest of them near Kazan. After the Cold War ended, the Russian government was amenable to handing them back in return for a payment, but Michael judged it would take millions of pounds to bring back to service, and not worth it.

Felizitas said of Michael: 'I believe he was the closest of the siblings to Alexander in character. He liked people to think he was doing good, that he was generous, even if it was all made up. He was insecure, probably from his education telling him he was very special and from one of the oldest Russian families, yet with no money. He didn't know how to treat people, but he could make fun of himself and see the humour in any situation. He eventually took up with a ballet dancer who had money, so at the end of his life Misha had what he'd always wanted – a Bentley and a chauffeur.'

Such is the complex legacy of Prince Alexander Sergeevich Obolensky. His parents Serge and Lubov were born in Imperial Russia in the 19th century. Today, they lie side by side in a cemetery in Gunnersbury, south-west London, displaced and to an extent destroyed by twists of history, and 90 miles from the military grave of their never-to-be-forgotten son.

APPENDIX

Alexander Obolensky's senior rugby career, chronologically – results of his first-class and other significant matches and the tries he scored. Alex's team in **bold**.

Season 1933–4

31 March 1934, Saracens 6 **Nottingham** 11, *One try.*
11 April, Worcestershire & Herefordshire 9 **Derbyshire** 8
14 April, Derby 16 **Nottingham** 14
21 April, Waterloo 28 **Nottingham** 5

Season 1934–5

16 October 1934, (Oxford) Colours 15 **Whites** 13, *One try.*
18 October, **Colours** 14 Whites 8, *One try.*
20 October, **Notts, Lincs & Derbyshire** 13 Warwickshire 30
22 October, **Brasenose College** 3 Oxford University Greyhounds 29
24 October, **Greyhounds** 24 United Banks 6, *One try.*
1 November, (Oxford) Varsity 26 **Greyhounds** 7
3 November, North Midlands 22 **Notts, Lincs & Derbyshire** 11
5 November, Llanelli 12 **Greyhounds** 6, *One try.*
15 November, Gloucester 18 **Greyhounds** 9, *Two tries.*
17 November, Leicestershire 9 **Notts, Lincs & Derbyshire** 18, *One try.*
24 November, **Rosslyn Park** 10 London Irish 3, *One try.*
29 November, **Oxford University** 12 Gloucester 8
1 December, **Rosslyn Park** 11 St Bartholomew's Hospital 8
3 December, **Rosslyn Park** 11 Oxford University 11
15 December, North of Ireland 9 **Oxford University** 10
17 December, Dublin University 3 **Oxford University** 0
26 December, **Leicester** 8 Birkenhead Park 12, *Two tries.*

28 December, **Leicester** 3 Manchester 0

31 December, **Rosslyn Park** 15 Fettesian-Lorettonians 8, *One try.*

26 January 1935, **Oxford University** 8 London Scottish 10

30 January, **Oxford University** 9 Edinburgh University 9, *One try.*

2 February, **Oxford University** 9 Richmond 8, *One try.*

6 February, **Oxford University** 3 Royal Air Force 3

9 February, **Oxford University** 3 Bristol 12

14 February, Worcester College 5 **Brasenose College** 28, Oxford Inter-College Cup, *Two tries.*

16 February, **Oxford University** 5 Harlequins 9, *One try.*

21 February, **Brasenose College** 12 Oriel College 7, Oxford Inter-College Cup semi-final, *One try.*

28 February, University College 19 **Brasenose College** 0, Oxford Inter-College Cup final

2 March, Blackheath 21 **Oxford University** 5

23 March, Pontypool 9 **Oxford University** 3

4 April, **Midland Counties** 29 Police Union 9, *Two tries.*

20 April, Bristol 11 **Leicester** 6, Easter tour, *One try.*

22 April, Plymouth Albion 3 **Leicester** 3, *One try.*

4 May, **Warwickshire, North Midlands & Notts, Lincs & Derbyshire** 13 East Midlands & Leicestershire 18, *One try.*

Season 1935–6

7 September 1935, **Leicester** 30 Bedford 11, *One try.*

14 September, **Leicester** 38 Penarth 0, *One try.*

19 September, **Midland Counties** 3 New Zealand XV 9

28 September, **Leicester** 26 Waterloo 9, *One try.*

5 October, Coventry 12 **Leicester** 11, *One try.*

12 October, **Rosslyn Park** 7 London Scottish 15, *One try.*

14 October, (Oxford) **Colours** 22 Whites 0, *One try.*

17 October, **Colours** 13 Whites 23, *Three tries.*

19 October, Old Merchant Taylors 3 **Oxford University** 0

24 October, **Oxford University** 12 Newport 0, *Two tries.*

26 October, **Oxford University** 24 United Services 0, *Two tries.*

30 October, (Oxford) **Varsity** 26 Greyhounds 5, *Two tries.*

2 November, **Oxford University** 20 Richmond 9

7 November, **Oxford University** 9 New Zealanders 10, *One try.*

9 November, Blackheath 8 **Oxford University** 0

14 November, **Oxford University** 16 Leicester 4, *Two tries.*

16 November, Harlequins 6 **Oxford University** 21, *Three tries.*

23 November, London Scottish 8 **Oxford University** 21, *One try.*

28 November, **Oxford University** 13 Major R.V. Stanley's XV 25, *One try.*

10 December, **Oxford University** 0 Cambridge University 0

16 December, Edinburgh Academicals 13 **Oxford University** 8

21 December, **England** 26 The Rest 12 (England Second and Final Trial) *Three tries.*

27 December, **Leicester** 0 Barbarians 0

4 January 1936, **England** 13 New Zealand 0, *Two tries.*

18 January, Wales 0 **England** 0

1 February, Richmond 20 **Oxford University** 3

8 February, Ireland 6 **England** 3

15 February, **Oxford University** 15 Harlequins 8, *One try.*

22 February, Gloucester 16 **Oxford University** 6, *One try.*

27 February, **Brasenose College** 33 Jesus College 3 Oxford Inter-College Cup semi-final, *Five tries.*

5 March, University College 10 **Brasenose College** 3, Oxford Inter-College Cup final, *One try.*

21 March, **England** 9 Scotland 8

22 April, Middlesex seven-a-sides, **Rosslyn Park** 10 Saracens 3, *Two tries.*

25 April, Middlesex seven-a-sides finals, **Rosslyn Park** 18 Beaumont Old Boys 5, *One try;* Sale 13 **Rosslyn Park** 5

Summer 1936
British & Irish Lions tour to South America
22 July 1936, Olivos 3 **Lions** 27, *Two tries.*

26 July, Argentina B 0 **Lions** 28, *One try.*

29 July, Pacific RAC 0 **Lions** 62, *Two tries.*

2 August, Unión de Litoral 0 **Lions** 41, *Two tries.*

5 August, Old Georgians 6 **Lions** 55, *Four tries.*

23 August, SIC/CUBA/Hindu Combined 0 **Lions** 44, *One try.*

Season 1936–7

23 September 1936, **Sandal** 0 Headingley 3

26 September, Durham County 3 **R.F. Oakes's International XV** 19, *Two tries.*

3 October, **Rosslyn Park** 11 Old Blues 3, *Two tries.*

15 October, (Oxford) **Probables** 29 Possibles 10, *One try.*

22 October, Newport 5 **Oxford University** 8

29 October, (Oxford) **Varsity** 14 Greyhounds 0, *One try.*

4 November, **Oxford University** 13 Leicester 16, *One try.*

28 November, **Oxford University** 3 Gloucester 15

30 December, **Blackheath Wednesday** 9 Kent Public Schools 6, *Two tries.*

2 January 1937, Bedford 34 **Rosslyn Park** 8, *One try.*

9 January, Gloucester 14 **Leicester** 12

23 January, **Oxford University** 17 London Scottish 15, *Two tries.*

10 February, **Oxford University** 23 Edinburgh University 3, *One try.*

13 February, **Oxford University** 15 Bristol 6, *One try.*

27 February, The Army 11 **Oxford University** 3

4 March, East Midlands 13 **Barbarians** 3, *One try.*

6 March, Blackheath 4 **Oxford University** 21

13 March, **Leicester** 9 London Welsh 0, *One try.*

30 March, Bath 17 **Leicester** 13, *One try.*

17 April, **Leicester** 9 Blackheath 4, *One try.*

Season 1937–8

14 October 1937, (Oxford) **Probables** 22 Possibles 6, *Two tries.*

21 October, Leicester 11 **Oxford University** 14, *One try.*

23 October, London Scottish 0 **Oxford University** 3

27 October, **Oxford University** 8 Newport 11

2 November, (Oxford) **Varsity** 22 Greyhounds 11, *One try.*

6 November, **Oxford University** 11 Richmond 11, *One try.*

9 November, **Oxford University** 6 Dublin University 3, *One try.*

13 November, Blackheath 19 **Oxford University** 21, *Two tries.*

20 November, Harlequins 18 **Oxford University** 11, *One try.*

25 November, **Oxford University** 8 Major Stanley's XV 9

27 November, Gloucester 10 **Oxford University** 8, *One try.*

7 December, **Oxford University** 17 Cambridge University 4

18 December, Probables 23 **Possibles** 11 (England Second Trial)

1 January 1938, England 13 **The Rest** 11 (England Third and Final Trial)

22 January, **Leicester** 9 Richmond 3, *One try.*

17 February, Christ Church 11 **Brasenose College** 8, Oxford Inter-College Cup semi-final

26 February, Northampton 12 **Leicester** 3

3 March, East Midlands 7 **Barbarians** 8

5 March, **Leicester** 6 Harlequins 11

9 March, Sussex County Rovers 0 **Greyhounds** 17, *One try.*

15 April, Penarth 0 **Barbarians** 8, *One try.*

18 April, Swansea 14 **Barbarians** 7

Season 1938–9

24 September 1938, **Rosslyn Park** 19 Harlequins 21

28 September, Bristol 3 **R.F. Oakes's International XV** 16, *Two tries.*

1 October, **Rosslyn Park** 13 Sale 13, *One try.*

8 October, London Scottish 18 **Rosslyn Park** 6

12 October, Old Cranleighans 0 **International XV** 21, *Two tries.*

15 October, Richmond 13 **Rosslyn Park** 21, *One try.*

22 October, Bristol 12 **Rosslyn Park** 3

27 October, Eastern Counties 15 **Middlesex** 6, *Two tries.*

29 October, Old Millhillians 3 **Rosslyn Park** 24, *One try.*

2 November, Surrey 10 **Middlesex** 10, *One try.*

5 November, **Rosslyn Park** 23 London Irish 6, *One try.*

16 November, **Middlesex** 6 Hampshire 17, *One try.*

23 November, Oxford University 16 **Major Stanley's XV** 6

26 November, **Rosslyn Park** 3 Richmond 16

30 November, Kent 9 **Middlesex** 30, *Two tries.*

3 December, **England** 17 Possibles 18 (England First Trial), *One try.*

10 December, United Services 22 **Rosslyn Park** 9, *Two tries.*

17 December, **Probables** 15 Possibles 19 (England Second Trial)

27 December, Leicester 8 **Barbarians** 6, *One try.*

2 January 1939, **Rosslyn Park** 11 Fettesian-Lorettonians 3, *Two tries.*

7 January, England 3 **The Rest** 17 (England Third and Final Trial), *Two tries.*

14 January, **Rosslyn Park** 3 London Scottish 8

28 January, Richmond 13 **Leicester** 21

11 March, **Rosslyn Park** 3 Birkenhead Park 15

18 March, **Rosslyn Park** 20 St Thomas' Hospital 3, *Three tries.*
25 March, **Rosslyn Park** 8 Moseley 17
1 April, Edinburgh Sevens won by **Co-Optimists**.
8 April, Cardiff 6 **Barbarians** 11
10 April, Swansea 12 **Barbarians** 3
15 April, Worthing Sevens won by **Rosslyn Park**.
22 April, Middlesex seven-a-sides finals, Richmond 11 **Rosslyn Park** 8,
    first round.
26 April, **Wavell Wakefield International XV** 22 Twickenham and
    District XV 6, *One try.*

Season 1939–40

30 September 1939, **Rosslyn Park** 11 Harlequins 5, *One try.*
18 November, Oxford University 3 **Major Stanley's XV** 8, *One try.*
9 December, **Rosslyn Park** 20 Combined Old Boys XV 3, *Two tries.*
16 December, **England-Wales** 17 Scotland-Ireland 3 (Services
    International), *One try.*
10 February 1940, The Army 27 **Empire** 9
24 February, **Rosslyn Park** 18 Harlequins 11, *One try.*
9 March, Wales 9 **England** 18 (Red Cross International)
16 March, **Oxford Past & Present** 13 Cambridge Past & Present 11
25 March, East Midlands 6 **London** 13

Major Teams Summarised:

	P	W	D	L	Tries
England	4	2	1	1	2
England XV	1	1	0	0	0
British & Irish Lions XV	6	6	0	0	12
Oxford University	44	20	4	20	29
Rosslyn Park	24	12	2	10	21
Leicester	17	8	2	7	12
Nottingham	3	1	0	2	1
Barbarians	7	3	0	4	3
Midland Counties	2	1	0	1	2
Notts, Lincs & Derbyshire	3	1	0	2	1
Middlesex	4	1	1	2	6
Totals:	115	56	10	49	89

NOTES

Chapter 3
1 John Hendy, *Blown to Eternity: The Loss of HMS* Princess Irene, 2015.
2 london-medals.co.uk.
3 *The Scotsman*, 10 January 1919.

Chapter 5
1 Dimitri Obolensky, *Bread of Exile*, 1999.
2 Lady Masha Williams, *White Among the Reds*, 1980.

Chapter 6
1 David Pinney, Trent College.
2 Geoffrey Nicholson and John Morgan, *Report on Rugby*, 1961.
3 *Trident*, Trent College school magazine, c. 1969. Article by Alec Goodrich.

Chapter 7
1 Report written by Geoffrey Bell.
2 *Trident*, Trent College school magazine.
3 Keith Briant and Lyall Wilkes (eds), *Would I Fight?*, 1938.

Chapter 8
1 Sir Charles J. Holmes, *Self and Partners (Mostly Self)*, 1936.
2 Richard Davenport-Hines, *An English Affair*, 2013.
3 J. Mordaunt Crook, *Brasenose: The Biography of an Oxford College*, 2008.

Chapter 9
1 Keith Briant, *Oxford Limited*, 1937.

Chapter 13
1 C.J. Oliver and E.W. Tindill, *The Tour of the Third All Blacks*, 1936.
2 U.A. Titley and Ross McWhirter, *Centenary History of the Rugby Football Union*, 1970.
3 Captain H.B.T. Wakelam, *The Game Goes On*, 1936.

Chapter 16
1 Phil McGowan, World Rugby Museum, Twickenham.
2 Geoffrey Archer, interview with author.
3 Wakelam, *The Game Goes On*.
4 Stephen Jones and Nick Cain, *Behind the Rose*, 2014.
5 Jones and Cain, *Behind the Rose*.

6 Wakelam, *The Game Goes On.*

Chapter 17
1 David Frost and David Lawrenson, *The Bowring Story of the Varsity Match*, 1988.
2 skegnessstandard.co.uk/news/when-the-royals-came-to-visit-us-1-1338385.

Chapter 18
1 Ruth Cahir, British Pathé.

Chapter 19
1 Wakelam, *The Game Goes On.*

Chapter 21
1 211squadron.org.
2 Larry Forrester, *Fly for Your Life: the story of Bob Stanford Tuck*, 1956.
3 Spitfiresite.com, April 2010.
4 Ray Holmes, *Sky Spy*, 1989.

Chapter 22
1 Magaly Rodríguez García, Lex Heerma van Voss and Elise van Nederveen Meerkerk (eds), *Selling Sex in the City: A Global History of Prostitution*, 2017.
2 *The Isis*, 4 November 1936, article by Alexander Obolensky.
3 gloucesterrugbyheritage.org.uk/page_id__228.aspx?path=0p3p17p.

Chapter 24
1 Family scrapbooks, Charles Percy, April 2018.
2 Family scrapbooks, Charles Percy, April 2018.

Chapter 27
1 Edward Beddington-Behrens, *Look Back – Look Forward*, 1963.

Chapter 28
1 Tom Neil, *Gun Button to Fire*, 1987.
2 Oxford University Archives.

Chapter 29
1 Aviva company archive.
2 Duff Hart-Davis (ed.) *King's Counsellor: Abdication and War, the Diaries of Sir Alan Lascelles*, 2006.

Chapter 31
1 Alan Evans, *The Barbarians: The United Nations of Rugby*, 2005
2 Barbarian FC (barbarianfc.co.uk).
3 Anne de Courcy, *The Last Season*, 1989.
4 *The Bystander*, 26 April 1939.
5 *Portsmouth Evening News*, 27 June 1936.

Chapter 32
1 kenleyrevival.org.
2 Alexandra Obolensky, interviews with author.
3 Richard Hillary, *The Last Enemy*, 1942.

4 battleofbritain1940.net and Royal Air Force Museum (rafmuseum.org.uk).

5 Forrester, *Fly for Your Life*.

Chapter 33

1 Tom Neil, *Gun Button to Fire*, 1987.

2 aircrewremembered.com/hartley-watson-rupert.html.

3 Edward Bishop, *Hurricane*, 1986.

4 Malcolm Barrass, interview with author.

5 Holmes, *Sky Spy*.

Chapter 34

1 Willard Largent, *The Royal Air Force Over Florida*, 2000.

2 aircrashsites.co.uk/pre-war-crash-sites-2/dsc_0001p-2.

3 Bishop, *Hurricane*.

4 Accident report file, National Archive.

5 skiesmag.com/news/16252-flying-a-legend-html.

Chapter 35

1 British Military Terminology, May 1943, US Army Military History Institute.

2 Accident report file, National Archive.

3 Bishop, *Hurricane*.

Chapter 36

1 militaryspeakers.co.uk/speakers/rory-underwood.

2 RAFCommands.com.

3 bfi.org.uk.

BIBLIOGRAPHY & REFERENCES

Arbenina, Stella, *Through Terror to Freedom*, 1929

Beddington-Behrens, Edward, *Look Back – Look Forward*, 1963
Bennett, Geoffrey, *Freeing the Baltic*, 1964
Bishop, Edward, *Hurricane*, 1986
Briant, Keith, *Oxford Limited*, 1937
Briant, Keith, and Wilkes, Lyall (eds), *Would I Fight?*, 1938
Buchanan, Sir George, *My Mission to Russia and Other Diplomatic Memories*, 1923
Bunin, Ivan, *Cursed Days*, 2000

Chester, R.H., and McMillan, N.A.C., *Centenary: 100 Years of All Black Rugby*, 1984
Chester, R.H., and McMillan, N.A.C., *Men in Black*, 1979
Churchill, Winston, *The Gathering Storm*, 1948
Collins, Tony, *The Oval World: A Global History of Rugby*, 2015
Cooper, Stephen, *The Final Whistle*, 2013
Crook, J. Mordaunt, *Brasenose: The Biography of an Oxford College*, 2008

Davenport-Hines, Richard, *An English Affair*, 2013
De Courcy, Anne, *1939: The Last Season*, 1989
Dunford, Penny, *A Biographical Dictionary of Women Artists in Europe and America since 1850*, 1989

Evans, Alan, *The Barbarians: The United Nations of Rugby*, 2005

Farmer, Stuart, and Hands, David, *The Tigers Tale: The Official History of Leicester Football Club 1880–1993*, 1993
Ferguson, Niall, *The War of the World: History's Age of Hatred*, 2006
Fitzpatrick, Sheila, and Slezkine, Yuri (eds), *In the Shadow of Revolution: Life Stories of Russian Women from 1917 to the Second World War*, 2000

Forrest, Denys, *Foursome in St James's*, 1982
Forrester, Larry, *Fly for Your Life: The Story of Bob Stanford Tuck*, 1956
Frost, David, and Lawrenson, David, *The Bowring Story of the Varsity Match*, 1988

García, Magaly Rodríguez, van Voss, Lex Heerma, and van Nederveen Meerkerk, Elise (eds), *Selling Sex in the City: A Global History of Prostitution*, 2017
Godwin, Terry, *The Complete Who's Who of International Rugby*, 1987
Goodyear, David, *'Tiz All Accordin': The Life of Peter Cranmer*, 1999
Griffiths, John, *Rugby's Greatest Characters*, 2009

Hart-Davis, Duff (ed.), *King's Counsellor: Abdication and War, the Diaries of Sir Alan Lascelles*, 2006
Hendy, John, *Blown to Eternity: The Loss of HMS Princess Irene*, 2015
Hillary, Richard, *The Last Enemy*, 1942
Hohenlohe, Prince Franz, *The G.I. Prince*, 1995
Holmes, Sir Charles J., *Self and Partners (Mostly Self)*, 1936
Holmes, Ray, *Sky Spy*, 1989

Jacoby, Charlie, *The East India Club: A History*, 2009
Jones, Stephen, and Cain, Nick, *Behind the Rose*, 2014

Largent, Willard, *The Royal Air Force Over Florida*, 2000
Leadbetter, F.W.B., *A Celebration of Trent College*, 2002
Logbook of the *Princess Margaret*, National Archives, Kew, 1919

Marie Louise, Princess, *My Memories of Six Reigns*, 1956

Neil, Tom, *Gun Button to Fire*, 1987
Nicholson, Geoffrey, and Morgan, W. John, *Report on Rugby*, 1961

Obolensky, Dimitri, *Bread of Exile*, 1999
Obolensky, Prince Serge Platonovitch, *One Man in His Time*, 1960
Oliver, C.J., and Tindill, E.W., *The Tour of the Third All Blacks*, 1936
Owen, O.L., *The History of the Rugby Football Union*, 1955
Owen, O.L. (ed.), *The Rugby Football Annual 1936–37*, 1936

Profumo, David, *Bringing the House Down*, 2006

Raymond, Boris, and Jones, David R., *The Russian Diaspora 1917–1941*, 2000

Richards, Huw, *A Game for Hooligans*, 2007

Roskill, Stephen, *Naval Policy Between the Wars. Volume I: The Period of Anglo-American Antagonism (1919–1929)*, 1968

The Russian Chronicles: A Thousand Years that Changed the World, 1990

Smith, Douglas, *Former People: The Last Days of the Russian Aristocracy*, 2012

Thomas, Clem, and Thomas, Greg, with Cole, Rob, *The British & Irish Lions*, 2016

Titley, U.A., and McWhirter, Ross, *Centenary History of the Rugby Football Union*, 1970

Wakelam, Captain H.B.T., *The Game Goes On*, 1936

Williams, Lady Masha, *White Among the Reds*, 1980

Websites

aircrewremembered.com

ancestry.co.uk

baltictimes.com

Barbarian FC (barbarianfc.co.uk)

battleofbritain1940.net

British Film Institute (bfi.org.uk)

British & Irish Lions (lionsrugby.com)

British Movietone (aparchive.com)

britishnewspaperarchive.co.uk

British Universities and Colleges Film and Video Council (bufvc.ac.uk)

deepbaltic.com

gloucesterrugbyheritage.org.uk

kenleyrevival.org

latvianhistory.com

Royal Air Force Museum (rafmuseum.org.uk)

spitfiresite.com

toffeeweb.com

211squadron.org

INDEX